Learning Online

At a time when more and more of what people learn both in formal courses and in everyday life is mediated by technology, *Learning Online* provides a much-needed guide to different forms and applications of online learning. This book describes how online learning is being used in both K-12 and higher education settings as well as in learning outside of school. Particular online learning technologies, such as MOOCs (massive open online courses), multi-player games, learning analytics, and adaptive online practice environments, are described in terms of design principles, implementation, and contexts of use.

Learning Online synthesizes research findings on the effectiveness of different types of online learning, but a major message of the book is that student outcomes arise from the joint influence of implementation, context, and learner characteristics interacting with technology—not from technology alone. The book describes available research about how best to implement different forms of online learning for specific kinds of students, subject areas, and contexts.

Building on available evidence regarding practices that make online and blended learning more effective in different contexts, *Learning Online* draws implications for institutional and state policies that would promote judicious uses of online learning and effective implementation models. This in-depth research work concludes with a call for an online learning implementation research agenda, combining education institutions and research partners in a collaborative effort to generate and share evidence on effective practices.

Dr. Barbara Means directs the Center for Technology in Learning at SRI International. Dr. Means is an educational psychologist whose research focuses on ways to use technology to support students' learning of advanced skills and the revitalization of classrooms and schools. A fellow of the American Educational Research Association, she is regarded as a leader in defining issues and approaches for evaluating the implementation and efficacy of technology-supported educational innovations.

Dr. Marianne Bakia is a senior social science researcher with SRI International's Center for Technology in Learning, where she leads research and evaluation projects that explore online learning and other educational technology policies and programs. Prior to joining SRI, Dr. Bakia worked at the Federation of American Scientists and the Education Unit of the World Bank.

Dr. Robert Murphy is a principal scientist with SRI International's Center for Technology in Learning, where he designs and conducts large-scale experimental and quasi-experimental evaluations of widely adopted educational programs and technologies. Prior to joining SRI, he was a research graduate fellow at the Institute for Policy Research at Northwestern University, a Rotary Ambassadorial Scholar at the University of Dublin - Trinity College, and a research engineer at United Technologies Research Center in East Hartford, Connecticut.

Learning Online

What Research Tells Us About Whether, When and How

Barbara Means,
Marianne Bakia, and
Robert Murphy

Center for Technology in Learning
SRI International

 Routledge
Taylor & Francis Group

NEW YORK AND LONDON

First published 2014
by Routledge
711 Third Avenue, New York, NY 10017

and by Routledge
2 Park Square, Milton Park, Abingdon, Oxon OX14 4RN

Routledge is an imprint of the Taylor & Francis Group, an informa business

Library of Congress Cataloging in Publication Data
Means, Barbara, 1949–
Learning online : what research tells us about whether, when and how /
Barbara Means, Marianne Bakia, Robert Murphy.
        pages cm
Includes bibliographical references and index.
    1. Internet in education.   2. Distance education.   3. Educational
technology.   I. Bakia, Marianne.   II. Murphy, Robert, 1962–   III. Title.
LB1028.3M415 2014
371.33'44678—dc23   2013036601

ISBN: 978-0-415-63028-3 (hbk)
ISBN: 978-0-415-63029-0 (pbk)
ISBN: 978-0-203-09595-9 (ebk)

Typeset in Times New Roman
by RefineCatch Limited, Bungay, Suffolk

Printed and bound in the United States of America by Publishers Graphics,
LLC on sustainably sourced paper.

Contents

List of Figures and Tables

Figures

Tables

Foreword

What Research Tells Us About Whether, When, and How

At a time when more and more of what people learn in formal courses and everyday life is mediated by technology, *Learning Online* provides a much-needed guide to different forms and applications of online learning. This book describes how online learning is being used in both K-12 (kindergarten through grade 12) and higher education settings as well as in learning outside of school. It describes the design principles, implementation, and contexts of use of particular online learning technologies, such as massive open online courses (MOOCs), multiplayer games, learning analytics, and adaptive online practice environments.

Learning Online synthesizes research findings on the effectiveness of different types of online learning, but a major message of the book is that student outcomes arise from the joint influence of implementation, context, and learner characteristics interacting with technology, not from technology alone. The book describes available research about how best to implement different forms of online learning for specific kinds of students, subject areas, and contexts.

Building on available evidence regarding practices that make online and blended learning more effective in different contexts, *Learning Online* draws implications for institutional and state policies that would promote judicious uses of online learning and effective implementation models. This in-depth research work concludes with a call for an online learning implementation research agenda, combining education institutions and research partners in a collaborative effort to generate and share evidence on effective practices.

Dr. Barbara Means directs the Center for Technology in Learning at SRI International. She is an educational psychologist whose research focuses on ways to use technology to support students' learning of advanced skills and the revitalization of classrooms and schools. A fellow of the American Educational

Research Association, she is regarded as a leader in defining issues and approaches for evaluating the implementation and efficacy of technology-supported educational innovations.

Dr. Marianne Bakia is a senior social science researcher with SRI International's Center for Technology in Learning, where she leads research and evaluation projects that explore online learning and other educational technology policies and programs. Prior to joining SRI, Dr. Bakia worked at the Federation of American Scientists and the Education Unit of the World Bank.

Dr. Robert Murphy is a principal scientist with SRI International's Center for Technology in Learning, where he designs and conducts large-scale experimental and quasi-experimental evaluations of widely adopted educational programs and technologies. Prior to joining SRI, he was a research graduate fellow at the Institute for Policy Research at Northwestern University, a Rotary Ambassadorial Scholar at the University of Dublin Trinity College, and a research engineer at United Technologies Research Center in East Hartford, Connecticut.

Preface

Individually and in collaboration, the three of us have spent literally decades studying efforts to use technology to support learning, to broaden opportunities, and to change practices within classrooms and schools. But nothing quite prepared us for the explosion of online learning resources, course providers, and venture-capital-backed companies descending on K-12 and higher education during the last five years.

Policy makers and education funders have asked us to conduct studies that will help them make better decisions about online education. Our efforts to meet their needs have encountered a number of challenges. The supply of solid empirical research on implementations of online learning is limited, especially at the K-12 level, and is always lagging behind the newest technology innovations that are sparking the greatest interest. Even defining what is meant by online learning has proved troublesome; the concept has fuzzy boundaries and terms are used loosely and inconsistently. Finally, in doing our own primary research on dozens of interventions incorporating online learning, we have confronted many challenges to undertaking high-quality studies, including the difficulty of studying technologies and implementation models that are constantly changing.

As we have continued to monitor the emerging literature on the effectiveness of online learning, we have been discouraged by the proliferation of polemics and advocacy pieces based on selective reporting of research findings, and the scarcity of articles and research syntheses offering a reasoned weighing of available evidence. Depending on which reports and media accounts you read, online learning portends either a golden age of educational access and personalization or the cynical degradation of teaching and learning in the name of profit-making and public education cost cutting.

It is exactly this absence of independent, unbiased syntheses of online learning research that motivated us to write this book. There is no set of definitive studies revealing whether or not using online learning is a good idea. And indeed, in this book we will argue that the debate needs to be framed in more specific terms. Moreover, as fast as the world of online learning resources is changing, educators will always have to make decisions about whether and how to implement the newest technology-based innovations in the absence of rigorous research on that innovation implemented in their own particular context. For this reason, decision makers have to depend on the "best available evidence." The online learning research base is, and will always be, imperfect. Educators and policy makers need summaries of the research evidence and help drawing reasonable inferences to inform the decisions they need to make in the absence of the perfect study.

This book offers a balanced reporting of available evidence that takes the reader beyond the question of whether online learning can be as effective as face-to-face instruction to examine the research base for specific design principles and implementation practices as they are used with different types of learners (for example, high versus low achievers). We describe the ways that online learning is being used in a wide range of contexts—in elementary and secondary schools, colleges and universities, and in the home and wherever else people have access to Internet connections.

We wrote this book with multiple audiences in mind. We have brought together research on the use of online learning across the spectrum from elementary school to university studies, to provide the most comprehensive review possible in a way that is useful for courses on the role of technology in learning and education. Chapters of the book would be useful also in educational leadership courses, methodology courses addressing meta-analysis, courses on the economics of education, and education policy courses.

Throughout, we address issues of practice and policy, drawing out the implications of the research for people who need to make decisions today, and who do not want to hear that "more research is necessary."

We delve into apparently contradictory studies concerning the effectiveness of online learning, making sense of the pattern of findings by looking more closely at the nature of the learning experiences and of the types of learners being compared. We note that many studies have fallen into the trap of treating the online aspects of a course or other learning experience as if they were self-contained, ignoring the broader context in which learning takes place and the relationship between online and offline learning activities.

Many studies focused on measuring impact do not even specify the essential features of the online experience they are investigating. In part, this neglect reflects the field's lack of a common conceptual framework and vocabulary—two gaps we attempt to fill by offering a framework and set of key design features for online learning.

This book provides a framework for thinking about the essential conditions that support online learning. We summarize empirical studies on the effects of designing those conditions into online systems. We also describe and discuss research on the use of online learning with learners who are vulnerable to school failure, examining the complex relationships among learning system design features, implementation practices, and outcomes. We conclude the book with a proposal for an online learning research agenda, addressing major gaps in the research base and potential points of leverage for significantly enhancing learning outcomes.

The research we summarize in this book is drawn from the work of hundreds of researchers using a wide range of methods. We also incorporate first-hand observations and insights we have gained in conducting many studies of K-12 and postsecondary online learning innovations ourselves.

Scholars who study transformational innovations, such as the national highway system and the Internet, note that their short-term impacts tend to be less than expected, but that in the long run they have broader effects than anyone could have anticipated. We are still in the early stages of harnessing the potential of online learning. While we cannot foresee all of its long-term effects, we are confident that they will be more positive if decisions are based on the objective analysis and interpretation of research evidence.

Acknowledgments

Numerous individuals and organizations have contributed to this work. We owe much to our many collaborations and discussions with other researchers in SRI's Center for Technology in Learning (CTL). We have benefited from the insights of too many CTL colleagues to name them all individually. It is truly a privilege to work with a group of more than 60 talented researchers dedicated to enhancing human learning and to investigating the ways that technology can support and enable better educational approaches.

Equally important have been the many conversations we have had with teachers and college faculty, who have welcomed us into their classrooms and shared the thinking behind their instructional strategies in the hundreds of interviews conducted in the course of decades of research. They have taught us that online interactions are just part of the learner experience and that we need to consider technology within the broader context of its use.

This volume draws on studies that the three of us have conducted for a range of sponsors, including the U.S. Department of Education, the Bill & Melinda Gates Foundation, Microsoft Partners in Learning, the Michael and Susan Dell Foundation, and the National Science Foundation. We are indebted to these organizations not only for their financial support but also for what we have learned through our interactions with their leaders and project officers, who schooled us in the issues that matter to policy makers. The interpretations and opinions expressed in this book are our own, however, and do not necessarily coincide with the views and policies of any particular organization that has sponsored our work.

Appreciation is due also to SRI International. This book would not have been possible without SRI's support in the form of a fellowship that provided me with uninterrupted time to finish the manuscript in the summer of 2013.

Finally, on a personal note, I am grateful to my husband, Richard Leask, for being my greatest cheerleader and for the many months when he took on more than his share of household and family duties so that I could write.

Barbara Means
Menlo Park, California
September 2013

Chapter 1

Introduction

Teachers and students in Taiwan have been sharing educational resources and lesson plans and offering educational courses through "159," a cluster of school Web sites that have reached more than 1.5 million students and over 1,700 schools. In one striking story, the online teacher of the year contest in EduCity was won in 2000 by the teacher of a popular Visual Basics course. Only after the award was announced did the students in the course learn that their online teacher was a 13-year-old boy younger than any of them.

Storefront West, a school in Volusia County, Florida, serves about 50 students who were unsuccessful in traditional high schools. Storefront West students typically take one or two courses a semester through a commercial online learning system, working individually on a desktop computer connected to the Internet. One or two teachers are available in the room where students are logged into their online courses. When students have questions, they turn on a light that signals the teacher in the classroom that they need assistance. The teacher works with students individually to address their questions.

Stanford University announced that one of its most popular computer science courses, Introduction to Artificial Intelligence, would be available online, without charge, in the fall of 2011. Online enrollees would view all lectures, complete homework assignments including computer programming, and take a midterm and a final examination. The course description cited solid understanding of probability and linear algebra as prerequisites. The university was astounded when 160,000 people from 190 countries around the world signed up.

Many different kinds of learners engage in online learning for many different purposes. More and more education institutions are either offering courses online or weighing the option of doing so. Many of the latter institutions are concerned about whether their students will be able to learn online or whether this is just another passing, techno-fad. This book describes today's landscape of online learning, key issues in implementing online learning for different purposes, in different contexts, and for different kinds of learners, and the research that bears on decisions of whether and how to implement learning online.

We will avoid overly simplistic generalizations about online learning "working" or "not working" and instead look for more detailed evidence about the circumstances under which different approaches to online learning are more and less likely to fulfill their intended purposes.

The technology and products available to use for learning online are changing rapidly as are the organizations providing and using these products and the ways in which online learning resources and systems are used. When we started writing this volume, few had ever heard of MOOCs—a topic that became inescapable for even the most casual follower of educational technology by the end of 2012.

Readers should understand that the empirical research base is lagging far behind technology innovations and the adoption of online learning. This book seeks to offer an objective, even-handed presentation of the research that is available and a conceptual framework to inspire additional research by clarifying some of the most pressing gaps in our knowledge about how best to harness online learning's potential.

We will emphasize research trends and issues that transcend individual products and that are likely to be with us long after the particular Web resources and products described here as examples have been supplanted by newer online offerings.

An Area of Rapid Growth

Most U.S. higher education institutions offer online courses (Parsad & Lewis, 2008), and enrollments in online courses have been growing faster than overall higher education enrollments in the past several years. In fall 2011, over 6.7 million students—roughly a third of all U.S. higher education students—were taking at least one online course (Allen & Seaman, 2013).

In the corporate world, according to a report by the American Society of Training and Development (ASTD), about 33 percent of training was delivered electronically in 2007, nearly triple the rate in 2000 (Paradise, 2008). By 2009, ASTD estimated that more than 75 percent of technology-based learning was delivered online (ASTD, 2010).

Although K-12 school systems lagged behind other sectors in moving into online learning, this sector's adoption of e-learning is now proceeding rapidly. Estimates of the number of U.S. K-12 students enrolled in fully online virtual schools range from 200,000 to 275,000 (Miron, Horvitz, & Gulosino, 2013; Watson et al., 2012). In addition, an unknown but very large number of K-12 students receive part of their instruction online while attending regular "brick-and-mortar" schools. Two district surveys commissioned by the Sloan Consortium (Picciano & Seaman, 2007, 2008) produced estimates that 700,000 K-12 public school students took online courses in 2005–6 and over a million students did so in 2007–8—a 43 percent increase in just two years. Wicks

(2010) estimated that there were 1.5 million K-12 course enrollments in 2009–10.

As of late 2010, 48 states and Washington, D.C. supported online educational programs, including state virtual schools that provided courses to supplement conventional offerings, state-led initiatives that provided schools with online resources and tools, and full-time online schools (Watson et al., 2010). The largest state virtual school, the Florida Virtual School (FLVS), had over 260,000 course enrollments in 2010–11.

Christensen, Horn, and Johnson (2008) predict that by 2019 *half* of all U.S. high-school enrollments will be online. That is a long way from the estimated 1.5 million online K-12 course enrollments in 2009–10 (Wicks, 2010), but the shape of the K-12 online learning growth curve from 2001 to 2010 now resembles the exponential growth we saw for school acquisition of computers from 1985 to 1995 and for K-12 Internet connections from 1995 to 2005.

Five states (Alabama, Florida, Idaho, Michigan, and Virginia) require a student to take an online course in order to earn a high-school diploma, as do a large number of districts (Evergreen Education Group, 2012).

What is driving this rapid growth in online learning? We see four, interrelated trends pushing the world in this direction.

First, as technology capabilities have expanded and information technology has become more affordable and mobile, people live more of their lives online. Why should people who schedule dinner reservations, stay in touch with friends, get experts' responses to their questions, and find their way through unfamiliar cities with online resources forgo such capabilities when they want to take a course or learn about a new field? Many parents and students are asking for online learning to supplement what is done in classes. In one survey, 43 percent of middle and high-school students identified online classes as an essential component of their ideal school (Project Tomorrow, 2011).

In states that now require students to take an online course to earn a diploma, the rationale is that they will need to know how to learn online because they will be required to do so in college and throughout their careers. In a world where the state of the art is advancing at an unprecedented rate, people will need to expand their skills repeatedly in order to stay employable.

The second impetus for online learning is the belief that it can address some of education's persistent and emerging challenges. These include the achievement gap and the rate at which students—especially poor and non-Asian minority students—leave high schools and colleges without a diploma. The graduation rate in the U.S. (77 percent) is below the Organisation for Economic Co-operation and Development (OECD) average and well below that of countries with the highest graduation rates (like Germany and Japan, with graduation rates of 97 percent and 95 percent, respectively). The average graduation rate in U.S. public schools was less than 80 percent in

34 states and of these, ten states graduated 70 percent or fewer of the students who were high-school freshmen in 2007–8 (Chapman, Laird, & Kewal Ramani, 2010).

Many districts and schools are turning to online approaches for students who have failed required courses or left school. Credit recovery programs, in which students take (online) courses that they failed previously in face-to-face classes, are probably the fastest growing segment in K-12 online education. One report estimated that among Florida students who took English I and Algebra I courses from FLVS during school year 2006–7, 40 percent of those in English I and 30 percent of those in Algebra I had failed the course previously (Bakia et al., 2011).

Emerging education problems that online learning can address include the shortage of highly skilled, qualified teachers, especially in science and mathematics. As Baby Boomers are reaching retirement age, over a third of this country's teachers are expected to retire in the next decade. Just replacing retiring teachers will require filling a third of a million slots a year for the foreseeable future. The problem is exacerbated by the fact that new teachers do not reach their full potential until they have had three to five years of experience, but half of all new teachers leave the profession within five years (Ingersoll, 2003). While we may be able to find enough young people who want to go into teaching, the question is whether we can find enough with the requisite talent, dedication, and knowledge base to teach a world-class curriculum and to work with the great diversity of America's students. Teacher availability and quality issues are particularly acute in rural areas and in mathematics and science. Wise and Rothman (2010) report, for example, that Georgia has only 88 qualified physics teachers for a state with 440 high schools. Without online education how could we make high-quality physics instruction available to any Georgia high-school student who wants it?

The third driver toward online learning is economic. Studies examining the costs of online learning compared to face-to-face instruction consistently find savings associated with the online option, although costs of both options vary widely, depending on the type of online learning, student–teacher ratio, and the amount of money put into developing online courses or modules. But education policy makers are not waiting for detailed cost analyses before trying online learning as a strategy for saving money. Online learning also provides opportunities to aggregate demand across rural communities that could not afford to hire teachers individually.

Industry has long realized the cost-savings potential of training a far-flung workforce online rather than paying for instructors or students to fly around the world for face-to-face training. Online approaches are especially attractive for kinds of training that are required by law because the online system provides documentation that all required parties have taken the training and embedded assessments can provide evidence that the material was mastered.

Through a process developed by the National Center for Academic Transformation, some higher education programs report that they have reduced personnel costs without cutting full-time positions or sacrificing student learning (Twigg, 2003; 2004). A reorganization of staffing models that relies on technology-assisted instructional activities (e.g., online quizzes with automated scoring instead of hand grading) and lower-paid instructional assistants who relieve faculty from relatively routine tasks allow faculty to focus their efforts on high-expertise aspects of instruction. In practical terms, these cost reduction strategies often translate into reducing the number of face-to-face meetings with full-time faculty as well as increasing student–faculty ratios.

In K-12 education, the economic recession and budget cutting that started in 2008 has led many school districts to consider online learning as a way to cut costs. Replacing classroom-based summer courses with online options has become relatively common. We are also starting to see districts turn to online learning for their regular program in response to budgetary pressures combined with other regulations. In Miami-Dade County School District, the nation's largest, labs for taking online courses were established in 56 schools during school year 2010–11 so that students could spend one class period there online. The district chose this option because state law capped the size of core academic courses at 24 students, and in cases where there were "extra" students needing a course but not enough to warrant another full-time position, the online option provided flexibility and cost savings. Charter schools too are turning to online learning as a way of controlling costs. Many of these schools are targeting students from low-income and under-served communities and providing a high-intensity program, with instruction for nine hours a day and sometimes on Saturday. Charter networks such as Rocketship and Carpe Diem are providing more learning time with fewer teachers by making extensive use of online learning.

And finally, one of the most important drivers for online learning derives not from necessity but from belief in its power to provide better learning experiences. Online learning offers the potential of individualizing the learner's experience so that he is always dealing with material at the right level of difficulty. By embedding brief assessments throughout, learning software can avoid repeating content that the learner has already mastered on the one hand and presenting material for which the student lacks necessary prerequisites on the other. A learning system can diagnose the current learning state of each student, and provide the instructor with both individual student information and summary data at the class level. Arne Duncan, the Secretary of Education, has asserted that it is difficult to see how the U.S. could possibly attain international standards in education achievement without using technology to support this kind of individualization. The U.S. Department of Education's 2010 National

Education Technology Plan (NETP) describes this vision of learner-centered instruction:

> technology is at the core of virtually every aspect of our daily lives and work, and we must leverage it to provide engaging and powerful learning experiences and content, as well as resources and assessments that measure student achievement in more complete, authentic, and meaningful ways. Technology-based learning and assessment systems will be pivotal in improving student learning and generating data that can be used to continuously improve the education system at all levels.
>
> (U.S. Department of Education, 2010b, p. xi)

At the same time that these motivations for online learning have fueled its growth, that growth has given rise to questions about the quality of learning experiences offered online. For example, some Florida parents expressed concern and displeasure when they were surprised to find out that their children would be taking one of their courses online (Herrera, 2011). Quality concerns are especially acute in the case of K-12 and higher education degree programs conducted entirely online. Some two dozen states have prohibited cyber-schools and high-school degree programs offered entirely online (Glass & Welner, 2011).

Considering the potential scale and impact of online learning, as well as the controversies surrounding it, research-based guidance regarding effective online learning practices and their implementation in different contexts is strongly needed.

Defining Online Learning

One source of disagreement about online learning practices and a major contributor to controversies around their effectiveness is the vast array of different practices referred to as online learning. Both information technology and education seem to spawn more than their fair share of jargon, and when you bring the two of them together, the result seems like a catch-phrase-of-the-year phenomenon. What we are calling "online learning" frequently goes by the name of "Web-based learning," "cyber learning," or "e-learning."

Although online learning has much in common with computer-based learning, distance learning, and open educational resources, we feel that it differs from these concepts in some important ways.

As we use the term, "online learning" refers to a learner's interaction with content and/or people via the Internet for the purpose of learning. The learning may be part of a formal course or program or simply something learners pursue for their own interests. We restrict our concept of online learning to learning that occurs with the purpose of finding out information or learning to do something, even if that something is how to play an online game. We do not include incidental learning that may occur in the process of pursuing other goals (for example, what might be learned about different products in the process of shopping). Both teacher-led instruction and resources designed to instruct without the presence of a teacher meet our definition of online learning if they are carried out over the Internet.

The Babson Survey Research Group has been conducting annual surveys on online learning in higher education for over a decade. It uses the proportion of course activity that is Web-based as its basis for describing online learning and its alternatives (Allen & Seaman, 2013). A "traditional" course presents content entirely through speech and text; no online technology is used. A "Web-facilitated" course employs the Web for delivery of up to 29 percent of the course content; a course management system or course Web page may be used to post the syllabus and assignments, but the course is essentially taught face to face with some Web supports for information access. At the other end of the spectrum, an "online course" presents 80 percent or more of its content online; in the prototypical online course there are no face-to-face meetings. Finally, the terms "blended" and "hybrid" are used interchangeably to describe a course where at least 30 percent of the content is delivered online but there are face-to-face meetings for at least 21 percent of the content.

Although we think the percentages used in the Babson Survey Group's work imply an unrealistic degree of precision in instructor and administrator reports, our own use of the terms "Web-enabled," "blended," and "online" corresponds with the essential concepts underlying that group's definitions. We use the term "fully online learning" in cases where all instruction and assessment are carried out using online, Internet-based delivery. In contrast, we call combinations of face-to-face and online learning experiences "blended learning." There are many forms of blended learning (also known as "hybrid" learning), which encompass all of the middle ground in the spectrum between fully face-to-face and fully online instruction (Graham, Allen, & Ure, 2005; U.S. Department of Education, 2010a; Watson et al., 2010).

Debates about the effectiveness, costs, and potential downsides of online learning often feature discussants talking past each other because of a failure to define their terms. For example, after our meta-analysis of the research on online learning was published, one of us participated in a call-in radio show. One of the callers, a community college instructor, took umbrage at the suggestion that blended learning could be more effective than conventional classroom teaching and insisted, "I put my PowerPoint slides online and it didn't make any difference!" We would call this a Web-enabled course, not online learning or blended instruction.

More Definitions

As we have defined it, online learning was not possible prior to the inception of the World Wide Web. Certainly, there were technology-based learning options much earlier. By the 1970s, Patrick Suppes and his colleagues at Stanford University were offering computer-based mathematics instruction that was the forerunner of many of the online math offerings we have today (Suppes, 1965). But computer- or server-based instructional offerings lacked the reach, affordability, and flexibility that are possible today with instruction taking place over the Internet.

Distance learning is a broader concept, as it encompasses any instruction in which the learner and the instructor are physically separated. Because distance learning includes other technologies, going all the way back to print-based correspondence courses, we treat online learning as a subset of distance learning rather than a synonym of it. But some of the research we will examine comes from the distance learning literature, and it remains an important source of insights.

Another important trend related to online learning is that of open educational resources. These resources, available over the Internet for free or at nominal cost, may include courses or course modules (the use of which we would consider online learning), but also may include course syllabi, lesson plans, and other instructional resources intended for use by instructors rather than for direct use by learners. (Though of course instructors can learn online too.)

Our definition of online learning differs from that of open educational resources in that it does not require that the learning experience be offered for free, and indeed, there are many for-profit companies that have become very active in providing online courses and credentials.

The Varied Terrain of Online Learning

The tremendous range and variety in online learning make the field difficult to encapsulate. There have been a number of efforts to delineate types of online learning (Horn & Staker, 2011; Watson et al., 2009), but we see the field as too emergent with too many new variations emerging every day to find a typology terrible useful. Instead, we offer a set of dimensions that can be used to characterize online learning and that readers can use when judging the relevance of various experiences and research studies for their own work. As illustrated in Figure 1.1, we propose characterizing online offerings in four dimensions: context, design features, implementation, and outcomes. Our ability to accumulate knowledge about the kinds of online learning experiences that produce desired effects for specific kinds of learners under a given set of circumstances would be greatly enhanced if every research report used these dimensions

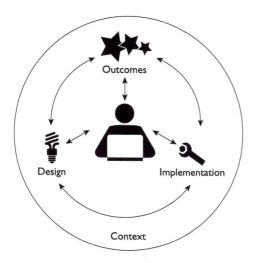

Figure 1.1 Four Dimensions of Online Learning

and an agreed set of more specific features within each dimension to generate comprehensive descriptions of the interventions they studied.

The set of essential online learning intervention features that have emerged from our own work are shown in Table 1.1. These features and terms will appear prominently in the chapters that follow.

Context

In describing the components of each dimension in our conceptual framework, we will begin generally with broad considerations and then move toward finer levels of detail. Under the dimension context, we consider first the *field of use*: whether the online learning application is intended for higher education, K-12 (primary/secondary) education, military or job training, or self-initiated learning. The resources we describe as "mixed field of use" are designed for use in more than one of these fields. A related dimension is the *provider* type: online learning is offered by district and state public K-12 education institutions (e.g., the Michigan Virtual School, Riverside Virtual School); for-profit vendors (e.g., K12 Inc., University of Phoenix); by public or private nonprofit higher education institutions (Arizona State University); other types of nonprofit institutions (National Geographic Society); government agencies (e.g., the U.S. Department of Energy's Online Learning Center); and by consortia of multiple organizations.

Third, we consider the *breadth* of the online offering: whether it is a full certificate or degree program, a formal course or training experience, a unit or

Table 1.1 A Conceptual Framework for Describing Online Learning

Context	
Field of use	K-12, higher education, postsecondary training, self-initiated, mixed
Provider	District, state, for-profit vendor, consortium, nonprofit higher education institution, other nonprofit, government agency, consortium
Breadth	Whole program, course, portion of course, brief episode
Learner's level of preparation	Weak, adequate, strong
Design features	
Modality	Fully online, blended, Web-enabled
Pacing	Independent mastery-paced, class-paced, mixture
Pedagogy	Expository, practice environment, exploratory, collaborative
Online communication synchrony	Asynchronous, synchronous, both
Intended instructor role online	Active instruction, small presence, none
Intended student role online	Listen and read; complete problems and answer questions; explore simulation and resource; collaborate with peers in building knowledge
Role of online assessments	Determine if student ready for new content, tell system how to support student, provide student and teacher with information about learning state, calculate student's risk of failure
Source of feedback	Automated, teacher, peers, mixed, none
Implementation	
Learning location	School, home, other, mixed
Co-located facilitator	Primary instructor, monitor and facilitator, absent
Student–instructor ratio	
Level of online student–content interaction	High, medium, low
Level of online student–instructor interaction	High, medium, low
Level of online student–student interaction	High, medium, low
Intended outcomes	
Cognitive	Declarative knowledge, procedural skills, problem solving and strategies
Engagement	Primary goal, secondary goal, not explicit goal
Productivity	Course pass rate, graduation rate, time to completion, cost
Learning to learn	Self regulation, new media skills

module within a course or training program, or a brief learning episode or "educational object."

A final, important component of the context dimension of online learning is the nature of the learners. Some important learner characteristics—average age and amount of prior schooling—are largely synonymous with the field of use. But other important learner characteristics include the *learner's level of preparation*, both facility with the basic skills of reading and mathematics and comfort with using technology. Other important learner characteristics include fluency in the language of instruction, sensory disabilities, and ability to regulate one's own learning.

Instructional Design

There is an almost infinite number of possible features for the design of an online learning experience, but our conceptual framework is limited to features that some research suggests influence the outcomes of online learning. First among these is what we call *modality:* the distinction between online, blended, and Web-enabled learning experiences discussed above.

Next, there is the *pacing* of instruction. Allowing students to begin learning and to proceed to the next learning module when (and only when) they have mastered the current module is a practice incorporated into many online learning systems, as it was in the computer-assisted learning systems of earlier decades. It is also possible to have a fixed or class-based schedule for when students are to be online and when learning components are supposed to be completed, much as the typical classroom-based course is run. Finally many instructors and online learning providers are experimenting with various strategies falling between these two pacing options, with some required times for online interaction or some completion deadlines but more flexibility than found in traditional classroom-based courses.

A related design feature is the *synchrony* provided by the technology used in the online learning system. In the earlier days of distance learning, some systems were designed to give learners in all locations the sense of being in the classroom, and they provided for synchronous (same time, different place) communication only. Other learning systems relied entirely on asynchronous (different time, different place) communication using materials posted online and discussion boards. Some researchers found that learning interventions using asynchronous communication were more effective than those using synchronous communication, but interest in the topic has receded with the dominance of modern, Web-based learning systems that support both synchronous and asynchronous interactions.

Describing aspects of the design dimensions becomes more complex as we move to consideration of the nature of the instructor and student roles. The intended *instructor role online* may be to lead instruction and conduct unscripted communication with students or may be primarily one of monitoring student progress and providing encouragement. In some cases the learner works directly with the online content and there is no online teacher at all, or an automated avatar takes on the role that an instructor might play in the classroom. The dominant intended *student role online* can vary markedly from listening or reading; to working on problems or answering questions; to exploring a set of resources, a simulation or game; to working with peers in a collaborative project. Most online courses try to support a mixture of several or all of these student activities, but it is usually possible to identify the role that will consume most of the student's time online.

Online courses usually incorporate assessments, and the emerging ability to analyze the learner's "click stream" is stimulating the creation of less obtrusive ways to get information about a learner's level of understanding and degree of engagement with the learning system without administering anything that looks like a conventional quiz or test (U.S. Department of Education, 2013). The *role of online assessments* will determine their design. In systems using mastery learning principles (also referred to as competency-based learning), the assessments are used to determine if the learner is ready to move on to new content. In more sophisticated adaptive systems, assessments may be designed to provide data that the system can use to determine how much to scaffold the student in future, for example, with more or less explicit hints. Assessments may be designed simply to provide a measure of student performance, which can tell the student and the teacher how much has been accomplished. Some learning systems combine assessments with software using predictive analytics to calculate the likelihood that the student will complete the course successfully in the time available.

A final feature of the design dimension is the feedback mechanisms built into the software. Immediate feedback supports learning and, for some types of questions and problems, scoring can be automated so that the system provides it. Other online learning environments are designed with the expectation that the instructor will be responsible for providing feedback on students' online work. Other systems provide supports for students to evaluate and provide feedback on each other's work, an area currently being explored by MOOC providers as a strategy for dealing with more open-ended assignments in online courses with extremely large enrollments.

Implementation

The third dimension in our model is implementation. No matter how a course or learning system has been designed, students may have different experiences depending on how it is implemented in practice. Typically, many decisions about implementation are made by schools or teachers, but some are made, at least in part, by students. The first feature under this dimension is the *learning location*, whether school, home, some other setting, or a mixture. A related feature is the presence and role of a *co-located facilitator.* In school-based implementations, this person may be the student's primary instructor with the online activities serving a secondary role or it could be someone who is in a learning lab with students learning online whose primary role is to make sure that the technology is working and that students stay on task. For home-based learning, a parent or other adult may assume one or both of these functions.

An important dimension of implementation from a cost-effectiveness standpoint is the *student–teacher ratio.* Some online learning applications are designed to preserve the typical ratio for the relevant grade level while others look to have several times the normal number of students per instructor in order to gain efficiency. The student–instructor ratio can be as low as 1:1 (online tutoring) and, with the advent of MOOCs, as high as hundreds of thousands to one.

Finally, regardless of the designer's intentions and what the online learning system technology will support, learning experiences get implemented with different levels of *student–content, student–instructor,* and *student–student interaction.* As we will describe later, these are some of the most influential aspects of online learning.

Outcomes

Finally, in describing and evaluating online learning resources it is important to keep in mind the intended outcomes. Most of the time we think about the *cognitive* outcomes valued by schools and colleges. But there are different kinds of cognitive outcomes and research and theory suggests that different kinds of learning experiences best enhance the different types, which can be described as declarative knowledge (e.g., learning the motor vehicle laws for your state), procedural skills (e.g., fluency solving algebra word problems), or problem solving and strategies for future learning (e.g., the split-half strategy for troubleshooting computer systems).

Another important category of outcomes has to do with the learner's affective responses and *engagement* in the online activity. For much self-initiated learning and for some of the activities selected by teachers, the extent of student engagement is valued as much as, or more than, cognitive outcomes.

From an education policy perspective, one of the most important classes of outcomes are *productivity measures.* These include things such as the course pass rate, a school's graduation rate, the time it takes a student to complete a program of study, or the costs of obtaining each course completion.

Finally, technology advocates believe that online learning experiences are vital for obtaining *learning-to-learn outcomes.* Two major classes of these outcomes dominate the literature. The first has to do with what is sometimes called self-regulation—the ability to plan and execute learning activities independently without needing someone else to tell you what to do and when to do it. Self-regulation skills include having an awareness of what you do and do not understand or know how to do and being able to set up and adhere to a schedule that meets completion deadlines. The other important class of learning-to-learn outcomes concerns the use of the new, Internet-based media themselves. As these media have become such a large part of our lives—socially and professionally—the mastery of online learning and communication skills has become a valued outcome in its own right.

Deconstructing the Rhetoric Around the Advantages of Online Learning

Proponents of online learning and the marketing of online products tend to focus on a set of practices that are easier to implement with technology and presumably linked to better learning outcomes. Some of the most frequently touted features and qualities are "personalized," "adaptive," "engaging," "game-like," "interactive," "media rich," and "providing immediate feedback."

Unfortunately for the people choosing to buy learning products and for practitioners attempting to redesign their instruction to incorporate online resources and activities, many of these terms lack clear, commonly shared definitions. A quick search for the definition of "personalized," for example, returns some very different descriptions:

- "finding the best ways to engage with people with different interests, passions, and ways of thinking"—principal Paul Lorette on his Ready for Learning blog
- "empower[ing] each student to learn the way they learn best—when, where, and how they want"—Pearson Learning Solutions Web site
- "providing adjustments to what is learned, the pace at which learning happens and the methods of learning based on students' needs and performance"—Desire2Learn Web site

The 2010 NETP of the U.S. Department of Education provides a somewhat more concrete definition of personalization: "In an environment that is fully personalized, the learning objectives and content as well as the pace may all vary" (U.S. Department of Education, 2010b, p. 12).

The NETP casts personalization as a more multi-faceted matching to learner needs and interests than *individualization*, which it defines as tailoring the pace of learning to each student, and *differentiation*, which it defines as varying the learning content or pedagogy to match learner preferences while keeping the learning objectives common across students. While these definitions serve to distinguish the three terms, they are not widely used in the field. Most often the term "differentiation" is used to refer to the practice of dividing students within a classroom into groups based on achievement level and giving them different learning objectives and content matched to their level.

Vendors often describe online learning products and courses as "personalized" because learners can advance at their own pace. Essentially, this feature is what was called "mastery learning" three decades ago. The content to be learned is organized into modules; modules are sequenced from what are presumed to be easier or more basic content to more advanced content; and learners begin with the module on the simplest skill or knowledge not yet mastered and then complete an assessment on which mastery must be demonstrated (typically by getting a set proportion of items correct) before moving on to the next module. The research literature suggests that mastery learning pedagogy can help low-achieving students but is not always effective (Kulik, Kulik, & Bangert-Drowns, 1990). High-ability students sometimes perceive mastery learning as boring. In the meta-analysis we did for the U.S. Department of Education, for example, the studies of online learning involving independent practice (which typically meant self-paced, mastery learning) produced weaker outcomes relative to conventional face-to-face instruction than did the other online pedagogies (Means, Toyama et al., 2013).

Because of the lack of agreement or common usage around the term "personalization," we prefer to use more specific descriptions of just what an online learning system does to tailor the provided experience to the individual. We also examine learning systems to ascertain the basis on which the system makes differentiations along these dimensions. Some systems rely on the teacher to determine the level of content and support each student should receive. Some administer a diagnostic test or assessment of learner preferences when learners first start with the system (U.S. Department of Education, 2010b). The most sophisticated learning systems perform "assessment on the fly" with the system itself using the learner's prior actions to determine the approach presumed to be the best fit for that learner (U.S. Department of Education, 2013), as described above in the discussion of the roles assessment may take within an online learning system.

Although promotional materials characterize qualities like personalization, gamification, and media rich as "research-based," the available supporting research typically is limited to a few very specific applications of some version of the principle, rather than evidence of a positive impact of the way the principle has been implemented in the particular product under consideration. Taking rich media, as an example, while marketing materials often equate the volume of media with courseware quality, the research literature actually suggests a much more complex set of design principles. In many cases, excessive use of multiple media can overload the learner or lead her to focus on superficial aspects of the media rather than the underlying content to be learned. (Some of the principles for making good media design choices that psychologists have derived from their research are discussed in Chapter 2.)

Clearly, there is a major gap between the loose usage of learning terms in everyday discussion and product promotion and the much more narrow, operational definitions required by research. Through this volume, we hope to arm the reader with the knowledge needed to make sense of, and to question, research findings and claims about online learning product features and outcomes.

The Contents of this Volume

Readers come to any book with a wide range of backgrounds and in pursuit of varying purposes. Some readers are likely to be interested primarily in online learning practices and research within a particular domain—be it higher education, life-long learning, or elementary and secondary education. Others will be concerned with cross-cutting issues, such as the best way to structure online instruction or the use of learning analytics. We have attempted to write chapters in such a way that each can stand alone so that readers can select those that are most pertinent to their own concerns.

Chapter 2 presents an overview of research on the effectiveness of online learning, drawing on an extensive meta-analysis that we conducted and on other meta-analyses and systematic surveys of the research literature. With the needs of institutional decision makers considering whether or not to support the provision of online learning options in mind, this chapter summarizes the best available evidence addressing not just the question of how outcomes of online learning compare to those of conventional classroom-based instruction but also the features of online and blended learning associated with stronger student outcomes.

Chapter 3 describes the major role that online learning is playing in higher (tertiary) education. It describes the complexities entailed in trying to compare the effectiveness of online and blended college courses relative to conventional, classroom-based courses. In addition, the origins, current practice, and state of research concerning MOOCs are discussed in this chapter.

Chapter 4 takes up the topic of the online learning that is all around us—learning that occurs outside of any formal education or training program. It includes a description and discussion of emerging research on online games as contexts for learning useful skills and concepts.

Chapter 5 describes how K-12 educators are blending online learning with classroom-based instruction. It describes different purposes and models for blending online and teacher-led instruction. The chapter concludes with a set of recommendations for the design of online learning resources for use in classrooms and for the implementation of blended learning models within schools.

In Chapter 6 we describe the fully Internet-based approaches of online universities and virtual schools, present available data on student performance in the courses and programs offered by these entities, and discuss the controversy surrounding their receipt of public funding.

Chapter 7 deals with the challenge of designing online and blended learning approaches that will be effective for less-prepared and less-independent students. This chapter includes a discussion of research-based principles for designing online learning activities, and should be of particular interest to instructional designers and those who will be teaching online or blended courses.

Chapter 8 takes up the issue of costs and benefits of online education and the potential for online learning to increase educational productivity.

We conclude with Chapter 9, which summarizes the main themes cutting across the preceding chapters and recommends an agenda for future research, data gathering, and data use.

Chapter 2

Research on the Effectiveness of Online Learning

Online learning inspires strong views both pro and con. Depending on which media accounts you attend to, the growing use of online instruction portends either a transformational increase in educational access and personalization (Collins & Halverson, 2009; Swan, 2003) or the cynical degradation of educational quality at public expense (Glass, 2009).

The purpose of this chapter is first to summarize available empirical research on the effectiveness of online and blended learning approaches, and second to describe why the field needs to move beyond studies that ask whether online learning "works" and address principles for designing and implementing online learning for different purposes, circumstances, and types of learners.

The Nature and Advantages of Meta-Analysis

We have bounded the subject for this volume to a great extent by limiting our discussion to research on learning online, rather than learning in general or all technology-assisted learning. But even within these boundaries, a description of all the research studies ever conducted would require an encyclopedia. Inevitably, we would end up selecting some studies to describe and others to leave out. Studies would use different methods and measure different outcomes and produce different findings. There would be no easy way to summarize what it all means or to know whether our compilation of studies and interpretation of their results were made without bias.

Meta-analysis is a well-developed technique for addressing this problem of summarizing the research literature in a way that is systematic, quantitative, and replicable (Smith & Glass, 1977). Meta-analysis entails defining the research literature of interest, searching for it methodically, and expressing each research study's outcomes according to the same standardized measure—the "effect size." An effect size is a standardized measure of the size of the difference between the averages for two groups or "conditions" being compared. Statistically speaking, this is the difference between the treatment and comparison group means divided by the pooled standard deviation. The advantage of using the standardized effect size metric is that it makes it possible to combine results across studies that examined different outcomes and used different measurement instruments.

Meta-analysis has a number of advantages:

- It requires an explicit and systematic process for reviewing existing research, thereby making the analyst's assumptions, procedures, evidence, and conclusions explicit.
- It provides a more differentiated and sophisticated summary of existing research than qualitative summaries or "vote-counting" based on statistical significance because it takes into consideration the strength of evidence from each empirical study.
- It produces synthesized effect estimates with considerably more statistical power than individual studies.
- It allows an examination of differential effects related to different study features (Lipsey & Wilson, 2001).

SRI's Meta-Analysis for the U.S. Department of Education

The U.S. Department of Education funded SRI to conduct a meta-analysis of studies of the relative effectiveness of online and face-to-face instruction. Our literature search and estimation of the average impact across studies relied on previously published research on fully online and blended learning interventions.

We conducted computerized searches of online research databases for the years from 1996 through July 2008 and supplemented these searches with a review of citations in prior meta-analyses of distance learning and a manual search of the last three years of key journals in online and distance education. These searches returned 1,132 abstracts from studies of online learning, which we then screened to see if they met our inclusion criteria (U.S. Department of Education, 2010a).

In contrast to many previous meta-analyses, we excluded studies of computer-based or distance learning that did not use the Internet, and we confined our analysis to measures of student learning and did not consider effects on students' perception of how well they learned or their liking for the online experience. To be included in our meta-analysis, a study had to:

- contrast instruction conducted wholly or partially over the Internet with face-to-face instruction
- measure student learning outcomes for both a treatment and a comparison group

- use a rigorous quantitative research design
- provide adequate information for effect size calculation.

From the 1,132 abstracts, 99 online learning research studies were identified that compared an online condition (either entirely online or a blended condition with online and face-to-face components) with face-to-face instruction and used an experimental or controlled quasi-experimental design with an objective measure of student learning outcomes.

Of the 99 studies comparing online and face-to-face conditions, 45 provided sufficient data to compute or estimate 50 independent effect sizes. The types of learners in the meta-analysis studies were about evenly split between students in college or earlier years of education and learners in graduate programs or professional training. The average learner age in a study ranged from 13 to 44, but only five studies with seven independent effect size estimates dealt with K-12 education.

The studies encompassed a wide range of learning content, including computer science, teacher education, mathematics, and languages, with medicine or health care being the most common subject area.

We computed the average difference between learning outcomes in conditions incorporating online learning and those employing business-as-usual face-to-face instruction. We computed an average effect size for the entire set of 50 contrasts and then separately for those involving fully online instruction and those contrasting blended learning with wholly face-to-face conditions.

Meta-analysis of all 50 effects found that, on average, students in conditions that included significant amounts of learning online performed better than students receiving face-to-face instruction by .20 standard deviations, a modest, but statistically significant, amount. However, the subset of studies employing blended learning approaches was entirely responsible for the observed online advantage: The online advantage relative to purely face-to-face instruction was significant statistically in those studies contrasting blended learning with traditional face-to-face instruction but not in those studies contrasting purely online learning with face-to-face conditions. The magnitude of the blended learning advantage was +.35, about one-third of a standard deviation.[1]

Other Meta-Analyses and Syntheses

Although our meta-analysis remains one of the most comprehensive looking exclusively at Internet-based learning outcomes, there have been a number of prior and subsequent research syntheses and meta-analyses.

Bernard et al. (2004) conducted a thorough and wide-ranging meta-analysis of distance education studies, involving "telecourses" where the instructor's class is broadcast to students in other locations as well as correspondence courses and Internet-based instruction. These researchers examined 699 independent effect sizes from 232 studies published from 1985 to 2001. Bernard et al. (2004) found an overall effect size close to zero for student achievement, meaning that on average studies comparing distance and classroom-based instruction found that students achieved equivalent amounts in the two conditions. Follow-up analyses, to be described below, found a small positive average effect for some kinds of distance learning and a small negative effect for other types.

Cavanaugh et al. (2004) conducted a meta-analysis on Internet-based programs for K-12 students. These researchers combined 116 outcomes of various types from 14 studies published between 1999 and 2004 to compute an overall weighted effect, which was not statistically different from zero.

Zhao et al. (2005) examined 98 effect sizes from 51 studies published from 1996 to 2002. Like Bernard et al.'s study, this meta-analysis focused on distance education courses delivered via multiple generations of technology for a wide variety of learners, and found an overall effect size near zero. However, the subset of studies contrasting blended learning approaches (estimated as 60–80 percent "media involvement" by the researchers) to face-to-face instruction did have an average effect that was significantly positive.

Sitzmann et al. (2006) examined 96 studies published from 1996 to 2005 that compared Web-based and face-to-face training for job-related knowledge or skills. The authors found that in general, Web-based training was slightly more effective than face-to-face training for acquiring declarative knowledge ("knowing that"), and equivalent to face-to-face instruction for acquiring procedural knowledge ("knowing how"). Those studies contrasting blended learning with purely face-to-face training found that the former was more effective for both kinds of learning outcomes.

Two recent meta-analyses, both coming out of GLASS (Games, Learning, and Assessment) Lab research funded by the Gates and MacArthur Foundations, examined the effectiveness of digital games and simulations. In studies comparing learning outcomes for time spent with digital games versus other instructional methods, games proved modestly more effective overall, with an effect size of +0.29 across 13 studies (Clark et al., 2013). D'Angelo et al. (2013) found a larger effect size for the use of online simulations; 36 studies measuring the effect of incorporating simulations into science instruction found an average effect of +0.67 on student achievement. It should be noted that many of the studies synthesized in these meta-analyses had used researcher-developed assessments of learning. Studies using researcher-developed assessments usually show more positive effects than those using standardized achievement test because the assessment and intervention are more likely to be closely aligned (indeed, in some cases they may be overly aligned).

Jaggers (2011) did not conduct a formal meta-analysis but she did compile a set of studies contrasting online and classroom-based courses and provide a "vote-count" summary of the number of effects favoring online versus face-to-face instruction. Jaggers looked for studies of full courses published in 2000 or more recently in Canada or the U.S. in which there was either random assignment to instructional condition or an attempt to control statistically for any pre-existing group differences. She identified 36 studies meeting her inclusion criteria. Eight of the studies had assigned students to instructional conditions at random; among these, six found no difference in learning outcomes, one favored the online condition, and one favored the face-to-face condition. Jaggers judged an additional five studies to be "relatively well controlled." Among these, one found no difference between conditions, one favored the online condition, and three favored the face-to-face condition. The remaining 20 studies were judged to be "less well controlled."[2] For these she reports that most showed positive effects of online learning or no significant difference between conditions but she did not provide details.

A meta-analysis of the effectiveness of 22 "next generation learning" projects bringing online learning components to bear in college courses (Means, Shear et al., 2013) found an average effect size of +.16, which was not significantly different from 0. Eight individual projects did have effects indicating a significant difference from outcomes obtained in conventional versions of the courses; seven favored the online or blended learning condition and one favored conventional instruction.

Overall, the preponderance of the meta-analyses suggests that purely online and purely face-to-face instruction usually produce statistically equivalent learning outcomes. Meta-analyses of studies comparing blended to purely face-to-face instruction generally find modestly better outcomes for the former, but, as in the simulation and gaming meta-analyses described above, the blended learning conditions in these studies typically involve instructional resources and interactions with no counterparts in the classroom-based condition. In the chapters that follow we will describe a number of individual studies comparing online and classroom-based course effects (e.g., Bowen et al., 2012). These individual studies do not, however, contradict the overall tenor of the meta-analysis literature described here.

Limitations in the Studies Available for Meta-Analysis

The review above suggests that the available evidence supports the conclusion that on average there is no significant difference between purely online and purely face-to-face learning and that there may be modest advantages for blended learning approaches. Despite the increasing volume of studies pointing to these results, we need to be cautious in their interpretation. The recent meta-analyses described in this chapter were more selective than earlier research syntheses in that they included only studies using random assignment or statistical controls for any pre-existing differences between students in the learning conditions being compared in a quasi-experiment. Even so, many of the studies available for inclusion in these meta-analyses have had other weaknesses.

Multiple Differences Between Instructional Conditions

A problem already alluded to is that in many of the studies reporting online learning effects, multiple aspects of instruction varied between the conditions being compared. In the set of studies we analyzed for the U.S. Department of Education, we coded studies for the equivalence of the content coverage and learning time in the conditions being contrasted. We found significant variation in effect sizes between those studies in which the curriculum and instruction were judged to be identical or nearly identical in the online and face-to-face conditions and those in which curriculum and instruction were judged to vary in the two conditions. Although the online effect was significantly positive for both subsets of studies, it was significantly larger for those studies where curriculum and pedagogy were judged to vary across conditions (Means, Toyama et al., 2013).

We noted also that within the subset of studies in our meta-analysis on blended instruction, the blended treatment typically involved more than simply putting some aspect of existing instruction on the Internet. Rather, the blended learning conditions tended to result from a redesign of instruction to extend learning time or promote greater engagement with content. The online activities in blended learning conditions were likely to involve additional instructional resources and activities that encouraged interactions among learners. In light of this confounding of instructional features and delivery medium, we have noted that the superior learning outcomes in blended learning conditions in the studies in our meta-analysis need to be interpreted with care (Means, Toyama et al., 2013).

Some researchers advocate for studies providing a "fair test" of the effectiveness of online learning by keeping everything (including the instructor, the instructional strategies, and all content) the same except the medium of information transmission.[3] Clark (1994) asserts that this is the right kind of design to test the effect of instructional medium and that when such a fair comparison is made, there will never be a difference between instructional conditions because it is instructional content and design, rather than medium, that determines learning outcomes.

We concur with Clark's assertion that the key variables are those of instructional content and design, and make that point in discussing our meta-analysis results (Means, Toyama et al., 2013; U.S. Department of Education, 2010a). However, we also agree with learning technology advocates that there are affordances of technology that cannot be replicated in conventional classroom-based instruction. The greatest promise of learning technology lies not in doing what we have always done better, faster, or more cheaply but rather in providing kinds of learning experiences that would be impossible without technology (Fishman & Dede, in preparation).

Rather than trying to compare the outcomes of the non-existent chimera of "online learning in general" to the equally under-specified "typical classroom," researchers would do well to focus their efforts on particular kinds of online learning experiences that capitalize on the things that technology is differentially suited to provide. Learning technology researchers provide different enumerations of these affordances, but almost everyone's list includes:

- the ability to render concrete visual representations of abstract concepts
- increased interactivity between the learner and the content to be learned
- immediate feedback for students and instructors
- customizability of the pace, content complexity, interface, and amount of scaffolding for individual learners
- ability to immerse the learner in complex, lifelike environments and challenges
- automated recording of detailed data of each learner's interactions on the learning system over time.

Many online learning resources combine a number of these affordances. Online simulations, for example, can not only illustrate processes that are too large, too small, or too fast or slow to be observed directly in classrooms, but can also enable learners to interact with the simulation, changing certain variables and observing how a single change is propagated throughout the system being modeled. The D'Angelo et al. (2013) meta-analysis described above suggests that such simulations have large effects on student learning.

By necessity, a study in which everything except communication medium is held constant between the online and the face-to-face condition is one in which the full power of technology is not being exploited. As Swan (2003) notes, "Trying to make online education 'the same' most likely will lead to less than optimal learning, when, in fact, online education has the potential to support significant paradigm changes in teaching and learning" (p. 3).

An experiment conducted by Figlio, Rush, and Yin (2010), which they describe as "the first causal evidence of the effects of live versus Internet-based instruction in a university course delivery setting" (p. 19), illustrates how impoverished the uses of technology are in such "fair test" studies.

Figlio, Rush, and Yin (2010) studied an undergraduate economics course normally taught in a Web-enabled fashion. The faculty member lectured in a large lecture hall several times a week, and teaching assistants conducted smaller discussion sessions once a week. In addition, students had access to what Figlio and his colleagues describe as a "rich web-based learning environment to supplement the class lectures" (p. 7). The class Web site contained links to videos of the instructor's lectures, online quizzes, past course examinations, and other resources. For their experiment, Figlio and his colleagues randomly assigned volunteer students to either attend lectures in the lecture hall or view videotapes of the lectures online. Access to the other Web resources for the course and to the teaching-assistant-led discussion sessions was the same for both groups. Hence, their experiment tested whether there is a difference between watching lectures "live" or over the Internet. While the study's results might interest some administrators wondering whether they could substitute online lectures for live attendance, they hardly test the potential of online learning to improve learning.

Differential Attrition Rates

Another methodological problem is differential attrition from online and classroom-based instructional conditions. Even if students in the two conditions are equivalent at the start of the experiment, if weaker students tend to drop out of online learning conditions, the experiment will be biased in a way favoring online learning. Unfortunately, many research publications do not report the attrition rates for the conditions being compared.

In the studies included in the meta-analysis we conducted for the U.S. Department of Education, for example, retention rates were available for only 30 percent of the comparisons. For those studies for which retention rates for both conditions were reported, seven had equivalent retention in the two conditions, four had better retention in the face-to-face condition, and four had better retention in the fully online or blended condition.[4] The length of instruction studied in the research we summarized was often less than a full course, however; retention rates for full courses are typically lower for online courses than for those that are based wholly or partially in the classroom (see the discussion of this issue in Chapter 7).

Brief Units of Instruction and Small Sample Sizes

Another limitation of some of the online learning studies available for meta-analysis is that they had relatively small sample sizes. Of the 50 comparisons in the U.S. Department of Education meta-analysis, for example, ten involved fewer than 50 students. Studies with small samples have less power to detect differences between different forms of instruction if there are such differences than do studies with more participants. One of the advantages of meta-analysis, however, is that it provides greater power for detecting effects.

In a related vein, 19 of the studies we analyzed involved instructional timeframes of less than a month. Researchers at Columbia University's Community

College Research Center (Jaggers & Bailey, 2010) point out that such short-term interventions may not represent the results for entire courses. Differences may not show up during a short intervention that would be apparent over a full academic term.

Part of the reason that few controlled studies of online and blended learning involve entire courses and large samples is because it is difficult to obtain permission to conduct such studies (Bowen et al., 2012; Figlio, Rush, & Yin, 2010). As a matter of policy, many colleges and universities will not allow students to be assigned to an online course section against their will, thus ruling out random assignment for any students except those who volunteer to let a researcher assign them to an online or face-to-face section at random. Figlio, Rush, and Yin (2010) found that a relatively small proportion of students volunteer under such circumstances, even when offered extra credit toward their course grade for doing so.

Looking Backward Rather than Forward

Meta-analysis has been described as a statistician's rearview mirror. The technique can be used only once enough studies addressing the same intervention or practice have been conducted and made public. Technology-based resources or instructional approaches used by only a few of the most adventurous institutions and instructors today may be commonplace tomorrow, as evidenced by the Khan Academy in K-12 education and MOOCs in the field of higher education. But impact studies on such new approaches were not in the published literature at the time we conducted our meta-analysis or wrote this volume. In a field as fast-changing as instructional technology, meta-analyses will always be subject to the criticism that they are looking backward rather than forward (U.S. Department of Education, 2013).

Variables that Moderate the Online Learning Effect

When the effect sizes being summarized in a meta-analysis are highly variable, as is the case with online and blended learning studies, analysts typically look for features of the studies associated with differences in effect size. Those features with a statistically significant association with effect size are called "moderator variables." Table 2.1 displays a set of instructional design dimensions that vary across different online learning implementations. A number of meta-analyses of online and distance learning effectiveness studies, our own included, have attempted to code the research studies on these dimensions and found that only a minority of research articles provide this kind of information. Research studies comparing online instruction to conventional face-to-face instruction or different kinds of online learning to each other can better serve

Table 2.1 Online Learning Design Dimensions

Dimension	Example values
Modality	Fully online
	Blended with over 50% online but at least 25% FTF
	Blended with 25–50% online
	Web-enabled FTF
Pacing	Self-paced (open entry and open exit)
	Class-paced
	Class-paced with some self-paced elements
Student–instructor ratio	≤ 35 to 1
	36–99 to 1
	100–999 to 1
	≥ 1,000 to 1
Pedagogy	Expository
	Practice environment
	Exploratory
	Collaborative
Instructor role online	Active instruction online
	Small presence online
	None
Student role online	Listen or read
	Complete problems or answer questions
	Explore simulation and resources
	Collaborate with peers
Online communication synchrony	Asynchronous and synchronous
	Asynchronous only
	Synchronous only
	None
Role of online assessments	Determine if student ready for new content
	Tell system how to support the student (basis for adaptive instruction)
	Provide student or teacher with information about learning state
	Input to grade
	Identify students at risk of failure
Source of feedback	Automated
	Teacher
	Peers

the field if they describe these features for all of the instructional conditions being compared (including classroom-based "business as usual").

Table 2.2 illustrates how the dimensions in Table 2.1 could be used to describe typical examples of three currently popular forms of online instruction (independent learning online, online community of learners, and MOOCs).

Table 2.2 Contrasting Forms of Online Learning in Terms of Instructional Design Features

	Independent online learning	Online community of learners	MOOCs[a]
Pacing	Self-paced; open entry and open exit	Class-paced with some self-paced elements	Class-paced with self-paced elements
Student–instructor ratio	Varies	~ ratio as FTF classes	1000s to 1
Instructor role online	Instructor not teaching online; may monitor progress and motivate students	Support students' knowledge building	Transmit knowledge
Student–student interaction online	Minimal or absent	Extensive	Varies, but typically limited
Pedagogy	Expository + practice environment	Collaborative and exploratory	"Bite-size" expository + practice environment
Student role online	Listen or read; complete problems or assignments	Explore; collaborate; complete assignments	Listen or read; complete problems or assignments
Role of embedded assessments	Determine if student is ready for new content; may be input to grade	Provide student with information; may be input to grade	Provide student with information; typically not input to grade (except for designated midterm and final assessments for the minority of students taking the MOOC for credit)
Source of feedback	Automated	Varies; may include automated feedback, teacher feedback, and peer feedback	Automated for close-ended questions and assignments; peer feedback for open-ended projects and assignments

[a] This description is based on the best-known MOOCs, those provided by Coursera and Udacity. Other forms of MOOCs, sometimes called "Canadian" or "cMOOCs," have quite different instructional practices, as discussed in Chapter 3.

It illustrates the tremendous diversity of experiences labeled "online learning." When such diverse treatments are compared to equally diverse conditions of face-to-face instruction, it is little wonder that relative learning outcomes vary from study to study.

To explore reasons why studies of the same phenomenon might find very different effect sizes, researchers conducting a meta-analysis code each study for variables that might influence the treatment's effect on the outcome under investigation. In the meta-analysis we conducted for the U.S. Department of Education, we were actually more interested in the moderator variable analysis testing the influence of different practices (such as incorporation of opportunities to communicate online with peers) and conditions (such as the type of school and subject being studied) than we were in the average effect size. We applied a coding scheme to each of the 50 contrasts in the meta-analysis, classifying them as a set of conditions, practices, and methodological variables that might moderate the effects of online learning.

One key practice, the blending of online and classroom-based instruction, proved to be very influential, as has already been discussed. We tested 11 other online learning practices as well, and only one of these attained statistical significance. This variable was the pedagogical approach used in the online instruction.

The dominant pedagogy used in the online condition in each contrast was coded as one of three types: expository (transmission through audio or text), interactive (working with peers online), or independent practice. We found that studies in which students worked collaboratively online and those in which they worked with online explanations or lectures (expository pedagogy) produced learning outcomes that on average exceeded those of students in the corresponding face-to-face control group. In studies in which the online activity consisted primarily of independent practice with online content, on the other hand, online students' learning outcomes were equivalent to, but not better than, those of students in the control groups.

When we analyzed the effectiveness of online learning under different conditions, there were no differences in effect size related to publication year, student grade level, or subject matter. Study design features such as sample size, whether or not the study used random assignment, and whether or not the same instructor did the teaching in the online and face-to-face conditions did not influence the effect size significantly either.

The earlier meta-analyses described above also included coding of studies for various features and testing of those features as moderator variables. Bernard et al. (2004) found a small but significant positive effect for what they called asynchronous distance education, which included Internet-based and correspondence courses, and a small but significant negative effect for asynchronous distance education, which included the telecourses and satellite-based delivery.

Cavanaugh et al. (2004) found no significant moderator variables in their meta-analysis of online learning in K-12 education. In contrast, the meta-analysis of online learning studies by Zhao et al. (2005) and the meta-analysis by Sitzmann et al. (2006), like ours, found stronger results relative to purely face-to-face instruction for blends of online and face-to-face elements. Zhao et al. also report that a medium to high level of teacher activity online is associated with better learning outcomes than is either teacher inactivity or a very high level of teacher direction online.

In a second meta-analysis published in 2009, Bernard and his colleagues applied a variant of the usual moderator variable analysis approach. Rather than coding each practice as present or absent in the treatment condition in each study, they looked at the conditions being compared and made a judgment as to which included more of the practice of interest. Their analysis included studies comparing different forms of online learning as well as studies comparing online to face-to-face conditions. They point out that in the former type of study, it is actually very difficult to specify which condition is the experimental treatment and which the control. For each comparison, they identified the condition that was stronger in each of three kinds of interaction: teacher–student, student–student, and student–content. They found that for each of these kinds of interaction, the instructional condition providing for more interaction produced stronger learning results. Of the three kinds of interaction, student–content interaction proved to be the most potent (Bernard et al., 2009). These findings are the basis for including these three types of interaction in our conceptual model for describing online learning (see Chapter 1).

Variables that have been found to moderate online learning effects should be measured and reported in future research. The heterogeneity of online learning effect estimates makes it clear that we are not dealing with a single "treatment" with consistent effects across settings and implementation regimens. To the contrary, the type of learning that is being fostered and the specific design of the online learning experience and the relationship between that experience and other learning opportunities appear to be important sources of variance.

Limitations of Moderator Variable Analyses

Research methods experts point out that finding that a variable moderates an effect (the effect is larger or smaller when the variable is present) does not mean the variable necessarily *causes* the effect. Moderator variables are simply features of the instruction, the circumstances under which instruction is undertaken, or aspects of the study design that are correlated with effect size. The correlation may exist because some third variable influences both the moderator and the outcome being measured as the effect.

For example, a negative correlation might be found between having the same instructor for blended learning and completely classroom-based conditions and the size of the online learning effect. The possible sources of this correlation are multiple. It could be that having the same instructor for both conditions leads to greater consistency of aspects of instruction unrelated to the inclusion of online components in the blended learning condition, thus serving to better isolate the effect of medium (as suggested, for example, by Figlio, Rush, & Yin, 2010). But it also could be the case that studies with the same instructor for blended and face-to-face conditions are most often done in institutional settings where there is not the option for assigning students at random to conditions, and these typically involve a single class in each condition. Such studies might be expected to have a lower probability of detecting a significant difference between conditions on the basis of their research designs, irrespective of the treatment being tried out in one course section.

Another example is the common finding of a correlation between the amount of time students spent using the online system (often termed "dosage") and the learning outcome or the advantage that online system users have relative to conventional face-to-face instruction. Developers typically reason that students or classes that use their online system to a greater extent reap more of its learning benefits. But in research designs with multiple classrooms wherein individual instructors get to make decisions about the extent to which their students use the online learning system, it is possible that instructors who see learning benefits as their students start using the online system (perhaps because there is a good match between the system and their students' proficiency level, preferred learning activities, or for some other reason) will choose to have their students use the online learning system more. The correlation between dosage and effect size per se does not tell us which of these variables, if either of them, is causing the relationship.

Obtaining research-based insights about how to design online or blended learning experiences is complicated further by the fact that many of the design features we might want to explore tend to be correlated with each other. As noted above, in our meta-analysis for the U.S. Department of Education, those studies in which the treatment condition included face-to-face instruction along with online learning also tended to provide treatment condition students with additional learning experiences that students in the control group did not have access to. This confounding of design features made it impossible to determine whether it was the blending of online and face-to-face media or the inclusion of more and more varied learning content that produced a treatment group advantage. From the standpoint of evaluating a specific course or instructional resource that will be reused with many learners, many practitioners may not care about which features are the "active ingredients" as long as they can count on good results. From the standpoint of building knowledge in the field, so that principles are available to guide future online learning design, this situation is unfortunate.

Some Claims to Watch Out For

Technology enthusiasts and providers of online learning products are predisposed to tick off a list of presumed advantages for online learning. We will discuss a few of them to illustrate the problem with using ill-defined terms and accepting overly simplified claims about what "research shows" at face value.

In Chapter 1 we described the lack of agreement or common usage around the term "personalization." Presented with the claim that a course or piece of learning software provides for personalized learning, the savvy consumer presses for details about just what varies from learner to learner and the basis on which that variation is achieved. Learning systems may provide different learners with different:

- pacing and time to learn (self-paced learning)
- learning objectives (let learners choose their course of study)
- content choices for specified learning objectives (e.g., opportunities to choose content to match learner background or interests while working on the same skills or concepts)
- content complexity or difficulty level
- pedagogy (e.g., a tutorial versus learn by doing)
- degree of learner control (e.g., fixed path through the content for some students while others get to choose their own learning sequence)
- types of scaffolding (c.g., hints suggesting what a learner might review versus providing the prerequisite piece of knowledge)
- nature and timing of feedback (e.g., information on whether the response was right or wrong versus information on what the learner might do to solve future such problems correctly).

The sheer size of this list (as well as the need for each of these terms to be defined) attests to the complexity of the idea of personalization.

In addition to the many features of the learning experience that can be customized to individual learners' needs or tastes, there are also multiple possibilities for how differentiations along these dimensions are made. Some systems let the learner choose different objectives, content, or pedagogy (usually referred to by a more user friendly term such as "mode").

Some systems are set up to give the student's teacher control of the level of content and support each student receives. Although letting the student or the teacher match instructional mode to the student's preference or perceived learning "style" sounds attractive, meta-analyses of this kind of matching suggest that it is a weak intervention at best (Aiello & Wolfle, 1980; Hattie, 2009; Slemmer, 2002).

Some systems administer a diagnostic test or assessment of learner preferences when learners first start with the system (U.S. Department of Education, 2010b). The most sophisticated learning systems perform "assessment on the fly" with the system itself using the learner's prior actions to determine the approach presumed to be the best fit for that learner (U.S. Department of Education, 2013, Chapter 2).

Another frequently touted virtue of commercially produced online learning resources and systems is their use of "rich media." Marketing materials often imply "the more media the better," but the research literature actually suggests a much more complex set of design principles.

Humans have separate channels for processing visual and verbal information (pictures and words), and learning can be enhanced by exploiting both channels, but humans can only process a certain amount of information at any one time. Further, the extent to which learning occurs and is retained is a function of the extent to which the learner actively engages with the material to be learned.

With these three characteristics of human information processing interacting, the results of any particular configuration of text, animation, voice over, and graphics becomes much harder to predict. In many cases, simple schematic diagrams are as effective as or more effective than more elaborate visuals. Mayer and his colleagues have demonstrated repeatedly that adding music, video clips, and the insertion of interesting facts to instruction on science phenomena actually reduces the effectiveness of instruction (Mayer, 2008).

Mayer has conducted meta-analyses on a number of theoretically grounded principles for multimedia instruction. He identifies five principles, each of which has been shown to improve learning in most or all experimental tests:

- coherence—reduce extraneous material
- signaling—highlight essential material
- redundancy—avoid adding on-screen text to narrated animations
- spatial contiguity—place printed words next to corresponding graphics
- temporal contiguity—present corresponding narration and animation at the same time.

But the only way to know whether the use of media in a particular online learning resource is in fact optimal is to try out different versions with learners.

Although promotional materials characterize qualities like personalization, game-like, and media rich as "research-based," the available supporting research typically is limited to specific applications of some version of the principle in interventions that may be quite different from those of the product being promoted. Potential adopters need evidence of a positive impact of the way the principle has been implemented in the particular product under consideration.

An implication of the gap between the loose usage of learning terms in everyday discussion and product promotion and the much more narrow, operational definitions used in research is that it is difficult to translate research into terms that make sense to practitioners and product designers.

Individual research studies involve particular instantiations of theory-based concepts, such as immediate feedback or spaced practice. The details of how these concepts are operationalized are important to researchers and can affect learning outcomes. Given the number of different ways in which an instructional design principle can be operationalized in different contexts, interpreting research investigating principles for designing online learning can be daunting.

One approach to dealing with this complexity is to promote a common set of terms and definitions organized as a hierarchy of terminology. Yaeil Kali of the Israel Institute of Technology and Marcia Linn from the University of California, Berkeley, have done this with their online design principles database. This resource was developed to support those engaged in designing learning environments in applying research-based principles and describing their products in terms of a standard set of features. As illustrated in Figure 2.1, from Kali and Linn (2010), the Design Principles Database classifies principles at three different levels of abstraction (see edu-design-principles.org). A *meta-principle* is a generalization based on the basic research literature about how people learn. A sample meta-principle would be "Make thinking visible." *Pragmatic principles* are more specific descriptions of how the meta-principle could be instantiated in a piece of learning software. Two pragmatic principles for "make thinking visible" are "Provide a visual overview of the inquiry cycle" and "Provide dynamic visual aids for the perception of

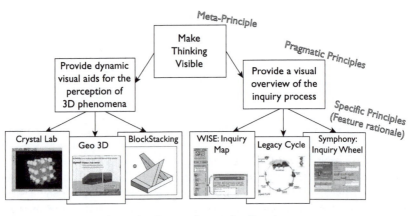

Figure 2.1 Example from the Design Principles Database

three-dimensional phenomena." For each pragmatic principle, the design principles database offers one or more *specific principles*, which are pointers to how that pragmatic principle was realized in specific applications (for example, three different visual representations for the inquiry cycle) for which there is evidence that the specific principle enhanced learning.

Researchers at the Pittsburgh Science of Learning Center (PSLC) make the case that online learning developers and researchers need to be applying research-based design principles not at the level of whole courses or subject areas but at the level of the specific knowledge components within a course. PSLC researchers have been working to identify different types of knowledge components and to test experimentally theory-based principles for supporting each of them within online learning (Koedinger, Corbett, & Perfetti, 2012). The PSLC researchers contrast their approach, which is organized around cognitive representations of the multiple knowledge components needed to achieve an instructional objective, with the more-familiar Bloom's taxonomy (Bloom, 1956), which is organized around the nature of the instructional objective per se. The approach taken at PSLC is illustrated in Table 2.3, which lists some of the instructional design principles they have studied and summarizes available research on the applicability of each to a range of knowledge components.

Time for Expanding Research on Design Principles for Online and Blended Learning

Given the rapid growth of online and blended learning, there is an urgent need and unprecedented opportunities for research on the effectiveness of these approaches for teaching different kinds of content to different kinds of students. The large variation in the estimates of effectiveness for different online and blended learning interventions tells us that all online learning is not equally effective, and the field needs to turn away from trying to justify the use of online learning in general, by showing that it can be as effective as face-to-face instruction, and concentrate instead on identifying and testing online learning design principles as applied to specific types of online learning and implementation models for specific types of learners under specified circumstances.

The online learning framework we presented in Figure 1.1 of Chapter 1 may be useful for organizing and summarizing the online learning literature, but it is not detailed enough to guide the design of learning technologies or research studies by itself. Our understanding of learning and educational practice would benefit from having more experimental tests of instructional design practices such as breaking didactic, lecture-based instruction into small segments (as carried out in the Khan Academy and the Udacity and Coursera MOOCs); providing immediate right and wrong feedback versus guiding

Table 2.3 Pittsburgh Science of Learning Center Instructional Principles

Instructional principle	Principle application	CV	FA	EA	AE	GR	CR	HS	PP	PC
Optimized scheduling	Selection of practice instances based on prior statistics and on each student's experience with each target knowledge component	+				+				
Timely feedback	Providing an evaluative response (e.g., correct or incorrect) soon after a student's attempt at task or step		+		+			+		
Feature focusing	Guiding the learner's attention ("focus") to valid or relevant features of target knowledge components	+	+							
Worked examples	Worked examples are interleaved with problem solving practice (as opposed to practice that is all problem solving)				+	+	+			?
Prompted self-explanation	Encouraging students to explain to themselves parts of instruction (steps in worked example or sentences in a text)			0	+	+			+	?
Accountable talk	Encouraging classroom talk that is accountable to accurate knowledge, rigorous reasoning, and the classroom community by using six talk moves (question and response patterns)									+

Source: Koedinger, Corbett, & Perfetti (2012).

Key: CV = Chinese Vocabulary; FA = French Articles; EA = English Articles; AE = Algebra Equations; GR = Geometry Rules; CR = Chemistry Rules; HS = Help-seeking Skills; PP = Physics Principles; PC = Pressure Concept
+ = Principle found to enhance learning of this type of knowledge component.
0 = Principle tested for this knowledge component and no effect found.
? = Principle tested with this knowledge component with inconclusive results.

students incrementally toward a correct answer; and applying different approaches to grouping online students for peer assessment activities. Ideally, the published research literature would feature many well-designed experimental studies of each of these practices, with individual studies involving different kinds of learning content and different kinds of online learners.

Impediments to the growth of such a literature include the fact that commercially produced digital learning products may not want to make experimental data public, especially if it contradicts marketing claims. There is also the issue that designing and developing online learning experiences are labor-intensive activities often performed under time pressure to be ready for the next academic term. People engaged in these activities are often disinclined to spend time searching the learning sciences literature or setting out to experiment with alternative instructional design principles.

The circumstances most conducive to meaningful research on how best to design and implement online learning appear to involve longer-term projects that explicitly bring together learning researchers, instructors, and technology developers with the expectation that the online instruction they produce will be used in multiple settings by multiple instructors and refined over time on the basis of learner data. Notable examples include Carnegie Mellon University's Open Learning Initiative, funded by the Hewlett Foundation, and the GLASS Lab, currently operating with funding from the Gates and MacArthur Foundations.

In addition to having more research testing learning principles within the context of online learning, the field also needs more careful documentation of the kind of learning being addressed and the nature of the learners involved in implementations of online and blended learning. Variability in learning content and learner types is important because most instructional design principles are effective under some but not all circumstances. An example is the principle of providing learners with "worked examples." Learning theory suggests that when learners are trying to acquire challenging new content (for example, how to simplify certain kinds of algebraic expressions), their information processing capacity may be taxed. Worked examples relieve the learner of trying to mentally perform some of the components of the new skill (such as multiplication, division, or finding the least common denominator) so that the learner can concentrate on the overall strategy for equation simplification. In a series of studies involving tutoring systems, researchers at Carnegie Mellon and elsewhere found that in the early stages of learning mathematics and physics content, the provision of worked examples facilitates learning (Sweller & Cooper, 1985). As learners gain expertise in the skill the worked examples no longer provide any benefit, however (Kalyuga et al., 2001).

By identifying the design principles used in online learning and systematically testing the efficacy of each principle for different types of learning, stages of learning, and types of learners, we should be able to greatly increase the effectiveness of online learning systems relative to today's systems built largely on developers' hunches. We will return to this theme in the conclusion of this volume, suggesting that the rush to put education online should not distract us from the tremendous potential for using the avalanche of empirical data being generated by online systems to advance our understanding of how to enhance learning for different kinds of learners, learning content, and circumstances.

Summary and Implications

Based on the overview of online learning effectiveness research in this chapter, we come to a number of conclusions concerning the current status of the field and the most productive avenue for further advancement.

It is clear that online instruction can be effective. In most meta-analyses of controlled studies comparing learning outcomes for online and face-to-face instruction, those who learn online fare as well as, and sometimes even better than, those experiencing the instruction in face-to-face format.

However, studies vary greatly in their outcomes, limiting the confidence that an educator or administrator can have in adopting an online approach. One cannot just assume that because online and face-to-face conditions have produced equivalent learning on average in several meta-analyses that a specific online course will be as effective as the classroom version of the course. There is no replacement for trying out the new online or blended course and collecting data on implementation and student outcomes.

Learning science research suggests that technology offers some distinctive benefits by providing concrete visual representations of abstract concepts; fostering interactivity; immersing learners in complex, lifelike environments and challenges; customizing the pace, content complexity, interface, and amount of scaffolding for individual learners; and maintaining automated records of each learner's actions on the learning system over time. Online learning research and development would do well to capitalize on these affordances and move toward amassing evidence around the relative efficacy of specific design principles.

Although MOOCs still operate predominantly outside the realm of credit-bearing college courses, they are clearly moving in that direction and foreshadow a time when certain courses will be used by large numbers of students from multiple campuses across multiple semesters. (See the discussion in Chapter 3.) As this trend materializes, it will become cost effective to invest more money in developing and refining such courses so that they are as good as we can make them. An implication is that greater resources should be put into the objective evaluation of the effectiveness of these courses and into studying implementation factors that influence effectiveness.

As individual courses are redesigned for teaching wholly or partially online, student learning outcomes in redesigned courses should be monitored and compared to the same outcome measures from previous or alternative versions of the course. We have a tremendous opportunity to examine and reflect on detailed data collected from online portions of instruction, but we need to combine these data with the results of external assessments of learning. Educational institutions that make this kind of ongoing evaluation and reflection a standard practice will be in a position both to reassure stakeholders that the move to online instruction is not putting students' academic success at risk and to further improve their classes and outcomes.

Notes

1 Cohen (1988) describes effect sizes of .20 as "small," .50 as "medium," and .80 as "large" for social science research. Hattie (2009), who has synthesized results of over 800 meta-analyses on variables related to educational achievement, suggests that an effect size of .40 represents a level "where the effects of the innovation enhance achievement in such a way that we can notice a real-world difference" (p. 17).

2 Although Jaggers provides examples of better and more poorly controlled studies, she does not report the criteria she used to classify studies.

3 Most learning technology researchers regard this as a fairly meaningless comparison (Kozma, 1994) since they regard the point of using technology as providing experiences that are not possible in conventional classroom instruction.

4 Looking just at the 11 contrasts with the largest positive effects for online or blended learning, retention rates were higher for the face-to-face condition in two, for the online condition in two, equivalent in the two conditions in two, and not reported in five.

Chapter 3

Online and Blended Learning in Higher Education

Colleges and universities have led the way in adopting online learning. Over the last decade, enrollment in online college courses has been increasing faster than enrollment in higher education as a whole (Allen & Seaman, 2013). Tertiary education institutions have advantages over elementary and secondary schools as contexts for Web-based learning because they have greater resources to invest in a technology infrastructure. In addition, they deal with more mature learners, who can be expected to do more of their learning independently without close monitoring by an instructor. Finally, experience with distance learning at institutions such as the Open University in the United Kingdom and Athabasca University in Canada provided proof points that learning at a distance could serve the needs of many students and yielded insights into how it could be implemented.

Factors Fueling the Explosion of Online Learning in Higher Education

Although higher education has been employing online learning to some extent since the advent of the Internet, in the last decade there has been a dramatic rise in Internet-based postsecondary enrollments. The number of U.S. college students taking at least one online course in school year 2011–12 was estimated to be 6.7 million, or 32 percent of all higher education enrollees (Allen & Seaman, 2013). This level of market penetration puts online higher education enrollments on track to meet the projection made by Christensen et al. (2011, p. 31) that half of all college students will be taking at least one of their courses online by 2014.

This increase in online enrollments is accompanied by an increasing perception among higher education institutions that online learning is central to their core mission. The Babson Survey Research Group has been surveying the chief academic officers of American colleges and universities about their online education practices since 2002. In the first year of the survey, less than half of these institutions reported that online education was critical to their future; by 2012 the proportion had risen to nearly 70 percent (Allen & Seaman, 2013). The surveys have documented also a trend toward greater confidence that online instruction is as effective as traditional face-to-face instruction. In the first survey conducted in 2002, 57 percent of responding chief academic officers said that online learning was either equal or superior to traditional methods in effectiveness. By 2012, that proportion had risen to 77 percent (Allen & Seaman, 2013).[1]

A number of different factors appear to have contributed to putting online learning into the higher education spotlight. First, the technology infrastructure—the systems that campuses can afford to purchase and the hardware devices that students bring to campus—reached a "tipping point," enabling course designers at many campuses to assume every student would have access to anything on the Web. Another enabler has been the increased supply of free or "open" learning management systems and learning resources and commercial products. This supply has been stimulated by a recent influx of both philanthropic and commercial investment capital into companies offering services, infrastructure, or content for higher education learning online. In addition, some of the for-profit postsecondary education providers, such as the University of Phoenix and Walden University, achieved tremendous year-to-year growth in enrollments during the first decade of the twenty-first century, putting pressure on public university systems to compete by offering courses and programs that met the needs of busy adults with home or work responsibilities.[2]

In the U.S., the increased activity of for-profit providers and venture capital investment in online learning systems and resources occurred at the same time that state budgets for higher education were being cut significantly (State Higher Education Executive Officers, 2013). Budgetary pressures led higher education administrators, governors, and legislatures to look for ways to continue to deliver higher education services but at lower cost. Many looked to online education as the way to escape their service-cost dilemmas.

In California, for example, Governor Jerry Brown has pushed for more online courses in the state's college systems as a means of reducing costs. Speaking before the University of California Regents, Brown asserted, "So there isn't the luxury of sitting in the present trajectory unless you don't mind paying ever increasing tuition" (Melendez, 2013). A bill that went before California's state legislature in 2013 called for the development of 50 online versions of the most highly oversubscribed required lower-division college courses. Students at the University of California, California State, or community college campuses would be able to take these online courses, or approved equivalent online courses from commercial providers or out-of-state colleges, if they were not able to get into the classroom-based course on their own campus.

Walsh (2011) quotes William G. Bowen, the former president of Princeton University, who said, "I think that present and prospective economic realities dictate that there be a serious rethinking of the way some forms of instruction are provided, especially in those parts of the public sector that have been hurt the most by funding cuts."

Taking a more international view, we are in a period of rising demand for higher education worldwide. Atkins, Brown, and Hammond (2007) assert that global demand for higher education cannot possibly be met without online learning. They illustrate the scope of this need with remarks by Sir John Daniels, former vice-chancellor of the Open University and CEO of Canada's Commonwealth of Learning. Daniels asserted that there are 30 million more people in the world qualified for a university education than there are places in higher education institutions. Daniels predicted that this number would soon grow to 100 million and estimated that fully meeting the worldwide demand for higher education would require *opening a major university every week.* Clearly, this level of unmet need cannot be satisfied with brick-and-mortar institutions of the same kind we have had for the last 300 years.

Finally, the spectacular enrollment numbers for MOOCs—with hundreds of thousands of people signing up to take a single online course—have triggered huge amounts of publicity and a "gold rush" mentality among colleges and universities eager to get in on the opportunity. Colleges feel they need to participate or risk being overshadowed by institutions with online offerings. One university president was even fired by her board of trustees, apparently for failing to move fast enough to implement MOOCs as other elite universities had done (Webley, 2012).[3] Both irrational exuberance and deep-seated fear concerning online learning are running high (Brooks, 2012; Christensen & Horn, 2013; Shullenberger, 2013; Yuan & Powell, 2013).

Influential Precedents

As noted above, learning at a distance, whether through televised lectures, radio, or more recently online courses, has had a presence within higher education for decades. But the rise of the World Wide Web and the emergence of Web 2.0 capabilities have brought learning at a distance from instructors into a new era. Harasim (2001) traces the origins of online courses both before and after the introduction of the World Wide Web.

While the invention of email and computer conferencing had launched an unprecedented level of social interaction, communication, and collaboration, the invention of the Web led to a phenomenal amount of self-publishing. Two basic models of online courses thus emerged: one based on collaborative learning and interaction, and the other based on publishing information online (course materials, lecture notes, student assignments, and so on). The second, based on the old model of transmission of information or lecture mode, seemed to flourish during the late 1990s, but then its weaknesses became evident. At the same time, new tools and environments customized for education based on educational interaction and collaboration were emerging (Harasim, 2001, p. 52).

Harasim's review highlights the difference between didactic or transmission views of instruction and pedagogies emphasizing collaboration and the joint construction of knowledge, both of which can be supported through Web technologies. At the close of the twentieth century, many learning technology researchers shared Harasim's belief that transmission forms of online learning would give way to more collaborate pedagogies.

But until relatively recently, online learning was confined to the periphery of the higher education system—to for-profit colleges, professional certification programs, a few non-selective "open" institutions, and offerings for military personnel stationed overseas, for example—rather than to the core higher education function of undergraduate degree programs. As long as online learning was confined to this peripheral space, it was unlikely to have a profound influence on the fundamental nature of higher education.

Open Courseware at the Massachusetts Institute of Technology

Starting early in this century, initiatives and new organizations emerged that would reconceptualize the role of online learning and exert pressure to bring it into the mainstream of higher education. One of these was the open courseware (OCW) initiative started by the Massachusetts Institute of Technology (MIT) in 2000. There had been several earlier attempts to put exemplary university teaching content online and make it available for a fee, but these had failed by the time of the dot-com bust (Walsh, 2011). MIT hoped to carve out a distinctive niche for itself in the online space, and given the interest of its faculty in open software (software that is available for free with its code modifiable and hence improvable by anyone around the world), there was a certain logic in making MIT course content available in an open form as well. MIT's Council on Educational Technology had, in fact, considered trying to create a revenue-generating online presence, but business consultants hired by the Council advised that such an endeavor would distract MIT from its core mission and would be unlikely to operate at a profit. Instead, the Council recommended putting MIT course materials on the Internet and making them open—freely available—to anyone (Walsh, 2011).

MIT's president, Charles Vest, took up the Council's recommendation with enthusiasm. Here was an altruistic idea that would inspire MIT faculty and give something to the world. Vest proposed that if MIT was going to engage in making its courseware open, it needed to be a campus-wide initiative involving all faculty and all courses to the largest extent possible. Vest appreciated the appeal of the open courseware idea and personally undertook an effort to raise funds from the William and Flora Hewlett and the Andrew W. Mellon Foundations.

In designing MIT OCW, the university was clear that it was putting course materials on the Web—syllabi, reading, lecture notes, and so on—not providing online instruction per se. Part of the rationale for this decision was a desire not to "dilute the brand" of MIT instruction offered to its own students on campus and part was a recognition of the fact that posting their course materials required much less of faculty than redesigning their courses as online instruction would. MIT expected that the major users of OCW would be faculty at other colleges and universities who would have access to the course content and supporting materials used at MIT and could incorporate these materials into their own courses (Walsh, 2011).

In 2001 MIT made content from an initial set of 50 courses freely available online. Another 500 courses were added during a second phase. Eventually, the number of OCW courses exceeded 1,200.

A survey of MIT OCW users conducted in 2009 found that usage was worldwide with 54 percent of OCW visits coming from outside the U.S. (Walsh, 2011). Contrary to expectation, only 9 percent of users were educators: 42 percent of OCW users described themselves as students, and 43 percent as "self-learners." Course content that MIT had expected to be taken up by and interpreted by faculty was instead being consumed directly by learners—an outcome totally in keeping with the emerging philosophy of resource sharing that came to be characterized as "Web 2.0."

From the beginning, MIT had hoped that its OCW initiative would serve as an example to other universities around the world. With a grant from the Hewlett Foundation, MIT launched the OCW Consortium in 2005. A decade later, more than 200 other higher education institutions from around the world had joined the OCW Consortium, each pledging to make at least ten of its courses available in open form (Smith, 2009). The biggest enthusiasm for joining the OCW Consortium came from Asian universities, however. U.S. institutions did not join in large numbers (Walsh, 2011).

The Open Learning Initiative

The development of open educational resources was nurtured by the William and Flora Hewlett Foundation, which during the tenure of Marshall ("Mike") Smith as Education Director, invested not only in OCW but also in a number of other initiatives. The Hewett Foundation's work in this area started in 2002, after a review of the educational content available on the Web judged it to be "alarmingly disappointing" (Atkins, Brown, & Hammond, 2007). One of the Hewlett Foundation investments that turned out to have the largest impact was the Open Learning Initiative at Carnegie Mellon University (CMU). Smith wanted to invest in additional open educational resources projects that would demonstrate the affordances of online learning. Discussions with the chief technology officer and provost at CMU gave rise to the idea of marrying the university's capabilities in designing and developing instructional systems with Hewlett's desire to see effective openly available online learning systems. An initial $1.9 million proposal for "Four Courses, Millions of Users: Creating a New Online Learning Paradigm" was funded in 2002 (Walsh, 2011).

In comparison to the OCW initiative, CMU's Open Learning Initiative (OLI) adopted a more ambitious goal—providing learning systems that would enable an independent learner working online to achieve the same learning outcomes as students at Carnegie Mellon. In doing this work, CMU could draw on its decades of work in cognitive science and intelligent tutoring systems, notably the series of cognitive tutors in subjects such as algebra and geometry developed by John Anderson and his colleagues (Koedinger & Corbett, 2006). Joel Smith, the director of the OLI, set forth the vision of interactive learning systems with designs based on learning research that would also generate data as students used them. The clickstream data generated by student use of the OLI learning systems would then be analyzed to provide direction for improving those systems. Joel Smith (as quoted in Lederman, 2006) pointed out that most digital learning resources "make shockingly little use of what is in fact the best information available to improve education: scientific results from research studies in the learning sciences."

The Open Learning Initiative, which to date has developed 14 online courses, is unusual if not unique in its course development processes. Because the courses were designed to provide everything a student would need to develop understanding and competency in the course material, each course would have to be redesigned. For each OLI course, the team doing this work comprised a faculty member representing expertise in the content of the course, a learning scientist, a software engineer, a user interface designer, and a project manager.

The OLI courses run on an interactive platform capable of adjusting course content to the individual student's needs as evident from that student's prior interactions with the system. Although the design varies across different courses, common elements include tutoring in which a concept and associated procedures are described and a practice environment in which the student works on a set of problems related to the tutorial. OLI's simplified versions of the kinds of tutoring systems CMU had created in the past are capable of scaffolding student performance on problems with hints geared to the particular student's current level of understanding. Some of the courses, such as chemistry, include interactive diagrams and "virtual laboratories" in which students can apply their understanding of concepts in simulated experiments.

The OLI course designers think of everything the student does online as a form of embedded assessment. The system is constantly gathering information about student actions—data that CMU researchers later analyze to look for places where many students get stuck or more generally, where learning does not unfold as one would expect based on learning theory and the developers' analysis of the subject domain. The courses also include short tests interspersed with the learning and practice activities. These tests are self-assessments designed to help students reflect on their learning rather than tests that serve as inputs into a course grade. Some of the assessment items call for reflections, such as "What was hardest to understand?"

Although the cost of developing an OLI course has dropped from the initial million dollars to something in the neighborhood of half of that (Walsh, 2011), the expertise and labor going into these courses is far from typical for the development of online college courses.

Four Major Trends in How Universities are Using Online Learning

We turn now to discussing what we regard as the four major trends in online learning as applied to higher education:

- self-paced, adaptive instruction and competency-based learning
- blended learning
- learning analytics
- MOOCs.

Self-paced, Adaptive Instruction and Competency-based Learning

One of the major selling points of digital learning systems is the potential for tailoring the learning experience to the needs and interests of the individual learner. The idea has great intuitive appeal, on the grounds of increased efficiency and in expectation that learning experiences at just the right level of challenge for an individual will increase engagement and persistence.

As noted in Chapter 1, the basic idea of having learners work through instructional content at their own pace has been around since the early days of computer-based instruction. Today, learning system providers are more likely to talk about "personalized" or "self-paced" rather than "mastery" learning, but operationally they usually mean the same thing.

On the surface at least, mastery-based approaches offer considerable efficiencies. Students do not need to spend time being instructed on learning objectives they have already mastered. Fast learners can proceed through course material much more quickly than a typical class of learners working in "lock step" (which means moving to new content only when the instructor determines that most students are ready). Learners who need more time can take that time and achieve the same level of mastery as their peers rather than being moved ahead when they are not ready. In contrast to conventional classroom-based instruction which holds time constant and lets level of mastery vary for different students, personalized learning systems seek to hold the level of mastery constant and vary learning time.

In the 1980s mastery learning approaches were used most often in the U.S. in compensatory education services for younger students receiving remediation in basic reading and mathematics skills. More recently, we are starting to see online learning systems resulting in greater use of mastery learning approaches in higher education as well as K-12. Mastery learning has particular appeal in remedial courses addressing mathematics and language arts skills that students should have attained prior to entering college and in mathematics and math-related subjects more generally.

A high-profile application of mastery learning for this purpose is the "emporium model" of mathematics instruction popularized by Virginia Polytechnic Institute and State University ("Virginia Tech"). Motivated by the desire to improve student performance in mathematics courses and to reduce costs, Virginia Tech set up a large open space with clusters of computers to serve as an "emporium" for mathematics learning. Currently housed in a 60,000-square-foot off-campus space that formerly served as a grocery store, Virginia Tech's Math Emporium serves over 8,000 students a semester. Equipped with 550 computers arranged in six-station hubs, the Math Emporium is open 24/7 for students wanting to work on their online math courses. Students use streaming video, audio, or text explanations of math concepts and then take online quizzes. Once they have mastered the content in all the quizzes, they take a test comprised of new mathematics problems on the same learning objectives. Students who would like personal assistance while working in the Math Emporium can get it from one of the instructors, graduate students, or advanced undergraduates who staff the Emporium 15 hours a day. Because fewer and less-expensive staff are used in the Emporium than in traditional lecture-based classes, the Math Emporium has reduced the cost of delivering math courses by 75 percent at Virginia Tech (Robinson & Moore, 2006). The university reports that students who took their mathematics classes through the Math Emporium do as well or better in more advanced mathematics classes as those students who took the classes in traditional classroom-based format (Robinson & Moore, 2006).

The emporium model for mathematics instruction has been adopted by other universities, reportedly resulting in larger proportions of their students earning a C or better in remedial or entry college-level mathematics courses (Twigg, 2011). The model is currently being expanded to 38 two-year or community colleges under the auspices of the National Center for Academic Transformation (Twigg, 2011).

A more general concept that subsumes mastery learning is that of *adaptive instruction*. A learning system is considered adaptive if it uses information gained as the student is learning with it, rather than pre-existing information such as the learner's age, gender, or prior achievement test score, to change the way in which the system presents instruction to better meet the learner's needs. Systems can be adaptive in the way they represent a concept (e.g., through text or diagrams or formulae), the difficulty level of the text or problems they provide, the sequencing of material, or the nature of hints and feedback given. While the mastery learning systems of the 1980s varied the pace with which students moved through a curriculum, they still had all students work through the same content in the same sequence. Newer adaptive learning systems with artificial intelligence capabilities are able to mimic the more complex variations in instructional styles that a human tutor would use with a student (Koedinger & Corbett, 2006; U.S. Department of Education, 2013). The Open Learning Initiative courses described above incorporate artificial intelligence techniques to make their instruction adaptive.

As education systems adopt individualized, mastery-based approaches to instruction, a very natural extension is the move into *competency-based* approaches to structuring learning and learning certification. Building a mastery-based instructional system requires specifying the content and the level of performance that students must master to complete the course and developing a valid, reliable way of assessing whether the stipulated competencies have been attained. If such assessments are in fact valid measures of competency attainment, one can then think about systems in which students can take the assessment any time they feel they are ready, much as student drivers choose when to take their driving test. Logically, what should matter is competency attainment, not the number of hours one sat in a classroom to attain it. Competency-based systems determine both a student's place in an education program and when the student has completed the program on the basis of the demonstration of competencies, rather than the number of hours of instruction or the month of the year.

Providers of online degree programs (see Chapter 6) are enthusiastic about competency-based approaches to documenting learning because such approaches free learners up from fixed timeframes for academic terms. Once the certification of learning is decoupled from time spent in the classroom, all kinds of new models of higher education become possible.

An early effort to provide competency-based education online was Western Governors University, which, as described in Chapter 6, offers degrees based on competency rather than seat time.

Under the Obama Administration, the move toward competency-based higher education has received encouragement from the federal government. In an interview with *The New York Times*, U.S. Education Secretary Arne Duncan highlighted the competency-based programs of Western Governors University (WGU) and said that in the future he would like to see them become the norm (Lewin, 2011).

Currently, a number of public higher education institutions are working to pioneer competency-based programs, an effort that requires overcoming the hurdles presented by accrediting processes and federal financial aid regulations that were written around the notion of measuring education by class hours (the "Carnegie unit").[4] In fall 2012 Southern New Hampshire University received approval from its regional accrediting agency for its proposed College for America, which offers online assessments of 120 competencies. There are no required courses in this program; rather, students attempt to perform the task associated with each competency and students' products are judged by faculty using a rubric for judging whether or not the performance provides sufficient evidence that the student possesses the target competency. Competencies are organized into three levels, from simpler to more complex, and a student may take as much or as little time as needed to perform the tasks at the required level of competency. Tuition is set at $2,500 a year, so a student could earn an associate's degree for as little as $1,250 if she could demonstrate all the required competencies in six months' time (LeBlanc, 2013).

The U.S. Department of Education subsequently approved Southern New Hampshire University's program for student receipt of financial aid based on direct assessment of competency rather than credit hour. The Secretary of Education, Arne Duncan, wrote:

> This is a key step forward in expanding access to affordable higher education. We know many students and adult learners across the country need the flexibility to fit their education into their lives or work through a class on their own pace, and these competency-based programs offer those features.
>
> (quoted in Lewin, 2011)

The Bill & Melinda Gates Foundation is another organization that has been trying to leverage online learning and competency-based programs to create new higher education structures with dramatically lower costs and better student graduation rates. The foundation has funded experimental programs within existing colleges and universities and start-up higher education institutions to develop "breakthrough delivery models" for cost effective higher education. One of the foundation's grantees, Northern Arizona University, has partnered with Pearson to provide competency-based undergraduate programs in computer information technology, business administration, and liberal arts, starting in 2013. Courses for these programs were redesigned around outcomes and competencies. The programs were designed for self-motivated learners who could test out some of the instructional units by demonstrating the target competencies on a pre-assessment. The program design allows students to start a course at any time during the year, with tuition set at a flat rate of $2,500 for six months.[5]

Blended Learning

A second major trend in higher education, as in K-12 education, is the use of blended learning approaches involving various combinations of online and face-to-face instruction. As Christensen, Horn, and Staker (2013) point out, such approaches allow higher education institutions and individual faculty to harness some of the advantages of online education without completely disrupting the normal course structure and faculty role. Blended approaches are often perceived as less threatening to faculty, as the instructor remains the course orchestrator, deciding what portions of instruction to provide through online systems and resources and how to use classroom time to best effect. As noted above, higher education is filled with diverse combinations of online and classroom-based learning activities, ranging from simply putting the course syllabus, assignments, and lecture notes online, to "flipped classrooms" with online videotaped lectures, to courses using online learning systems not only to introduce concepts but also to provide students with practice environments and immediate feedback. These latter two approaches call on students to do much of their learning independently, outside of class, and often enable fewer hours to be spent in the classroom.

Such has been the case with the OLI statistics course as its implementation has evolved over time. Originally, Carnegie Mellon designed OLI statistics with the idea that it would be a standalone resource that would enable students to learn introductory statistics on their own, at their own pace. When the Hewlett Foundation challenged the OLI to demonstrate the efficiency of the course relative to regular classroom-based instruction in statistics, however, the OLI team chose a blended learning approach. Students still met with their statistics instructor, but they worked with the OLI software between classes. The instructor had the data from students' interactions with the OLI system to use in identifying those areas where students were having the most difficulty and was able to then tailor classroom explanations and examples around those confusions. An early implementation of this blended model at Carnegie Mellon resulted in students acquiring the introductory statistics competencies to the same level as, or a higher level than, that attained by students in an ordinary class—while doing so in half the time (Lovett, Meyer, & Thille, 2008).

Keeping college faculty employed is not the best justification for moving to blended rather than fully online conditions, however. Just as hybrid cars provide the extra speed and range of gasoline power when needed, blended learning is a hybrid innovation that can use the instructor's face time with students to address nuances of understanding that are not well represented in the software. There is also considerable power to the faculty member's importance as a role model and inspiration, including modeling the kinds of language, reasoning, and argumentation that are appropriate in the field. In Chapter 7, we will suggest that these functions, which are still better performed by humans than by even the most sophisticated learning software and avatars, appear to be particularly important for students with weak educational backgrounds.

When EDUCAUSE, the nonprofit organization promoting the use of technology in higher education, issued a request for proposals to use technology to transform student outcomes in higher education, the great majority of the proposals it received, and most of the 29 it chose to fund, called for blended rather than fully online models of instruction (Means, Shear et al., 2013). Many of these projects involved making a set of resources and expertise available to faculty wishing to redesign their courses to use blended learning (grants to Abilene Christian University, Bryn Mawr College, Cerritos College, the Missouri Learning College, OhioLINK, and the SUNY Learning Network). Other projects developed specific online resources for use in blended learning courses. One grant supported the implementation of *SimSchool*, a game-like environment that uses simulations of classroom situations that can be incorporated into teacher training courses. A grant to Carnegie Learning supported development of a collection of games designed to support students' math fluency and strategy development for rapid decision making in procedural areas. The games were designed to be incorporated into developmental mathematics classes. Similarly, a grant to the University of Massachusetts supported implementing their *Wayang Outpost* online environment in college mathematics classes. *Wayang Outpost* was designed to support students' mathematics learning by having them apply math in the context of "adventures" in a virtual environment, complete with "learning companions" who provide affective encouragement as students progress through the material.

Learning Analytics and Data Mining

As college students are making greater use of interactive online learning systems, they are also generating detailed data about their learning process. Data collected by interactive online learning systems can be aggregated across large numbers of students and then analyzed to identify patterns and trends.

Generally, educational data mining looks for new patterns in data and develops new algorithms and/or new models, while learning analytics applies known predictive models in instructional systems. However, the two terms are often used more or less interchangeably in non-technical circles. The annual *Horizon Report* for higher education, produced by the EDUCAUSE Learning Initiative and the New Media Consortium, first listed learning analytics as one of its top six technology trends to watch in 2011. Predicting that widespread use of learning analytics was four to five years in the future, the 2011 report explained its potential significance:

> Learning analytics promises to harness the power of advances in data mining, interpretation, and modeling to improve understandings of teaching and learning, and to tailor education to individual students more effectively. Still in its early stages, learning analytics responds to calls for accountability on campuses across the country, and leverages the vast amount of data produced by students in day-to-day academic activities.

> While learning analytics has already been used in admissions and fund-raising efforts on several campuses, "academic analytics" is just beginning to take shape.
>
> (Johnson et al., 2011, p. 28)

The 2013 edition of the *Horizon Report* placed learning analytics two to three years in the future and noted:

> This year, the rise of big data was the subject of discussions across many campuses, and educational data scientists all over the world are beginning to look at vast sets of data through analytical methods pioneered by businesses to predict consumer behaviors.
>
> (Johnson et al., 2013, p. 24)

Learning analytics, and the related field of educational data mining, borrow many of the techniques developed by Web-based businesses such as Amazon, Google, and Netflix. While the latter seek a better understanding of their customers in order to better tailor their online experiences in ways that will maintain engagement, and ultimately lead to sales, applications of these techniques in education have a different set of priorities. A brief published by the U.S. Department of Education (Bienkowski, Feng, & Means, 2012) characterized the kinds of questions addressed by learning analytics as:

- When are students falling behind in a course?
- When is a student at risk for not completing a course?
- What grade is a student likely to get without intervention?
- What is the best next course for a given student?
- Should a student be referred to a counselor for help?
- When are students ready to move on to the next topic?

The first five of these questions pertain to predicting student success—or calculating risk of failure—and this focus dominated learning analytics in higher education in its early years. The overarching goal was to monitor and predict students' learning performance with an eye toward spotting potential issues early enough to be able to intervene before a student failed a course or failed to complete a program of study (EDUCAUSE, 2010; Johnson et al., 2011). This capability has become of increasing interest to colleges and universities as their student retention rates have come under intense scrutiny by government entities providing higher education funding.

The University of Alabama provided one of the early examples of applying data analytic techniques to predicting and enhancing student retention. Graduate students in a data mining course were given copies of the university's data records for students who entered in 1999, 2000, and 2001 (with individuals' personal identifying information removed). The graduate students were challenged to develop statistical models predicting which students would fail to return for their sophomore year based on data in the administrative records. The resulting model used variables such as highest college admissions test score, distance from the university to home, university grade point average, and number of credit hours earned (Wu, n.d.). The university has been able to take this model, developed using data from past student cohorts, and apply it to incoming freshmen to identify the 150–200 students each year with the highest likelihood of failing to return for their sophomore year. This information is shared with academic advisors and faculty so that they can make an extra effort to reach out to these students and provide counseling and other assistance (Wu, n.d.).

Learning analytics are also being applied at the course level. A prominent example of this kind of application is Purdue University's course *Signals* system (Arnold, 2010).

Purdue wanted to have a way of identifying student risk on the basis of up-to-date information so that it could respond to risks associated with acute events such as an illness, breakup of a relationship, or family issues. The university had been having faculty report midterm grades through a campuswide system for some years, but had found that this information came too late and was too general to indicate the type of support needed in time for a struggling student to succeed in the course. Purdue wanted a system that would provide more information about student behaviors in the course and that could distinguish between students who were trying and failing and those who were not putting in the effort (Arnold, 2010).

Mining data from the university's course management system, its student information system, and faculty grade books, *Signals* applies an algorithm that produces a high, medium, or low risk classification for each student. Using information on what a student has done in a course (for example, the number of log ins, time on the learning system, and number of assignments completed) as well as administrative data, *Signals* can provide warnings as early as the second week of the semester (Arnold, 2010).

Instructors using *Signals* post each student's risk level (the red, yellow, or green signal) on their learning management system entry page. Many students institute corrective action (e.g., spending more time with the learning system or completing homework assignments) in response to receiving a yellow or red signal. For students with medium or high risk, faculty can send email messages or text messages, schedule face-to-face meetings, or make referrals to an academic resource center. *Signals* provides faculty with sample email messages that they can edit or send to students as written.

Researchers involved with *Signals* report that students in course sections using *Signals* have consistently had higher grades than their peers in sections that did not use the predictive analytics (Campbell & Arnold, 2011). Moreover, analysis of data on students who entered in fall 2007 and experienced courses with *Signals* found that their likelihoods of still being in college four years later and of earning a degree within five years were significantly higher than those for previous student cohorts (U.S. Department of Education, 2013).

The University of Wollongong in Australia was an early user of learning analytics with its Social Networks Adapting Pedagogical Practice (SNAPP) system. This work builds on insights from data mining of student behavior in online courses, which has revealed differences between successful and unsuccessful students (as measured by final course grades) according to such variables as level of participation in discussion boards, number of emails sent, and number of quizzes completed (Macfadyen & Dawson, 2010). The SNAPP software application identifies the number of posts and replies made by each student, including who replied to whose message, the topic of the discussion, and the length of posts and replies. SNAPP software provides faculty with sociogram-type visualizations of these data, helping them identify students who are disconnected from their class peers as well as students who are brokering information for others (Johnson et al., 2011; Wu, n.d.).

Another application of learning analytics applied to data from online learning systems is to create feedback loops for improving the course. Analysis of online learning data can reveal deficiencies in the characterization of the content to be learned, such as failure to specify all of the prerequisites for a certain skill or concept, inadequate criteria for mastery, confusing directions or assessment items, and so on (Graf & Kinshuk, 2013; U.S. Department of Education, 2013).

Massive Open Online Courses

The initial, largely unheralded genesis of MOOCs was an extension of the altruistic ideology behind open education resources described above. Stephan Downes, a research officer at the National Research Council Canada, and George Siemens, a researcher at Athabasca University, decided to make the online learning theory class they were co-teaching at the University of Manitoba available to anyone in the world, regardless of whether they could afford college tuition (Parry, 2010). Over 2,300 people availed themselves of the opportunity to join the 25 University of Manitoba students taking the course. Weekly readings were posted on a wiki, and the instructors emailed a daily newsletter highlighting key points to all students. About 150 of the 2,300 students participated actively in online discussion forums; some student groups self-organized face-to-face meetings. There was no top-down control of where, how, or to what extent students interacted around the course content. Various groups of students interacted using the discussion forum feature of Moodle, an open-source course management system, or through Twitter, Ning, Second

Life, or blogs. Papers and a final project were required and evaluated only for those students taking the course for credit (Parry, 2010).

Siemens (2012) contrasts the MOOCs pioneered in Canada and at Brigham Young University and the University of Florida with those that came later out of Stanford and edX, referring to the former as "cMOOCs." According to Downes and Siemens, the instructional philosophy behind the Canadian cMOOCs reflects connectivism, a philosophy of open learning through collaborative online networks. Rather than conveying a body of instructor-developed content in top-down fashion, the cMOOCs seek to seed online discussions and collaborations through which the networked community of learners will build knowledge and understanding. It is for this reason that cMOOC participants are free to share material and collaborate using any technological tools they like.

Siemens calls the newer MOOCs that burst on the scene in fall 2011 and led *The New York Times* to call 2012 "The Year of the MOOC" (Pappano, 2012) "xMOOCs." One commentator described xMOOCs as emerging "at the inter-section of Wall Street and Silicon Valley" (Caulfield, 2012). While the original xMOOCs shared with cMOOCs the notion of free worldwide participation in a course without credit, they differed in employing a course management plat-form, in many ways not unlike Blackboard or Moodle, and instructor-led instruction in a traditional hub-and-spoke model. Nevertheless, there are some distinctive, characteristic features of xMOOCs that emerged from the predilections of the Stanford faculty who began the xMOOC movement.

In the summer of 2011, Stanford University research professor Sebastian Thrun and Peter Norvig, Google's Director of Research, began planning the course Introduction to Artificial Intelligence, which they would co-teach that fall. Thrun and Norvig wanted to use the course to explore a better way to extend high-quality instruction to large numbers of students at no cost. Thrun sent out an email announcing that this class would be offered to anyone free of charge. *The New York Times* picked up the news, and it "went viral."

Norvig had expected 1,000 students to sign up for the online version of the course, which would be offered also in face-to-face format for Stanford students. The more optimistic Thrun predicted 10,000 online enrollments, without really believing that prognosis himself. Both instructors—and Stanford—were amazed when 160,000 people from 190 countries signed up to take the course online. Online students were not offered Stanford college credits, but those who successfully completed all course requirements would get a "letter of accomplishment" signed by the instructors.

Thrun and Norvig acknowledged MIT's role in leading the effort of high-prestige universities to make course materials available for free online. But they both felt that the MIT online materials were too dominated by videotapes of hour-long university lectures (Leckhart & Cheshire, 2012). Thrun and Norvig did not think this was the best strategy for engaging online learners;

they regarded the Khan Academy's five-minute videos as closer to the mark. In addition, Thrun and Norvig wanted to preserve some elements of the assignment deadlines and synchronous interactions among people in a face-to-face class. Accordingly, they chose to use very short pieces of videotaped explanations (about a minute in length) as one of the professors sketched out an idea, followed by interactive exercises that asked the online student to respond to questions about what he had just seen. Students might respond by choosing one of several options or by entering a value right on the same drawing. Responses were scored for accuracy automatically so that the student could get immediate feedback. Online students could also submit questions, and artificial intelligence software sifted through the submissions to identify the most common questions, which Thrun or Norvig then addressed in future videotaped segments. Online and Stanford-based students did the same homework, due every Friday, and took the same exams. Peer-to-peer interaction was achieved through online discussion forums. Some 2,000 volunteer translators helped translate the course materials into 44 languages (Thrun, 2012).

The Introduction to Artificial Intelligence course will be remembered as a landmark in the move to open access to higher education, but Thrun and Norvig viewed it as a pilot effort. Norvig points out that the 160,000-person enrollment numbers are somewhat misleading; many of the people who signed up for the course never did anything with it again (Norvig, 2012a). Three weeks into the course, there were 45,000 students participating online—still more students than Stanford's entire student body. Of those online students, 21,000 ended up successfully completing all of the course requirements and 3,000 completed a "basic" track with less programming.

And what of the 200 students taking the course at Stanford? Thrun notes that by the end of the term, the face-to-face lectures were attended by only about 30 students (Thrun, 2012). Most of the Stanford students preferred the online short videos and associated exercises.

When it came to students' performance in the course, Norvig describes the distribution of points for online and Stanford students as being overall quite similar (Norvig, 2012b). Stanford students had a slightly higher mean, and there was more variance among online students. Thrun points out that the 248 students with perfect scores were all taking the course online (Salmon, 2012). Norvig speculates that this may be because Introduction to Artificial Intelligence was the only class some of the online students were taking, and they could spend a lot of time to get things just right. Some cynics suggested that there may have been some online cheating.

In January 2012 Thrun launched a Web-based start-up using the same learning platform as the Stanford artificial intelligence course. He named his new enterprise Udacity—a combination of "university" and "audacity." By the fall of 2012 venture capitalists had ponied up $21.5 million to fund Thrun's start-up, according to *The Wall Street Journal* (Clark, 2012).

At roughly the same time, two other Stanford professors, Daphne Koller and Andrew Ng, announced the formation of another MOOC start-up called Coursera. Unlike Udacity, which concentrated on mathematics and information technology subjects, Coursera announced its intention to work with all kinds of higher education content. Coursera received $16 million in venture capital funding in April 2012 and announced its partnership with four elite universities (Stanford, University of Michigan, Princeton, and the University of Pennsylvania). By fall 2012, Coursera was offering 100 courses. By the end of 2012 another 29 universities had agreed to partner with Coursera and by April 2013, the anniversary of the company's founding, the Coursera Web site boasted 3.2 million users of its courses.

Although it started like Udacity by offering its courses for free on a non-credit basis, Coursera moved quickly to open up options for its MOOC participants to receive college credit. It began talking to the American Council on Education (ACE) about reviewing five of its first courses to certify them as being on the college level. In spring 2013 the ACE recommended that its member colleges and universities accept these courses (Algebra, Pre-Calculus, Calculus, Genetics and Evolution, and Bioelectricity) for transfer credit. ACE course approval opened the door for students to receive credit for course completion, but students taking one of these MOOCs for college credit would have to pay to have their examinations proctored by ProctorU, a company that connects students and proctors through Web cameras, and to petition for credit from the specific college or university they attend. ACE subsequently reviewed four of Udacity's courses for credit as well.

The MOOC providers' move into offering courses for era was apparent in new partnership with political support from the California governor's office and financial support from the Gates Foundation, Udacity, and San Jose State University (SJSU) struck a deal to develop and implement a set of MOOCs on that state university campus. The experience with one of these MOOCs, that for teaching remedial mathematics, is described in some detail in Chapter 7.

In addition to the two Stanford MOOC spinoff companies, 2012 also saw the establishment of edX as a joint project between the MIT and Harvard University to offer free online courses on a massive scale on their own MOOC platform. The nonprofit edX has tended to portray itself as the more academic, deliberate player in the MOOC sector using the tag line "take great online courses from the world's best universities." EdX was able to draw on an even larger set of resources than the Stanford startups, with MIT and Harvard pledging $30 million each to establish the nonprofit organization. Subsequent partners have included the University of California, Berkeley, the University of Texas system, and a host of U.S. and international partners (Australian National University, TU Delft, Ecole Polytechnique Fédérale de Lausanne, Georgetown University, McGill University, Rice University, the University of Toronto, Wellesley College, Kyoto University, Seoul National University, Berklee

College of Music, Boston University, Cornell University, Davidson College, the University of Hong Kong, the Hong Kong University of Science and Technology, Karolinska Institutet, Université Catholique de Louvain, Peking University, Tsinghua University, Technische Universität München, the University of Queensland, and the University of Washington). For each edX course they want to develop, university partners can choose one of two relationships with edX: they can either use the edX platform as a free learning management system and develop the course on their own (later giving edX a cut of any revenue generated by the course) or they can team with edX in developing the course, paying edX for its design and production services (and also giving edX a share of any revenue ultimately generated by the course).

Although maintaining the idea of offering MOOCs for free to students not seeking college credit, edX appears poised to engage actively with students who do want college credit. It has contracted with Pearson VUE so that MOOC students can use any of that company's testing centers around the world. It has also licensed one of its MIT-developed courses, "Circuits & Electronics," to SJSU, where it has been used for a blended course taken by 85 tuition-paying students.

These MOOC startups have developed course platforms that are similar in many ways to commercially available platforms like Blackboard or Desire2Learn (Watters, 2012). The biggest difference technologically is around assessment capabilities. The xMOOCs incorporate automated scoring of students' homework and responses to test questions. Coursera also has technology supports for peer grading and feedback. The MOOC startups differ from companies like Blackboard or Desire2Learn also in that they offer the faculty member teaching a MOOC extensive assistance in the design and development of course materials. The MOOC companies will take responsibility for filming lectures, editing and segmenting the video, and will work with faculty members to develop the embedded assessments as well as graphics and animations that enliven course content.

In the United Kingdom, 20 universities have come together to build on the online instruction experiences of the Open University to offer MOOCs starting in the 2013–14 academic year. The courses will be offered through Future Learn, which has been established as an independent company.

In contrast to other online courses in higher education, the original xMOOCs did not use personalized instruction, adaptive learning features, or blended instruction. Recall that Thrun and Norvig wanted their Stanford artificial intelligence MOOC to have many of the cohort-pacing features of classroom-based instruction. The xMOOCs are characterized by very short segments of direct instruction or demonstration followed by brief skills assessments that can be scored automatically. They are designed not only to accommodate large numbers of users but also to leverage the massiveness of their audience. Learners can post questions for their classmates to respond to. Coursera asserts that because of the large number of users and their distribution in time zones around the world, the average question receives an answer within 22 minutes (Koller & Ng, 2012).

As the xMOOC companies have gained experience in course outcomes and trying to obtain faculty buy-in, they have departed from their initial concept of instruction offered totally online and started moving to blended models of instruction. After the developmental mathematics MOOC piloted at SJSU in spring 2013 resulted in a drastic drop in student pass rates, a blend of MOOC-based and classroom-based instruction in developmental mathematics was tried out the following summer.

Some observers see supporting education in the developing world as the major potential contribution of MOOCs (Liyanagunawardena, Williams, & Adams, 2013), and blended learning versions appear most likely to take hold in those settings as well. In Rwanda, the new Kepler University has opened with a design based on using MOOCs supplemented by classroom sessions with local instructors.

It should be remembered that MOOCs are in a very early stage of evolution. Colleges and universities are just starting to gain experience with them, and research on how they operate and their effects on learning is just now under way (see the MOOC Research Hub at www.moocresearch.com/).

To gain another perspective on where MOOCs may go in the future, we return to Peter Norvig, Google's director of research and one of the instructors of the Stanford Introduction to Artificial Intelligence MOOC that triggered so much attention. An idea about improving the MOOC experience came from Peter Norvig's response when we asked him what he would do differently if he were offering another MOOC:

> I think the main thing to focus on is better community. Our discussion forums went pretty well, but could be better. I think it would be useful to have a sense of community that goes beyond a single class. The Beach Boys don't sing "be true to your course," and courses don't have colors and mascots. But schools do, and students feel they belong to a school, and they gain something from that belonging and contribute. It would be great to build that online. Then the students who perform well in one class would expect to be teaching assistants in the next; the community would contribute to each other over time.
>
> I'd also like to find a way to have more branching, not just a linear sequence with everyone going at the same pace. We'd like to practice mastery learning, but we also benefit from having people stick together synchronously. I would like to find a way to balance these.
>
> (Norvig, 2012b)

It should be remembered that despite all the media attention, MOOCs had a relatively limited footprint in higher education in 2012. According to the Babson Survey Research Group, only 2.6 percent of U.S. higher education institutions were offering MOOCs that year and only another 9.4 percent described themselves as engaged in planning to do so (Allen & Seaman, 2013). Moreover, the vast majority of MOOC participants were not enrolled students taking the course for credit.

Evidence of Effectiveness

With all this activity around online courses in higher education, a natural question is how well do students learn from these courses? Are cohort-based MOOCs using a broadcast model more or less effective than mastery-based learning systems? How important is it to have a face-to-face component supplementing learning activities that occur online?

Unfortunately, we do not yet have a straightforward answer to any of these questions. The meta-analysis we conducted for the U.S. Department of Education suggested that blended approaches typically have an advantage over conventional face-to-face instruction while purely online courses produce equivalent learning outcomes. However, that meta-analysis did not include any courses developed after 2008.

More recently, we had the opportunity to examine outcomes for a variety of online learning interventions funded by the Bill & Melinda Gates Foundation through the Next Generation Learning Challenges (NGLC) initiative. The first wave of grants awarded under this initiative went to interventions designed to improve student outcomes by applying one or more of four technology-based strategies: blended learning, learning analytics, open courseware for a core academic course, or experiences to promote deeper learning. The rationale behind the grant-making was that the "pockets of innovation" in colleges and universities typically do not spread to improve outcomes at scale, in part because of a "not invented here" attitude on the part of higher education institutions and in part because the inventors of new approaches lack funding and prior experience in bringing innovations to scale. The question the foundation asked us to address as evaluators for this set of grants was whether or not the student outcomes achieved on the campus originally developing the innovation, or wherever it had first been used, could be replicated on multiple campuses with larger numbers of students.

For a variety of reasons, few of the NGLC projects set up random-assignment experiments to provide a rigorous test of the effectiveness of their online learning innovations. In some cases, technology-based and conventional versions of a course ran concurrently so that student outcomes could be compared. More often, the best data available were course outcomes for the newly designed course compared to those for the same course taught in prior years to different student cohorts (and not necessarily by the same instructor). Hence, the individual projects' reported outcomes could easily be confounded by differences between the students taking the two versions of the course or by differences in instructors that have nothing to do with the NGLC interventions. Nevertheless, when taken in aggregate, the outcomes provide a portrait of the experiences that colleges and universities are having with online learning.

The core student outcome measure for the NGLC innovations was "course success rate," defined as the proportion of enrolled students passing the course with a grade of "C" or better. Overall, the NGLC innovations led to student course outcomes on a par with those of instruction as usual (Means, Shear et al., 2013). This outcome was interpreted positively by those projects that were able to demonstrate cost savings either for the institution offering the course or for students who were freed from the requirement to purchase a text-book because they could use open educational resources. In addition, there were no differences on average in course success rates for low-income and other students (Means, Shear et al., 2013), a reassuring finding in light of some earlier studies of success rates in online community college courses (Jaggers, 2011).

As one would expect, despite the average finding of "no significant difference," the different NGLC projects varied considerably in their impacts.

Of the 22 projects that supplied data that could be used to calculate an esti-mated effect, eight had statistically significant effects. Of these eight effects, seven favored the course redesigned to incorporate online learning and one favored the original version of the course before technology was introduced. An examination of subsets of the projects found that the developmental and gateway mathematics courses redesigned to incorporate online learning on average had significantly positive effects on student outcomes. Average out-comes for redesigned English and humanities courses, on the other hand, were negative.

With respect to the evaluation's central question Means and her colleagues found that on average, student outcomes in courses redesigned to incorporate online learning were more positive than those in the prior courses on the campuses where the redesign effort was initiated, but not on other campuses to which the new course design or course design process was spread (Means, Shear et al., 2013).

The evidence of effectiveness provided by individual NGLC projects was not of the highest caliber. As Means et al. point out, in most cases course grades and completion rates for the courses redesigned to incorporate online learning components were compared to those for the same course without those com-ponents, without statistical correction for any differences in the characteristics of students in the two course versions.

Other studies of the effectiveness of online learning in college courses include the experiment by Figlio, Rush, and Yin (2010) described in Chapter 2. These economists argue that a fair test of the relative effectiveness of online learning requires not only random assignment of students to online and face-to-face conditions but also that the same instructor teach both versions of the course using exactly the same materials and approach. The conditions contrasted by Figlio et al. were two versions of a course with the only difference being whether or not the lectures were watched over the Internet or in the classroom. Few technology proponents would expect a difference in learning outcomes for such a weak manipulation, and indeed there were no statistically significant differences between the two groups in terms of performance on course examinations. Figlio et al. went on to examine differences between the two conditions for different student subgroups defined by race, gender, and prior college grade point average. They found that male students, Hispanics, and students with below-average grade point averages did better if they were assigned to the live-lecture condition than they did in the online lecture condition. The authors conjecture that Hispanic students may still be learning English and consequently have some difficulty understanding the videotaped lectures and that males and lower-achieving students may be more prone to procrastination and last-minute cramming when given the option of listening to lectures whenever they want. In discussing their findings, Figlio et al. strike a warning about higher education's rush to embrace online learning:

> Our strongest findings in favor of live instruction are for the relatively low-achieving students, male students, and Hispanic students. These are precisely the students who are more likely to populate the less selective universities and community colleges. These students may well be disadvantaged by the movement to online education and, to the extent that it is the less selective institutions and community colleges that are most fully embracing online education, inadvertently they may be harming a significant portion of their student body.
>
> (Figlio, Rush, & Yin, 2010, p. 21)

Some of the details of student behaviors documented by Figlio and colleagues cast doubt on the relationship between the course's lectures and learning as measured by course examinations. More than one-third (36 percent) of the students assigned to attend lectures in person actually went to less than 20 percent of those lectures (Figlio, Rush, & Yin, 2010, p. 14). A footnote provides a further bit of context: "It is also the case that many of the students who are observed rarely coming to class might actually not ever view the lectures at all. The university has several competing lecture note-taking services that are extremely popular with students." Students in both the Internet-based and the live-lecture conditions may in fact have relied on these notes rather than the lectures themselves, a common strategy among college students that works quite well with some kinds of tests. In any case, the Figlio, Rush, and Lin study illustrates the complexities of implementing experimental studies of college courses and the complexities of interpreting impact findings from experiments conducted in the messy real world of education institutions.

More recently ITHAKA, a nonprofit organization providing research and consulting to help higher education institutions using technology, ran a set of randomized trials comparing learning outcomes of the OLI statistics course with those of conventional classroom-based statistics at six public university campuses (Bowen et al., 2012). Students who signed up for introductory statistics on these campuses were invited to participate in the study for a modest reward (either a gift card or a free electronic textbook), and those who agreed were assigned at random to the treatment or the control condition. In the treatment condition, students used the OLI statistics course and met face to face with an instructor once a week in order to have the opportunity to ask questions and receive personalized assistance if they needed it. Students in the control condition received the regular version of the course (which varied from campus to campus and was not described by Bowen et al. (2012), beyond the statement that it met for three to four hours a week). All students completed a test of statistical literacy and a survey about their backgrounds at the beginning of the course, and all students on a particular campus took final examinations, which included a common set of statistics questions that were scored as one of the learning outcomes for the experiment. Other outcomes examined by the study were scores on the re-administration of the statistical literacy test at the end of the course and earning a passing grade. The results were quite straightforward: students in the blended learning condition with OLI did just slightly better than students in the control condition, but there were no statistically significant differences between the two versions of the course overall or for any student subgroup. This latter finding is important in light of the interpretations made by Figlio, Rush, and Yin (2010) and Jaggers (2011) that low-income, less well-prepared students, Hispanics, and males may suffer when courses are taught online. (See Chapter 7 for a more extended treatment of this issue.)

Importantly, among the 605 students participating in the ITHAKA study, more than half came from lower-income families, more than half had parents who had not attended college, about a third were African American or Hispanic, and over 40 percent were male. Of the 64 statistical tests for differences on study outcomes for particular student subgroups, only five attained statistical significance. (Testing for the significance of differences with a 95 percent confidence level, one would expect one out of 20 or three to four of these contrasts to be statistically significant merely by chance.) Four of the statistically significant contrasts favored the OLI treatment group and one favored the traditional face-to-face instruction group, but there was no consistent pattern for the subgroup or outcome for which statistically significant results were found. Although it involved only a single online course and only university students and therefore should not be assumed to generalize to all online instruction or to community college or younger students, the Bowen et al. (2012) study is the largest rigorous study of a specific online learning course we have been able to find in the literature.

As of this writing, no experimental tests of the effectiveness of MOOCs relative either to other forms of online instruction or to conventional classroom instruction have been published (Liyanagunawardena, Adams, & Williams, 2013). The very idea of taking people willing to learn through a MOOC and then assigning them to either that condition or some other form of instruction is fundamentally at odds with the open "take all comers" philosophy of the MOOC movement. But that philosophy may well get diluted over time and, as described above, we are starting to see courses that use the platform of one of the MOOC companies or university consortia but do not necessarily conform to the classic MOOC features of no credit, no in-class instruction, and assessment feedback derived entirely from automated or peer scoring.

Some MOOC critics point to the MOOCs' broadcast (one-to-many) communication approach and dismiss them as new wrapping on a thoroughly discredited transmission model of education (Leddy, 2013). Others express concern about the low proportion of learners actually completing all of the activities in a MOOC (Fujimoto & Cara, 2013). Not surprisingly, the for-profit MOOC companies have down-played course completion rates, which tend to be less than 20 percent, preferring inspirational stories about individuals facing adverse circumstances whose lives were improved by successfully completing a MOOC (see Daphne Koller's TED talk or Sebastian Thrun at www.ted.com). Moreover, MOOC proponents point out that the whole idea of a MOOC is to make learning experiences available to anyone who wants them, regardless of whether or not they intend to complete all the course assignments or to try to better themselves academically or professionally on the basis of a MOOC completion certificate.

One of the first detailed, scholarly descriptions of an xMOOC design and delivery experience was that by Belanger and Thornton (2013) who documented Duke University's experience with its first MOOC, Bioelectricity: A Quantitative Approach, offered through Coursera. Developed by biomedical engineering faculty member Roger Barr, this free eight-week course launched in September 2012 as part of Duke University's Online Education Initiative.

Over 12,000 students from 100 countries signed up for the Bioelectricity course, but only 3,576 responded to Coursera's "getting to know you" questionnaire and only 8,000 logged in during the first week of the course. Among those who responded to Coursera's questionnaire, only a third resided in the U.S. and two-thirds already held a bachelor's or advanced degree. The course included two distinct series of quizzes: the first series contained multiple-choice questions and the second involved quantitative problems requiring numeric solutions. Students were given as many attempts to take a quiz as they wanted, and their grade was based on their best score regardless of number of attempts. In the end, 313 students completed the course with either a "basic" certificate or a "certificate of distinction," depending on their quiz performance.

This example illustrates the complexity of trying to provide a fair measure of course completion rates for different kinds of courses. The completion rate for Duke's Bioelectricity MOOC could be cited as anything from 2.6 percent to 25 percent, depending on the denominator one selects to use—the number of original sign-ups, the number of learners who ever logged onto the course, or the number successfully completing both quizzes in the first week of the course.

Reported completion rates for other MOOCs include 5 percent for MIT's first MITx course (Gee as quoted in Watters, 2012); 14 percent for Thrun and Norvig's Introduction to AI; and just over 2 percent for Coursera's Social Network Analysis class (Levine as quoted in Watters, 2012). A broader data set is described by Kolowich (2013a) in his discussion of the results of a survey of MOOC instructors conducted by the *Chronicle of Higher Education*. An online questionnaire was sent to every MOOC professor the journal could identify—184 of them—and 103 responded. Among those professors whose MOOC had finished running, the average reported course completion rate was 7.5 percent, with a median of 2,600 course completions (Kolowich, 2013a).

As MOOC defenders point out, it is not really fair to compare completion rates for individuals who enroll in MOOCs for all kinds of reasons, including curiosity about the experience, with those for regular college courses with students taking them for college credit (Koller et al, 2013). Coursera's founders and several colleagues recently published an article in which they disaggregate data for several different categories of learners in a number of their MOOCs (Koller et al., 2013). One MOOC instructor asked her students to respond to a survey before the course started, indicating their reasons for taking the course. Only a third of those who signed up actually took the survey, but among them 63 percent said that their intention was to complete all of the course requirements so that they could earn the certificate of accomplishment. By the time the course ended, 24 percent of these students had successfully completed all components of the course compared with just 2 percent of the students who either declined to take the survey or indicated on the survey that they did not plan to do all of the course assignments.

Another data point described by Koller and colleagues was for a MOOC using a new Coursera option, called Signature Track, which for a small fee employs identity verification technology and allows the MOOC completer to get a "university-branded credential." Since they were paying money for Signature Track, these students could be construed as committed to finishing the course, and 74 percent of them did so, which is in the range of many university courses, and is far higher than the mere 9 percent of all the students who signed up completing the MOOC requirements.

We can expect a lot more information about MOOC completion rates for different kinds of students and courses to emerge over the coming years.

Course completion rate comparisons will be more fair when students in MOOC and conventional versions of the same course all come from the same population and all take the course for credit.

Early results leaked to the press from SJSU's pilot Udacity MOOCs are not encouraging (Fujimoto & Cara, 2013). The percentage of SJSU students earning course credit with a C or better in the spring 2013 MOOCs was 44 percent in college algebra and 51 percent in statistics (compared with usual rates of 74 percent in classroom versions of both courses). In the developmental mathematics course for students who had already failed the course the prior semester, the results were even more discouraging: only 29 percent of SJSU students earned the required C or better in this course, compared with its usual completion rate of 80 percent when taught as a classroom-based mastery learning course with online math practice and assessment software.[6]

Limitations of Available Research Evidence

As noted previously, the research base on the effectiveness of online learning in higher education is limited. With new technology capabilities and new players in the learning platform and course content spheres coming on so rapidly, careful research simply cannot keep up with events. By the time a rigorous study is designed, implemented, analyzed, and reported, the available technology has moved to a new level.

Moreover, university traditions and institutional research boards make it difficult to conduct adequately powered random-assignment experiments on alternative teaching approaches. Most campuses feel that it is inappropriate to require a tuition-paying student to take a course in an online format if that student does not wish to do so. Those wishing to conduct an experiment contrasting different versions of online and blended learning typically have to work with just that subset of the students signing up for a course who agree to be randomly assigned to an instructional condition. Information on the past academic achievement of the students volunteering to participate in the experiment is sometimes withheld from researchers by institutional research offices concerned with student privacy.

When random-assignment experiments or quasi-experiments are conducted, the attempt to establish a fair test can by stymied by different course retention rates in the conditions being compared. The high rate of non-participation among those who sign up for MOOCs is the extreme example, but in online courses generally, there is a significantly higher dropout rate than in traditional college courses (Jaggers, 2011). If 80 percent of the students in an online section of a course decide to discontinue, comparing the performance of the 20 percent who stick it out with that of students in a traditional section of the course where only 10–15 percent drop out leads to biased estimates of relative effectiveness.

Finally, in most cases colleges and universities introduce online and blended courses or sections without seriously examining student performance results. Campuses tend to perform a gross "gut check" on course completion rates and consider an online or blended course a success if pass rates are the same as or higher than those in previous years, without controlling for student characteristics or other aspects of the new course.

Given the amount of learning online occurring in colleges and universities today, there is tremendous untapped potential for exploring the nature of learning and sharing evidence-based best practices and online learning resources across institutions. We believe that universities could do much more to design courses and course implementation procedures to support evaluation of learning outcomes with different instructional models.

Looking Toward the Future

We close this chapter with a discussion of the implications of "MOOC mania" for the future of online learning in higher education and of higher education itself.

Today's MOOCs are unlikely to be the last word in online higher education. They are still in their infancy and the organizations that have mounted so many of these courses so quickly are almost sure to find problems in their initial designs and implementations but also to be a fertile source of innovative ideas for improving the MOOC experience.

We believe that it is important that we not judge the effectiveness of MOOCs or any other online learning model solely on the basis of course pass rates that depend largely on assessments of short-term memory of content. We need to take a broader look at performance on learning transfer tasks (How do students who achieve "mastery" within an online learning system perform on related problems that are not built into the learning system? How do they perform in the next course in a course sequence?) Ultimately, we would like to have data on impacts on employability and job performance as well. Addressing these questions will require a significant investment in longitudinal research. We believe that the issues at stake justify such an investment.

Hill (2012) argues that the biggest impact of MOOCs on higher education may turn out not to be the MOOC technology platforms and instructional models themselves but rather the greater prestige and legitimacy given to online learning because of association with the elite institutions developing and running MOOCs. At the same time, MOOCs are stirring debate about what higher education will be like in the twenty-first century, the role of different kinds of higher education institutions, and the nature of college faculty positions.

Some observers predict that the main influence of MOOCs in higher education will come from the emerging trend for less-selective colleges and community colleges to use MOOC platforms and the MOOC resources developed by elite universities (Christensen et al., 2011). We believe that if this trend grows, it will be in the form of blended learning designs. Faculty resist "teaching someone else's course" and will want to put their own stamp on a course even if it is based on a MOOC developed by and featuring some other professor. MOOCs are likely to evolve in ways that allow instructors using a MOOC developed elsewhere to do some tailoring and selecting of the MOOC content. And hopefully, instructors using a MOOC developed by someone else will focus on using classroom time with their students for more interactive activities rather than for information transmission.

The instructional model could look something like the one tried out by Stanford University in engineering education decades ago. Hewlett Packard employees in Santa Rosa, California, who wanted to take Stanford engineering courses but could not come to Stanford's campus watched videotapes of the engineering professors' lectures in small groups facilitated by an on-site "course coordinator." The groups discussed the content of the lectures and replayed parts they found confusing. Jim Gibbons, Stanford's dean of the school of engineering at the time, pioneered this "tutored video instruction" approach, which actually resulted in the remote students scoring higher on the course examinations than did those attending the lectures in person at Stanford, even though they had lower Scholastic Assessment Test (SAT) and Graduate Record Examination (GRE) scores than Stanford's residential students (Gibbons, Pannoni, & Orlin, 1996). In this model, both the faculty member giving the lectures and the on-site instructor guiding group discussion play important roles in supporting students' learning. We expect that Kepler University in Rwanda will employ a similar model, but using MOOC resources instead of videotaped lectures.

Some of those who foresee this future for online learning in higher education express concern that such practices will lead to fewer faculty positions at the less selective colleges and public universities (Shullenberger, 2013). They may well be right. Reducing the number of positions (or the compensation level for positions) is not going to be popular with faculty associations, but unfortunately it is essential to cutting costs in a labor-intensive industry like higher education (Bowen & Lack, 2012).

Blogger Audrey Watters (2012) raises a slightly different point about the potential effect of MOOCs on higher education: Since tuition attached to high-enrollment lower-division courses of the kind now being turned into MOOCs has traditionally subsidized the upper-division advanced courses with lower enrollment, how will the latter be funded in a MOOC-rich higher education system?

Heller (2013) raises a different concern. In addition to reducing the number of faculty positions, widespread use of a few highly regarded MOOCs for popular undergraduate courses could lead to the homogenization of the content taught in introductory courses in fields such as philosophy, psychology, or political science—a trend that eventually could undermine the diversity of thinking in these fields and the quality of intellectual life.

At the same time there are potential silver linings in the greater incorporation of well-crafted online courses (both MOOCs and adaptive non-MOOC courses such as those from the Open Learning Initiative). Instructional design is actually a field in its own right, with a set of principles and techniques, and an empirical research base. Perhaps more importantly, the last three decades have witnessed some remarkable advances in the learning sciences (Bransford, Brown, & Cocking, 2000; Koedinger, Corbett, & Perfetti, 2012), providing a clearer understanding of how people learn and how assessments can be designed to advance learning rather than merely to measure its outcomes (Pellegrino, Chudowsy, & Glaser, 2001). Most college faculty have no background in any of these areas. So even apart from the inefficiency stemming from the fact that all faculty members design their own courses, there is the fact that we are not optimizing higher education because we are not using all of the available expertise to design optimal learning experiences. Faculty members who have taught MOOCs report that the process of developing and teaching these courses has led them to re-examine their subjects and their teaching approaches in ways that will benefit their campus-based students in the future (Kolowich, 2013a).

The active collaboration between faculty, learning scientists, and technology experts, as modeled by a number of the MOOC providers as well as by the OLI, has promise for producing better courses. As it becomes respectable to be a faculty member using online learning systems and resources developed by others, we may see a new emphasis on faculty skill in leading classroom discussions, modeling how experts think and talk in the field, and being able to inspire students. Ultimately, undergraduates would be the chief beneficiaries of such a development.

Notes

1 The same series of surveys suggests that university faculty are not necessarily buying in. As late as 2012, only 30 percent of chief academic officers reported that their faculty see the value and legitimacy of online learning (Allen & Seaman, 2013).
2 This interest in online education as a potentially lucrative business opportunity is not limited to the U.S. In Brazil, the for-profit distance learning company Anhanguera is valued at $1.4 billion (Barber, Donnelly, & Rizvi, 2013, p. 34).
3 Subsequently, she was re-instated after strong demonstrations of support from faculty, alumni, and students, some of whom spray painted "GREED" on the columns of a campus building (Webley, 2012).
4 The Carnegie unit for measuring college credit, which is based on the number of hours spent in the classroom, has come under increasing criticism in recent years. In December 2012 the Carnegie Foundation for the Advancement of Teaching announced that it had received funding from the Hewlett Foundation to study the

past, present, and future role of the Carnegie unit in education. In a press release the foundation states "as expectations for schools and students have risen dramatically and technology has revealed the potential of personalized learning, the Carnegie Foundation now believes it is time to consider how a revised unit, based on competency rather than time, could improve teaching and learning in high schools, colleges, and universities."

5 See http://www4.nau.edu/insidenau/bumps/2012/7_9_12/pl.html (accessed May 26, 2013).

6 In the two mathematics MOOCs that were taken also by students outside of San Jose State for a whole range of purposes, the completion rate for non San Jose State students was just 12 percent (Fujimoto & Cara, 2013).

Chapter 4

Interest-Driven Learning Online

Most research on online learning has focused on learning in formal programs—either school courses or formal training programs. Yet most of our learning—online as well as in the physical world—actually occurs outside of formal settings. Learning happens not just in formal courses during our school years but "life-long and life-wide" (Bransford et al., 2006; Ito et al., 2013). Many of our waking hours are spent in some kind of learning—sometimes to better cope with or enrich our everyday lives, sometimes with the goal of strengthening our odds of succeeding in formal education programs, sometimes with the goal of making ourselves more employable or eligible for professional advancement, and sometimes just for fun.

People have always engaged in all of these types of out-of-school learning, but now with the increase in Internet access and the explosion of online learning and education resources, opportunities have greatly increased. For larger and larger segments of the world's population, Internet-based resources and applications are a major part of everyday learning, amplifying not just online access to information but also the ability to acquire new skills, find an audience for one's work, and connect with geographically dispersed fellow learners and mentors. On *YouTube EDU* a section for life-long learning sits next to those for K-12 schools and higher education. The life-long learning section contains videos on a host of topics, ranging from conducting a marine pest survey to setting up a virtual biotechnology lab to poetry readings to songs about science. People are using Web resources to learn everything from dishwasher repair to programming languages to how to dance the Harlem Shake. Internet-based learning in informal settings outside of school or formal training programs has become a major part of modern life.

Collins and Halverson (2009) make the case that the emergence of near-universal Internet access and plentiful free or low-cost computer-based learning resources is giving rise to a new era of learner-driven, life-long education. Just as schooling replaced apprenticeship as the dominant mechanism through which society passed on essential skills and knowledge in the nineteenth century, Collins and Halverson predict that technology-enabled self-initiated learning will one day displace formal schooling. In the new era they envision, learning will happen in multiple venues, be computer-mediated, and focus on generic skills such as problem solving, communicating in multiple media, and being able to find learning resources when you need them rather than on having a standard body of knowledge in your head. Regardless of whether or not formal schooling gets displaced as Collins and Halverson predict, there is ample evidence that formal schooling and training programs are not the only learning game in town.

Increasingly, policy documents are acknowledging the importance of learning outside of school and throughout the lifespan. The most recent National Education Technology Plan (NETP) from the U.S. Department of Education (2010b), for example, explicitly sets the nation's goal as providing the infrastructure and opportunities to learn any where, any time, and throughout the lifespan—something much broader than the goal of providing technology in K-12 schools that was the focus of earlier NETPs developed in 2000 and 2008. A recent report by the OECD calls for the recognition of competencies gained through non-formal and informal learning (Werquin, 2010).

Several commentators (Conner, 1997–2013; Sefton-Green, 2010) have suggested placing informal learning into the conceptual landscape defined by two dimensions—one dealing with the extent to which the learning is planned and structured and the other dealing with the setting. Sefton-Green (2004) describes a continuum of settings with formal settings such as schools or training programs on one end, through intermediate categories such as museums, clubs, and camps, to the totally informal settings we think of as everyday life, in which we interact with family, friends, and passers-by. His other dimension involves content, with organized curriculum at one end of the continuum and "casual" learning at the other, as illustrated in Figure 4.1.

In contrast to the last chapter and Chapters 5–8, which deal with formal settings and planned instruction, this chapter focuses on settings outside of school and on types of learning that are voluntary and often loosely structured. We provide examples of self-initiated learning occurring outside of classrooms, organizing their presentation according to the primary motivation driving the learning activity. We then discuss what we see as an emerging trend to try to connect school and informal learning activities in order to leverage the interest and persistence that learners show in informal settings for school-based learning. This discussion is followed by a description of research studies that have examined the learning outcomes of self-initiated informal learning activities and a cautionary note on applying research conclusions drawn from studies of informal learning to the design of formal learning environments. Finally, we take up the question of whether the "digital divide" is greater in self-directed learning than in school-based technology-based learning.

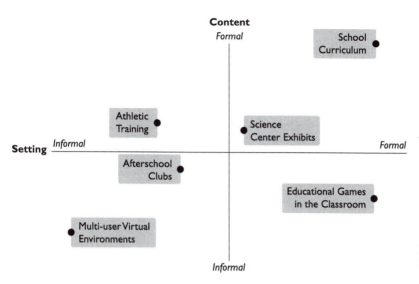

Figure 4.1 Learning Across Informal and Formal Settings

Diverse Goals for Self-Initiated Online Learning

Any categorization of intentional daily learning activities is bound to be something of an oversimplification, with some experiences spanning categories. Keeping this caveat in mind, we nevertheless have developed a taxonomy of types of self-directed, self-initiated online learning that we use to structure our description of how people use Web-based learning resources for out-of-school learning. Our categories, based on the major goal or intention motivating the learner, are:

- episodic learning to satisfy curiosity
- learning as entertainment
- learning for better living
- learning for professional advancement
- learning to reinforce or substitute for formal instruction.

Episodic Learning to Satisfy Curiosity

People have always been curious, but that curiosity was much harder to satisfy before the Internet, modern search engines, and *Wikipedia*. Many people lived in settings where there were no local experts and few books to tell them about the reproductive behavior of mollusks, the Coptic religion, or the way in which pi was discovered. One of the fundamental changes wrought by the Internet age is the increase in people's ability to find information on their own. We are much less reliant on experts or books located in the same physical space as we are. An Internet connection puts "all of the world's knowledge" at our fingertips.

Since the advent of modern search engines, the curiosity that has always been a human characteristic can be indulged rather than suppressed. As soon as someone says, "I wonder . . ." the next response is "Why don't you *Google* it?" For those who would like some help integrating information about a specific topic, *Wikipedia*, the online free encyclopedia, contains over 4 million entries (in English) contributed, reviewed, and edited by a worldwide legion of volunteers. Under the auspices of the Wikimedia Foundation, a nonprofit organization established to run Wikipedia and related wiki-based open education projects, additional wikipedias have been developed in 285 languages other than English. Languages other than English for which Wikipedia contains over a million entries are (in order of size) Dutch, German, French, Swedish, Italian, Spanish, and Russian.

We use the phrase "episodic learning" to describe short-term, intentional, low-stakes exploration and information seeking on the Internet.[1] These episodes are distinguished from learning for better living, professional advancement, and to reinforce formal instruction by the fact that they serve no obvious instrumental purpose—at least in the short term. Episodic learning has no obvious utility; it provides the learner with knowledge that is "nice to know."

The products of episodic learning online may be largely forgotten in a matter of months or days, or they may stick with the learner and be built on through more planned investigations of related material, which is one form of learning for pleasure, as described later in this section.

Some Web developers have tried to assemble miscellaneous information likely to appeal to the curiosity of broad groups of users. The Web site *HowStuffWorks*, for example, offers a smorgasbord of information on topics such as "Are figs really full of baby wasps?" and "Why do we have eyebrows?"

More typical is the interweaving of online resources with offline daily experiences and simple human curiosity. For example, one of us has a summer cottage on a remote, small piece of land called Breezy Point (not the Breezy Point on Long Island famous for the damage done to it by Super Storm Sandy). The widow living in the cottage next door had explained that her husband had named the point several decades earlier at the behest of his mother who had once played a role in a play called "Breezy Point." A framed copy of a playbill from that performance, put on by the church guild in a small town in 1909, hung in the neighbor's cottage. Inspection of the small type revealed the name of the playwright as Mary Barnard Horne. At this point, offline and online information seeking merged: a quick online search that night revealed that a play called *Breezy Point* was written in 1898 by one of America's first woman playwrights and netted a copy of the *Breezy Point* script, scanned by Google and available from the Harvard University library.[2]

Such situation-driven learning serves no obvious practical purpose but clearly enriches our lives. Through such activities, we gain a fuller appreciation of the world and, through the accumulation of such experiences over time, we can accrue social capital and an expanded sense of our own knowledge resources. As Renninger (2000) points out, interest-driven learning combines the affective and the cognitive aspects of our nature.

Learning as Entertainment

When you ask a young child to explain which things are "school" and which are "fun," the answer you get is essentially that "fun things are what I do that nobody makes me do." By this definition, self-initiated learning is always fun. Our category of learning as entertainment is a bit narrower, however. In this category we place learning activities undertaken without the expectation that there will be any tangible short- or long-term benefit other than pleasure. Important subcategories of online learning for entertainment are online games; Web 2.0 opportunities to create and share content; and the online opportunities provided by museums, civic groups, and clubs.

Extended Involvement With Topics of Interest

According to a December 2012 survey conducted by the Pew Internet and American Life Project, 81 percent of American adults use the Internet. Among Internet users, 84 percent report looking online for information about a hobby or interest. In contract to the situation-driven, brief learning episodes that comprised our first category of self-initiated learning, this category of online learning involves activities that people perform repeatedly. Crowley and Jacobs (2002) studied young children who developed what they called "islands of expertise" around specific topics, such as trains and railroads, through information seeking on the Internet as well as in other venues. Gee (2013) uses the term "passionate affinity spaces" to describe interest-driven Web sites where people discuss, interact around and produce things related to particular interests such as favorite animals, historical periods, anime, robotics, or fan fiction.

The Internet's extraordinary power to support self-initiated learning in a virtually infinite array of specific topic areas is related to what marketing people call the Internet's "long tail" (Anderson, 2004). No longer does a topic need to attract enough learners to warrant mass media; Internet distribution makes it cost effective to post information that only a very few people, perhaps scattered geographically around the world, will ever attend to. As

Web 2.0 tools allow people without programming skills to create and post Internet content, information and learning resources are no longer limited by the number of professional content producers or their judgment about what will attract a significant audience. As a consequence, our ability to become knowledgeable about very specialized topics that interest us has been magnified exponentially.

In addition to its role as a source of information, the Internet can provide models of others who are expert in the topic of interest and enable the learner to communicate with distant experts. Web 2.0 tools allow us to go beyond receiving interesting information on the Internet to becoming producers of content that reflects our interests and creativity. As Gee (2013) explains, "Digital tools . . . allow people to collaboratively engage in their own designs, critique, and discussions of news, games, media, science, policy, health, civic participation, or any other domain or topic one can imagine" (p. 8).

As people use the Internet to pursue information and communicate about these topics they become more and more knowledgeable about them. Over time, such self-initiated learning can lead to real expertise. A number of scholars are examining the role of online learning activities in developing expertise that becomes incorporated into the learner's sense of identity. In their book *A New Culture of Learning* (2011), Thomas and Seely Brown write about three kinds of learning: "learning about" and "learning to do," which are the focus of formal schooling and training, and "learning to be," which can occur when learning for fun leads to sustained engagement. The ethnographic work of Mimi Ito and her colleagues (2009) illustrates how out-of-school experiences involving use of technology can foster what Thomas and Seely Brown call "learning to be." Ito and colleagues offer numerous examples of how an accumulation of knowledge about a given area, such as Japanese anime, can become an important part of a young person's emerging identity, in turn creating the motivation for more learning. Barron's (2006) studies of young people's interest-driven learning emphasizes the connections between online and offline learning activities as well as the role of family and peers in creating opportunities for building knowledge over time.

Online Games as Entertaining Learning Activities

A subcategory of learning just for fun that has become increasingly popular, and an increasing focus of scholarship over the last decade is engagement with online games, especially multiplayer games and elaborate virtual environments. Here is an activity that often involves learning a specialized vocabulary, mastering use of novel online tools, and formulating mental models of a complex system. Online games can be challenging and require many hours of practice to achieve expertise, and yet millions of people not only voluntarily commit their time to this endeavor but also pay money for the privilege of doing so, even paying real money to obtain virtual artifacts that will enhance their online game experience.

Gee (2009) describes the essential attributes of games and their connection to learning, "Digital games are, at heart, problem solving spaces that use continual learning and provide pathways to mastery through entertainment and pleasure" (p. 67). The most obvious learning that occurs is simply how to play the game, but games may also call on learning content (e.g., Trivial Pursuit), skills, values, and conceptual content. Commercial games like *Civilization* and *Sim City* can be thought of as having "serious" subject matter (history, culture, and the environment). But regardless of its topical focus, gaming involves figuring out rules that can be used to one's advantage to accomplish goals that one is 'personally and emotionally' attached to. Gaming is always about problem solving, but unlike school assignments targeting problem solving skills, in gaming the problem solving is 'integrated with self interest.' Games provide a sense of "microcontrol" by giving the player power over movement and actions of an avatar or other game components at a fine-grained level of detail, leading to a sense of power and "embodied cognition." The player feels that his body is part of the virtual world of the game. Well-designed games lead players to induce the game's patterns and rules in order to prepare themselves for more advanced levels of the game. Games capitalize on the learning principles of ample practice and immediate feedback.

One of the best-known examples of an online game that attracts sustained engagement and serves as a "passionate affinity space" is *World of Warcraft*, a multiplayer game that 10 million people pay subscription fees to play. Players choose characteristics of their avatar and explore a complex world in which they can learn trades, slay monsters, and acquire possessions, working either singly or in teams (Steinkuehler & Duncan, 2008).

The Transition to Becoming an Online Content Producer

Dawley (2009) describes a typical trajectory in informal learning communities such as those engaged in multi-user virtual environment games as having five stages (identify, lurk, contribute, create, and lead). The entry point is often lurking, watching others play, followed by engaging in the simplest of online game interactions, both of which are informed by the examples set by more experienced participants. Sometimes players also receive explicit mentoring or tips from fellow players. As new players gain expertise in navigating the virtual environment and playing the game, they also gain recognition from other players; often they begin making modifications in the environment or add elaborations to the game. At this point, they may also become mentors for less-experienced players.

Gee (2009) highlights the intellectual accomplishments of large networks of amateurs working with smart digital tools. He asserts that they often outperform the credentialed experts in making predictions of solving problems. As examples he cites the fan-developed "sabermetrics," which proved more accurate than the statistics kept by professionals in predicting baseball outcomes and the discovery of the protein structure of an AIDS-causing monkey virus in just ten days by amateurs using the online game *Foldit* (Marshall, 2012).

Online Learning in Designed Settings

Museums, planetariums, and cultural organizations of all kinds have become important sources of creative and engaging technology-based learning content both within their physical walls and online. Content designers in this field think first about attracting the attention and interest of the museum goer or online browser and then about finding ways to extend and deepen the learner's engagement over time.

Some highly imaginative uses of technology to support learning have come from museums and science centers. The Museum of London, for example, has developed mobile phone apps to enhance a user's exploration of the city (museumoflondon.org.uk). The *Streetmuseum* app takes advantage of the phone's global positioning system (GPS) and camera to enable the user to see historical images from the museum's collection for the location where she is standing. The user can tap the app's information button to learn about the historical event the image represents. For those visiting key Roman sites in London, *Street Museum Londinium*, created through a collaboration with the History Channel, provides a more immersive experience. At historic locations such as the site of the Roman amphitheater at Guildhall, users can see recreations of the kinds of activities that would have occurred there, complete with sound effects. By using a finger to "dig" on the mobile's screen or simply blowing on an iPhone, users can excavate virtual representations of Roman artifacts, such as coins, pottery, and leather clothing that have been found at that site.

Another example from the U.K. is the Planet Science Web site (planet-science.com) with its teasing headlines ("Are your eyes playing tricks on you?" and "A gruesome sight as a giant eyeball washes up on a Florida beach"), science comics, and wacky (but scientifically sound) experiments.

The National Research Council recognized the importance of learning out of school in its report *Learning science in informal environments* (National Research Council, 2009). In discussing science learning opportunities in designed environments such as museums, aquariums, planetariums, and environmental centers, the report references the phases of interest development proposed by Hidi and Renninger (2006). They describe a trajectory through phases of situational interest triggered by information that is incongruous or surprising (like the giant eyeball featured on Planet Science) or of personal relevance; longer-term situational interest maintained through involvement in meaningful tasks; and then the emergence of what they call "individual interest" and its extended pursuit. Hidi and Renninger's concept of individual interest depends not on environmental triggers, but rather on activities that the individual will seek out and engage in repeatedly over time. This trajectory resembles those described by Ito and colleagues (2010) and by Dawley (2009) for youth's online participation and online games, described above. Designed environments have been fairly successful in engendering situational interest; their challenge is to move their visitors into sustained meaningful engagement and potentially the development of lasting individual interest.

One strategy for doing so is to engage interested people in genuine scientific or cultural activities, both of which can be supported through online learning resources. Since Christmas Day 1900, the Audubon Society has organized a Christmas Bird Count. It started with observers at 25 locations in the U.S. and Canada. Since moving to the Internet in 1998, the Bird Count has grown and extended its coverage of the globe; there are now 2,200 sites "from above the Arctic Circle to the waters of the Drake Passage off the Tierra del Fuego" (birds.audubon.org). Because the data are now available on the Internet, those who have contributed bird sites and other interested people can explore the data themselves to pursue questions about the prevalence of specific species or shifts in their location over time in response to changing weather patterns. Having people upload their observational data to a shared online database also makes it possible to have automated checking for potential entry errors, increasing the quality of the data and its usefulness to scientists, which in turn increases the meaningfulness of the citizen–scientist partnership.

Taking Courses for Enjoyment

Beyond the desire for online help for doing well in school, there are also many people who enjoy education and welcome the opportunity to add a course taken online purely for pleasure. In analyzing the people who use courses from the OCW Consortium, MIT found that as many users (43 percent) described themselves as "self-learners" as described themselves as "students" (42 percent). Among the latter group, the most commonly cited reason for using OCW was "enhance personal knowledge."

Learning for Better Living

In addition to episodic learning and learning for fun, both of which we have characterized as intrinsically rewarding learning for its own sake, people also engage in a vast amount of instrumental Internet-supported information seeking and learning. Many of the activities of daily living can be enhanced by learning how to do them better or where to get resources to make them easier.

Online learning can support better living by helping people learn how to maintain their homes or gardens, find recipes or learn advanced cooking techniques, acquire how-to tips or language skills for foreign travel, and understand and improve their own health.

The Web site *videojug* was designed for this kind of learning; it encourages us to "get good at life" by taking advantage of its 60,000 free videos and guides in areas spanning beauty and style, family and careers, do-it-yourself and home, sports and outdoor, and technology and cars.

The *Duolingo* website and associated smartphone applications offer free language instruction in Spanish, English, French, German, Portuguese, and Italian.[3] *Duolingo* was founded by CMU professor Luis von Ahn and one of his graduate students, using funds from von Ahn's MacArthur "genius award" and a grant from the National Science Foundation. *Duolingo* reported achieving 3 million users by May 2013—just 11 months after its launch in June 2012.

For cooks (or gourmets), there is *Epicurious*, a Web site with recipes, interviews with famous chefs, and articles on food preparation and restaurants that was launched by Condé Nast in 1996. In 2009 *Epicurious* released a mobile app. The Condé Nast Web site stated in July 2013 that 8.6 million people use *Epicurious* every month and that the *Epicurious* app has been downloaded 6.9 million times. That is a lot more people than ever attended the Cordon Bleu cooking school!

But cooking Web sites have nothing on those devoted to health. The *Yahoo! Health* Web site receives an estimated 21.5 million unique visitors a month, and the *National Institutes of Health* and *Web MD* are not far behind with 20 million and 19.5 million monthly users, respectively.

Although the aforementioned websites were produced professionally, there are even more better-living resources offered online by volunteer enthusiasts. By making it possible for people without high levels of technical skill to be developers of Internet content, Web 2.0 has released a flood of person-to-person instruction and advice giving, much of it provided with little or no monetary exchange.

Often this learning is done in a just-in-time fashion. Your fancy European dishwasher is not draining properly. You know the repairman will charge hundreds of dollars just to come look at it. You look online and learn about a common problem with this brand. There is even a link to a YouTube video demonstrating how to repair it yourself. More and more people are turning to the increased access to information, demonstrations, and encouragement available online to learn how to do new things. In contrast to school-based learning in which the learning objectives are typically set by someone else and the learner may not see the relevance of the learning content, this kind of just-in-time learning is self-initiated and of obvious value to the learner.

One popular Web site, *Skillshare*, brings together people who have a skill they are willing to teach online and learners who are willing to pay a modest fee (say $20) to take a skills class. Featured classes in July 2013 included "Meatball Making with the Meatball Shop," "HTML and CSS from Scratch," "Rock Poster Design," and "Illustrating Your Favorite Runway Looks." People who sign up for classes watch video lessons, produce a project, and receive feedback from peers. A learner can start any time after a "class" has launched and has ongoing access to the class resources with no end date.

The *Instructables* Web site appeals to the "maker culture," providing a place where people can share photographs and instructions on how to make all kinds of things from a radio-controlled World War I tank to homemade sparklers to a decorative wall vent cover.

And finally, for those who are not sure what they need to learn to improve their lives, the Marc and Angel Hack Life site offers *50 Things Everyone Should Know How to Do* (www.marcandangel.com/2008/06/02/50-things-everyone-should-know-how-to-do/).[4]

Learning to Increase Professional Opportunities

The faster change of pace and shorter half-life of specific skills training that characterize our information technology driven economies are well documented (National Academy of Engineering, 2004; Smerdon, 1996). The U.S. Department of Labor (2003) estimates that the average American worker will change jobs nine times or more before the age of 32. Today's state-of-the-art technical skills will be outmoded in less than five years, and to stay current people need to be adding to their skill set throughout their careers. In addition, information technology skills are in demand, and many employers in the IT industry care more about what prospective employees can do than about their educational pedigrees, creating what are arguably the best opportunities for upward mobility in the world today.

A number of major technology companies have been offering online training for technical certification for entry-level information technology jobs for years. Cisco started the Cisco Networking Academy in the late 1990s to provide standardized training for working with its networking equipment. Cisco was motivated to provide this training by reports from customers who were buying its equipment and then reporting that they could not find people qualified to maintain the networks. The Cisco Networking Academy is offered in conjunction with schools, either high schools or colleges, and courses are taught by Cisco-certified instructors. The courses use blended learning formats with online course elements such as simulations and interactive tools as well as online assessments with immediate feedback. *Cisco Packet Tracer* is an online simulation that students use to create and troubleshoot virtual networks, without any of the costs or risks that building real networks would entail. The online game *Cisco Aspire* presents students with realistic business and networking scenarios and challenges them to make decisions and complete projects for virtual clients.

Students who complete a Cisco Academy course and pass a proctored examination receive industry certification. With 10,000 academies in 165 countries, the Cisco Networking Academy has provided learning opportunities to over 4 million students.[5] Cisco has reported that two-thirds of 1,500 alumni of the Cisco Academy responding to a survey said they had found at least one job as a direct result of their Cisco training, and 20 percent said they had obtained a higher-level job than they could have gotten without the training (Littlefield, n.d.).

Oracle Academy offers a similar program but with more emphasis on "twenty-first-century skills." Courses include Introduction to Computer Science, Advanced Computer Science, and Enterprise Business Applications. Microsoft Learning provides training to prepare for certification examinations for the full array of Microsoft products. Learners can take the training online with a virtual instructor.

Other players are now joining IT companies in providing online training in computer programming languages, Web design, and entrepreneurship. The MOOC company Udacity was founded in 2012 with an emphasis on cutting-edge computer science skills and the precept that its courses, while not earning credits from an education institution, would be attractive to employers. When he announced that he was leaving his Stanford professorship to found Udacity, Sebastian Thrun described his motivation, "My real goal is to invent an education platform that has high quality to it . . . that enables students . . . to be empowered to find better jobs" (NPR interview quoted in *Fast Company*, 2012).

After co-teaching the MOOC on Artificial Intelligence at Stanford, Thrun selected advanced topics for the first two Udacity courses: how to build a search engine and how to program a self-driving car. In October 2012 Udacity's course coverage was described as computer science, mathematics, general sciences, programming, and entrepreneurship, all areas with economic value in the workplace. Thrun argues that technology is moving so fast that universities cannot keep up with workforce demands because their faculty do not have the latest technical skills.

Udacity's original business model called for offering its MOOCs for free and obtaining revenue by charging modest fees for taking certified examinations and accepting referral fees from employers eager to hire the best of the MOOC graduates. In an April 2013 interview with *PandoDaily*, Sebastian Thrun explained that companies such as Google, AutoDesk, and Microsoft were funding the development of Udacity courses to teach skills, such as HTML5 (the programming language for mobile Web applications), that are in short supply in the labor market (Lacy, 2013). Although Udacity has developed classes in subjects as far afield from computer science as psychology and developmental mathematics, computer science continues to be Udacity's focus.

While no other online learning provider may have as strong an emphasis on cutting-edge technology skills as Udacity, many companies are trying to leverage online learning to close the general gap between the skills people have and those employers are looking for.

The U.K.-based firm General Assembly, for example, provides training on entrepreneurial as well as technical skills, covering topics such as developing a business plan, data visualization for business, rapid prototyping, and branding your business. In addition to its classroom-based courses in London, Berlin, and Hong Kong, General Assembly offers scheduled online courses taught by business professionals at a modest price (typically one hour for $25).

Another U.K. player is LearnRev, a start-up company providing online courses on widely applicable workplace skills such as negotiating, running a meeting, and financial modeling (Barber, Donnelly, & Rizvi, 2013).

An instructionally sophisticated resource in this field is *CoreSkills-Mastery*, an adaptive online course designed by Apprion. *CoreSkillsMastery* addresses both basic workplace skills, including both mathematics, reading, and writing skills, and non-academic but equally important competencies in the areas of motivation, persistence, and problem solving (EdSurge, 2013). *CoreSkillsMastery* teaches these skills in the context of realistic workplace situations. Many of the questions students are asked to answer are open-ended. Students giving a wrong answer receive feedback that goes beyond indicating that their answer was incorrect to provide a diagnosis of the "thinking error" that likely led to that answer (EdSurge, 2013). *CoreSkillsMastery* is designed for use by a teacher working with secondary, college, or adult students. The courseware keeps track of each student's daily activity and provides the teacher with information on students who are not putting in the needed amount of time or who appear to be stuck. Apprion makes *CoreSkillsMastery* and the associated teacher resources available to schools for free. In 2012–13 several dozen traditional and charter high schools, community colleges, and adult education programs implemented *CoreSkillsMastery* on a pilot basis.

In addition to enhancing employment prospects, self-initiated online learning has become an important tool also for people with jobs who want to be able to do their jobs better or improve their prospects for promotion. The experience of one of our spouses typifies this situation. Currently in charge of in-house training for a Silicon Valley company, she enrolled in the University of Pennsylvania MOOC on gamification offered through Coursera. She did not need an education credential but wanted to see if there were concepts or techniques for gamification that could be applied to the internal job training developed by her company.

Representative, hard data about the characteristics of people signing up for MOOCs are hard to come by, but information about enrollees in specific

MOOCs suggests that they are primarily well-educated people interested in learning something new, rather than individuals seeking an initial tertiary degree. A survey of students enrolling in one of the first Stanford MOOCs, a course in machine learning offered by Andrew Ng (who went on to become one of the founders of Coursera) found that half of the students were professionals employed in the tech industry (Watters, 2012).

Self-initiated Learning to Reinforce Formal Education

Another group of voluntary online learners consists of students enrolled in formal courses at a school or college who are initiating learning activities online in order to obtain assistance and additional learning resources to help them do well in those courses.

Online One-on-One Tutoring

Online learning resources can supplement the information and practice opportunities provided in a course. Students who find their professors' or teachers' explanations of a concept difficult to understand (or who missed class) are turning to online resources on the same topic for help. Providing this kind of assistance to students was the original goal for creating the Khan Academy videos. The explosive growth in the number of students receiving tutoring from Sal Khan, from one cousin to ten cousins and family friends to 100,000 students viewing the YouTube videos a month to 6 million users a month (Noer, 2012), illustrates how many students feel a need for such help (or have parents who see the need). As a high-school student interviewed by PBS NewsHour in connection with a 2010 talk Sal Khan gave at her school explained,

> The teachers are good, but they can't go at a pace that's . . . like perfect for everyone . . . I like the concept of knowing something in class but actually going back [using Khan Academy videos] and pushing pause or rewind and actually getting a deeper understanding of it.

Worldwide, many parents seek private tutoring to help their children keep up and excel in school. A 2011 report by Global Industry Analysts, Inc. predicted that the private tutoring market would exceed $100 billion by the year 2017. Many students, especially teens, prefer to receive their tutoring online. The largest provider of online private tutoring, Tutor.com, acts as a marketplace where independent tutors can offer their online services. Although tutors from all over the world are now coaching students online, the online tutoring market has been a poster child for the "flat world" global economy. In high-wage countries, such as the U.S. and the U.K., the price of a private tutor is beyond the reach of many families. Entrepreneurs figured out that by providing private tutoring over the Internet, a company could offer much better rates by using tutors from a country with lower wages. As an English-speaking country with a large educated population, India quickly became the source of a large proportion of the online private tutoring for the U.S. and U.K. markets. Growing Stars, founded in 2000 with a base in Kochi, India, employs a set of online tutors, all of whom hold a master's degree in the subject being tutored as well as a teaching credential. TutorVista.com, based in Bangalore, India, offers unlimited tutoring in 30 subjects for a flat monthly fee.

Homework Assistance

Another way that learners initiate learning to support their success in school is by seeking online help for completing their homework. *HippoCampus* is a website devoted to homework help resources for elementary and secondary school students. *HippoCampus* provides access to collections of open education resources, such as the Khan Academy videos and exercises, and the Phet science simulations. Students who are having difficulty with a homework topic can use online resources related to that topic to sharpen their understanding.

For those looking for human interaction rather than course-related resources, the Internet can give students an alternative peer community or study group. OpenStudy, a company started in 2010 as a spinoff of the Georgia Institute of Technology and Emory University, leverages social networking to support learners working with online courses, such as those of the OCW Consortium. The site is free to users who are matched up with others working on the same course in a kind of virtual, global study group. The idea is that by assembling large groups of students from around the world, there will be a peer available to help you no matter what time of day or night you are studying. When users have a question, OpenStudy sends it to the appropriate user group. Users can earn OpenStudy badges by providing helpful answers to other students. By 2013, OpenStudy was reporting over 500,000 unique visitors to its site per month.

Using Out-of-School Time for Academic Learning

Another way in which online learning is reinforcing more formal, school-based instruction is by providing experiences that target academic content but are interesting and entertaining enough that students will be willing to use them on their own time at home or in afterschool programs. Policy makers have come to regard afterschool time as an untapped resource for advancing educational achievement, especially for elementary and secondary students who lag behind their peers academically.

Online immersive environments and "serious games" are often cited as promising approaches for enticing students to spend more time learning. University and nonprofit organizations have developed a number of virtual environments and games with educational content, largely under the sponsorship of the National Science Foundation. Some of the games developed by for-profit companies also have enough educational content that afterschool programs promote their use.

Whyville is a multi-user virtual environment online game designed for players between ages 8 and 15. It was developed by a company created by a California Institute of Technology professor and his students with the explicit purpose of testing whether a simulation-based game could produce valuable educational outcomes. *Whyville* players use online tools to develop avatars to represent them as they move through *Whyville*'s virtual spaces, which include a beach, stores, city hall, and different planets. *Whyville* was one of the first online environments to use virtual currency: players earn "clams" by engaging in the science activities embedded in the *Whyville* environment. They can use the clams to purchase more elaborate face parts for their avatar, furniture, things they can "throw," and other objects and services to enhance their lives in *Whyville*. Yasmin Kafai and her colleagues at UCLA performed extensive research on what "tweens" do in *Whyville*, including students engaging in this online experience as part of an afterschool club.

Kafai (2010) describes one of the more popular science activities, a hot air balloon race, in which the player moves the hot air balloon by burning fuel and releasing air and attempts to drop a bean bag on top of a target on the ground, by attending to the balloon's position on a coordinate graph and the variables of temperature and wind vectors. Some of the games are designed for multiple players. In smart car races, for example, each player designs a path of light (hopefully, using principles of light, mechanics, and transfer of energy) to guide her car with light sensitive tires to the finish line in competition with another player who has designed her own path.

WhyPox is a science game designed for the entire *Whyville* community. Every year, there is a virtual epidemic of WhyPox, which has two disturbing symptoms—the avatar of an infected player breaks out in pimples and online chatting is disrupted because the words the infected player inputs are replaced with "achoo." Players can go to *Whyville*'s virtual Center for Disease Control to obtain information about past epidemics, make predictions about the epidemic's spread, and apply tools to try to stem the spread of the disease.

In another community game, the *Whyville* beach was contaminated by Red Tide. Players took virtual water samples, analyzed the samples in a virtual laboratory, and then took action to try to discourage the algae blooms (Kafai, 2010).[6]

Connecting Self-Initiated and Formal Learning

Many educators are enthusiastic about the idea of leveraging the online activities their students love for classroom learning, and some of the more noteworthy of these efforts will be described in Chapter 5. But there are built in tensions between the two. The self-initiated learning that appears to develop the highest level of expertise and identity among accomplished learners occurs gradually over an extended time period and offers learners choices about what and how to learn (National Research Council, 2011; Richards, Stebbins, & Moellering, 2013). Schools, on the other hand, are typically organized around having everyone in a class learn the same things and, in the U.S. at least, prioritize covering a broad range of content over in-depth experience in a single area of intense personal interest.

While some researchers are studying self-initiated learning in the home or other natural spaces, others have found it useful to seek out (and sometimes to create) settings that children and youth attend voluntarily but where adults or older learners can provide some resources and social supports for learning. These so-called "third spaces" possessing characteristics of both formal and informal contexts, such as afterschool or recreation center programs, camps, or museum-based programs, are not constrained to follow any particular curriculum and can provide opportunities for interest-driven learning over a considerable time span. These spaces combine an educational mission with varying degrees of free choice and structured support for learning.

One of the largest and longest-lived efforts to provide young people with digital learning experiences in a third space is the Computer Clubhouse, established in 1993 as a joint effort of the MIT and the Boston Children's Museum (Rusk, Resnick, & Cooke, 2009). With support from Intel and other donors, the Computer Clubhouse has grown from a single site in Boston to a network of over 100 clubhouses worldwide. The Computer Clubhouse's focus is providing a safe, engaging place to learn with information and communication technologies for inner-city, low-income youth. Inspired by the response of students to a museum Lego-LOGO exhibit, the Clubhouse founders scanned the programs available for young people in the Boston area and found that although there were afterschool programs in which students could play educational computer games, there were no free programs that supported young people in designing and developing their own projects using technology.

The Clubhouse design reflects the constructionist philosophy of MIT professor Seymour Papert (1993). People construct rather than receive new knowledge, and learning occurs best in the context of designing something that is personally meaningful. At Computer Clubhouses, young people have access to technology tools for Web publishing, digital music and video creation and editing, computer programming, and robotics. They also have the support of volunteer mentors who can inspire and support them. Most Computer

Clubhouse participants attend the program at least once a week, and half of them attend every school day (Gallagher, Michalchik, & Emery, 2006).

Another prominent example of a third space using online learning is the Digital Youth Network (DYN) in Chicago. DYN offers two-hour weekly afterschool sessions for students in Chicago middle and high school, during which students are challenged and supported in creating digital media products that reflect their character and surroundings. DYN mentors help students acquire skills in creating their own movies, music videos, and commercials. An important component of DYN is Remix World, a private social learning network on which DYN students from all the partner schools can share their products, comment on each other's work, and participate in blogs and discussion threads (Kennedy Martin et al., 2009).

The advantages of third spaces as sites for learning that prepare young people for the interdisciplinary thinking needed to address issues of the twenty-first century were highlighted in research by DeVane, Durga, and Squire (2009). They chose to study what students learn playing the game *Civilization* in an afterschool setting because academic classes in specific subjects do not combine ecological, economic, and political concepts in the way that the game does. Science teachers likely would view time students spend working with economic and political concepts as a diversion, and economics teachers would be apt to feel the same way about devoting class time to biology. Those who design learning activities for third spaces can focus on what will interest and foster intellectual development in their students rather than covering a broad set of mandated curriculum content.

At the same time, third spaces can have drawbacks as learning sites if their activities are not well designed and implemented. Many afterschool settings are staffed by a combination of volunteers and low-paid staff with no training on how to select or design learning activities or how to guide students in ways that support their learning as they engage in those activities (Lundh et al., 2013). Some of the early research on student learning with educational computer games found that students often play the games in ways that circumvent the educational content, preferring to use the game for entertainment, for example, by purposely answering questions incorrectly if a wrong response leads to an amusing explosion.

Research on the Effectiveness of Self-Initiated Online Learning

We are accustomed to thinking that the effectiveness of learning activities is measured as competency demonstrated on some kind of assessment. Assessments play an important role in formal learning, but it should be remembered that many kinds of informal online learning have very different kinds of goals. The percentage of people who are using Internet resources to satisfy their curiosity who find the information they are looking for may be a more suitable measure of effectiveness than any knowledge test. The number of times people who are turning to online activities as a source of entertainment return, the amount of time they spend on each visit, and their willingness to pay money for the experience all attest that the online experiences are fulfilling their goals.

Other types of informal online learning, such as those designed to improve our lives, have goals whose attainment we might be able to measure, but in most cases, the difficulty of obtaining the data would outweigh the benefit to be derived. We do not know how many people have learned how to do home repair tasks from the Internet, for example, or how competent they have been when they attempted those tasks. But if people keep returning to the Internet to get home repair tips, they are "voting with their clicks," and for many situations, online usage rates and reviews are reasonable evidence of effectiveness from the consumer's standpoint (U.S. Department of Education, 2013).

In the area of online learning to support professional advancement, providers are more inclined to publicize testimonials from individuals who obtained good jobs than to publish overall employment statistics for those who used their materials and services. And even if they do publish statistics, there is no way to know what percentage of the individuals would have got the same kinds of jobs without the online learning experience.

In contrast to formal education, most informal learning activities of the sorts described in this chapter do not receive public funding, and hence there is less pressure to provide evaluation findings. Exceptions are the non-formal environments such as museums, planetariums, and afterschool programs, which may receive government funding to support their educational missions. For a long time the value of such activities was largely accepted as a given, and programs presented attendance rates as evidence of their worth. More recently, cash-strapped governments and philanthropic organizations have started demanding evidence that people are not just engaging in activities in these settings but that they are learning something from them, and providing this kind of evidence is a challenge very much on the minds of the nonprofit organizations providing publicly and philanthropically funded informal learning experiences.

Organizations that support informal learning opportunities point to the basic incompatibility between the nature of informal learning and the requirements of rigorous educational research designs. Controlled educational studies require samples of learners experiencing contrasting learning treatments, each of which is defined and implemented in a standard fashion and all of which intend to produce the same learning outcomes. The specification of outcomes and treatments by the researcher, as required by experimental research designs, is antithetical to the self-initiated and emergent qualities of informal learning. Moreover, controlled studies require that all participants take before and after assessments of knowledge or skill, an activity that many individuals given free choice will decline to undertake (National Research Council, 2011; Squire & Durga, 2013). The attempt to study and document the outcomes of many kinds of informal learning could destroy the very phenomenon we are hoping to study.

Scholars of informal learning have tended to eschew controlled experiments and instead use case study methods and comb records of online activity for evidence of changes in individuals or groups that suggest that learning has occurred. Qualitative studies of informal research have explored theoretical issues, such as the development of online identities or the emergence of online communities of learners.

Much of the literature on designed informal learning environments appeals to basic research on human learning as warrants for their design principles. For example, research shows that extrinsic and intrinsic motivations produce equivalent learning outcomes on simple tasks, but that intrinsic motives lead to better performance on creative or complex tasks (Utman, 1997). Zuckerman et al. (1978) have shown that letting learners choose the tasks they will work on and the amount of time to devote to them, as is common in informal, self-initiated learning, produces greater intrinsic motivation. By extrapolation, informal learning advocates reason that self-chosen learning activities will lead to the development of greater competency in complex, creative endeavors. Such competencies are sometimes described as "twenty-first century skills," and include problem solving, collaboration, and communicating effectively through new media.

Jenkins (2006) has written extensively about the importance of new media skills that involve collaboration and networking as well as the use of online tools. Jenkins describes learning gained through engaging in the participatory culture of online communities around hobbies, media creation, politics, and other topics of individual interest. Jenkins provides a list of new media skills defined not as the particular technologies people know how to use (which are likely to change rapidly as technology advances) but rather as cognitive competencies, as shown in Table 4.1. He argues that we should not leave acquisition of these skills entirely to young people themselves, however, because of differences in access to technology and social supports for using it, limitations in the ability to examine media critically, and the need to inculcate young people with a set of ethics around new media use. Jenkins asserts that young people are more likely to acquire these new media skills through afterschool programs and participation in online communities than through school-based instruction.

Rather than conducting controlled experiments to compare learning outcomes in informal settings to those in alternative interventions, researchers studying informal learning have generally relied on observational and descriptive studies, surveys, or pre-post single-group research designs.

Table 4.1 New Media Skills

Skill	*Defined as the ability to ...*
Play	Experiment with one's surroundings as a form of problem solving
Performance	Adopt alternative identities for the purpose of improvisation and discovery
Simulation	Interpret and construct dynamic models of real-world processes
Appropriation	Meaningfully sample and remix media content
Multitasking	Scan one's environment and shift focus as needed to salient details
Distributed cognition	Interact meaningfully with tools that expand mental capacities
Collective intelligence	Pool knowledge and compare notes with others toward a common goal
Judgment	Evaluate the reliability and credibility of different information sources
Transmedia navigation	Follow the flow of stories and information across multiple modalities
Networking	Search for, synthesize, and disseminate information
Negotiation	Travel across diverse communities, discerning and respecting multiple perspectives, and grasping and following alternative norms

Source: Jenkins (2006, p. 4).

Steinkuehler and Duncan (2008), for example, pulled a random sample of close to 2,000 discussion posts on *World of Warcraft* and analyzed them to look for cases in which the player cited evidence or data to back up a claim (28 percent of posts) or used systems reasoning to describe how game components and processes interact (58 percent).

Brennan (2012) interviewed 12-year-old students and their teachers using *Scratch* in their classrooms. Students described their enjoyment of *Scratch* as a means of self-expression, while teachers cited their reasons for introducing *Scratch* to their students as the desire to promote creativity and problem-solving skills. Brennan interpreted students' descriptions of their multiple cycles of trying *Scratch* programs out, seeing them fail to achieve the desired effects, and then revising them as evidence that *Scratch* experiences build persistence. Brennan also describes ways in which young *Scratch* users support each other's learning. The *Scratch* Web site contains numerous online tutorials, created by students to show other users how to achieve specific effects. Students also support each other's learning by providing feedback on each other's products.

Neulight et al. (2007) used pre- and posttests of students' understanding of disease transmission to investigate what sixth graders learn from participating in the WhyPox epidemic simulation in *Whyville* described above. They found a doubling of the proportion of students using correct biological principles to reason about the spread of infectious diseases.

Plass et al. (2009) studied the impact of *Peeps*, a gaming environment designed with the goal of increasing girls' interest in computer science. *Peeps* players receive a female avatar and influence game play by using their programming skills to make their avatar dance with the inhabitants of the virtual world. In a research study conducted in a sixth-grade classroom, four sessions of *Peeps* play appeared to increase students' sense of efficacy around computer programming but not to have any effect on programming skills.

Squire and Durga (2013) reported that students using an enhanced version of the game *Civilization* in an afterschool club developed a systemic perspective linking topics such as food shortages, agricultural policy, trade restrictions, and ecology. None of these studies used a control group permitting comparisons of outcomes for the time spent with the online game to other uses of time.

Attempts to study the impact of self-initiated and informal online learning rigorously face severe challenges. In addition to the risk of undermining the most powerful aspects of the phenomenon one is trying to study, alluded to above, there are three challenges to doing rigorous empirical research in this area:

- For many of the kinds of learning outcomes that researchers want to study and that designed learning environments hope to foster, there are no existing outcome measures with known validity and reliability.
- The individuals for whom data are available are often not representative of the entire population using the online learning resources.
- By definition, people engage in self-initiated learning only as long as they want to, and this may not be enough time to accrue any learning benefits, and especially not the kinds of competencies that have been observed for the most active users and participants in online communities.

The first of these challenges, access to an appropriate measure of the intended learning outcomes, is less of a problem for studies of the effectiveness of self-initiated learning to enhance or substitute for formal education experiences. We will describe a recent example of an evaluation of such a resource in order to illustrate the severity of the other two challenges.

Vesselinov and Grego (2012) undertook a study of the free online language learning website, *Duolingo*, with sponsorship from the company. Although this study did not use a control group, it provided for a point of comparison by administering a Web-based adaptive assessment of Spanish used by many colleges for placing students into the appropriate semester of study. Cut-off scores for semesters 2 through 4 of college Spanish were well established for this test and could be used in interpreting the progress made by learners using *Duolingo*.

A notice on the *Duolingo* website, made visible to users who registered for Spanish instruction, offered a $20 gift certificate to qualifying learners willing to take a Spanish placement examination before starting their *Duolingo* study and then again after two months. The invitation page was viewed by 727 people, of whom 556 completed a short required survey describing their backgrounds and reason for wanting to study Spanish. The characteristics of this group of volunteers are described in the top row of Table 4.2.

Table 4.2 also describes the researchers' subsequent steps to remove volunteers who would not be appropriate for the study and to draw a random sample of sufficient size to determine learning effects.

Study participants were urged to spend at least 30 hours on the *Duolingo* website during the two months the study was being conducted and received weekly notices of the time they had spent.

At the end of the eight-week study period, the researchers examined the website's backend usage data for the study participants. Only a quarter of them had spent the recommended 30 or more hours on the *Duolingo* website. People who had spent less than two hours on *Duolingo* over the eight-week period were eliminated from the data set on the grounds that they had not made a serious effort to participate. Even this very low bar (two hours out of the recommended 30) resulted in removing 115 people from the study sample, illustrating the third challenge listed above, the difficulty obtaining samples with enough exposure to the self-initiated online learning to have reason to expect significant learning impacts.

As shown in Table 4.2, the final group of 88 people whose assessment results were analyzed by Vesselinov and Grego differed from those who initially volunteered (as well as from the general population), illustrating the issue of representativeness.

The average amount of time study participants had spent with *Duolingo* was 22 hours across the eight-week study period, but the range of study times was fairly broad. A fourth of the participants spent between two and eight hours; another fourth spent 30 hours or more, with one individual putting in 133 hours.

Vesselinov and Grego argue that given the vastly different amounts of time spent by these self-initiated learners, the appropriate learning outcome is assessment score gain corrected for time spent. Accordingly, they computed the number of points gained on the placement examination per hour spent with *Duolingo*. Using this calculation, they estimated that the average person knowing no Spanish could make the equivalent of a semester's worth of progress in the language by spending 34 hours using *Duolingo*.

Although this statistic seems impressive, it should be remembered that despite being urged to spend 30 hours on the website, fewer than one out of eight of the 203 randomly selected study participants actually spent this much time

Table 4.2 Duolingo Informal Learning Evaluation Sampling and Attrition

Stage of research	Sample size	Sample characteristics
Viewers of Spanish instruction website willing to take Spanish assessment before starting Duolingo and after 2 months in return for a $20 gift certificate take a brief online survey	556 volunteer and complete survey	Average age: 30 % white: 75 % female: 46 % with a graduate degree: 17 % working full time: 46 % students: 29
Researchers screen out volunteers under 18, those whose first language is not English, those of Hispanic origin, and those with an IP address outside the U.S. or unintepretable	386 meet all eligibility requirements	
Researchers select a random sample calculated to be large enough to detect learning effects	211 selected at random	
Researchers screen out those placing in Semester 4+ on the Spanish pretest	203 participants of whom 75% place in Spanish Semester 1	
After 8 weeks researchers screen out those who have spent less than 2 hours total using Duolingo	88 participants with 2 or more hours of Duolingo use in the 8-week period	Average age: 35 % White: 82 % Female: 50 % with a graduate degree: 27 % working full time: 55 % students: 9

over the two months the study was ongoing. Another way of looking at the study findings is that 11 percent of the participants gained a semester or more of Spanish placement from pretest to posttest.

The *Duolingo* study was conducted thoughtfully, and the organization is to be commended for evaluating their product's effectiveness and making the data public. At the same time, the evaluation illustrated just how difficult it is to do this kind of research well.

Issues Around the Digital Divide in Self-Initiated Learning

Getting the full benefits of the kinds of Internet resources and capabilities for informal and life-long learning described in this chapter requires access to appropriate computing devices and broadband connections. Not long after the introduction of the World Wide Web made the Internet a convenient tool for non-software experts to find information, policy makers began to worry about the "digital divide" between those who did and those who did not have access to these resources (U.S. Department of Commerce, 1995). There are multiple views about what should be measured as part of the digital divide, but there does appear to be a growing consensus that being able to access information on the Internet is a lower level of digital participation than having the tools and supports (technological and human) to create content for the Internet (Fishman & Dede, in preparation; Jenkins, 2006; Warschauer & Matuchniak, 2010). Some prefer the term "digital inclusion" to signal that the central issue is one of participation in online activities including content creation, not just access to devices and networks per se.

In 2012, according to the Pew Internet and American Life Project (Rainie, 2012), 81 percent of U.S. adults used the Internet at least occasionally, but that does not mean that their homes had the broadband access needed to take advantage of the kinds of out-of-school learning opportunities described in this chapter.

Many people point to the increasing proportion of the world's population, including low-income, African American, and Hispanic communities within the U.S. that now owns mobile phones with Internet access. In the U.S. it is estimated that 77 percent of youth have a mobile phone, about a third of which are smart phones (Richards, Stebbins, & Moellering, 2013). The United Nations agency focused on information and communications technology, the International Telecommunications Union, estimated that in 2013 there were 89 mobile cellular subscriptions for every 100 people in the developing world (International Telecommunications Union, 2013).

We do not see these trends as closing the digital divide, however. Many of the mobile phones used in less-developed countries either do not support Internet access or the owner is unable to pay monthly data service fees. Even when mobile phones do support Internet services, they appear to be more suited to information access and social interactions than to supporting complex learning interactions and content creation. Although an increasing number of learning-oriented games and practice applications are available for mobile phones, few would argue that phones are the ideal platform for an online course or for content creation.

People of different income levels and educational backgrounds have different levels of access to powerful computing devices and broadband Internet access within the U.S., and in countries of different levels of national wealth (Anderson & Ainley, 2010). Warschauer and Matuchniak (2010) have provided an extensive review of statistical data and descriptive research on technology access and use in more- and less-privileged communities within the U.S. They caution:

> With home access to computers and the Internet slowly but steadily increasing, policymakers may also believe that youth will learn whatever they need to know about technology in home environments, under the myth that all youth are digital natives ... who can effortlessly absorb advanced media skills on their own or from friends, thus making community centers redundant. We hope that this review has demonstrated the naiveté of such beliefs and the necessity of providing enhanced social support, such as that offered in youth media programs, if we are to seriously tackle inequity in use of technology and the outcomes associated with such use.
>
> (Warschauer & Matuchniak, 2010, p. 218)

With respect to digital divide trends, Gee (2009) goes even further, arguing that the digital divide is growing, not shrinking, because those with greater literacy skills and more access to supports for learning how to use new technologies are obtaining larger and larger learning benefits not available to people of limited means. He suggests that the most empowering aspect of digital participation lies in the Web 2.0 capabilities to create or modify online content. Gee asserts that young people from less-privileged backgrounds have less opportunity for this kind of activity because of the combination of limited reading and writing skills and lack of access to mentoring (Gee, 2009, p. 13). Similarly, Warschauer and Matuchniak (2010) describe the importance of the "social envelope" surrounding technology use—the support of peers and family members who can serve as role models, mentors, and technical support for more advanced uses of technology.

Warschauer (2012) goes even further, citing evidence that students who do not have this supporting social envelope for using technology for learning tend to use their computing devices and Internet access for activities such as playing simple games or searching for celebrity sites, which may undermine rather than enhance educational attainment.

These trends have motivated efforts to create "third spaces," such as clubs and community centers, with rich technology resources and the necessary human supports for using them in ways that support learning. These efforts are one strategy for providing increased online informal learning opportunities for people who otherwise would not have them in the home or at school and who lack the resources to take advantage of fee-charging venues. There is some evidence that such a strategy can be effective. In one study, sixth-grade DYN participants in Chicago described themselves as fluent users of a greater variety of technology tools than did a sample of more affluent Silicon Valley students in grades 6–8, with greater access to technology at home and at school (Barron et al., in press).

Conclusion

In considering the shortage of rigorous quantitative research demonstrating learning outcomes for self-initiated online learning activities, it should be remembered that the kinds of outcomes typically measured in research studies are beside the point for many of these activities. Many of these learning activities are highly idiosyncratic, undertaken just in time to increase our enjoyment of what we are viewing on an excursion or satisfying a momentary curiosity. Many of the more enduring informal learning activities, such as participation in online communities with people with like interests or playing multiplayer online games, are undertaken for pleasure. They are learning, but the participants think of them as fun. Developers of these online communities and games measure their success by the number of people who use their system, the length of their engagement with the website, and the number of repeat visits. If the goal is interest and enjoyment, these are surely relevant measures of success.

Elsewhere we have argued for an expanded view of the research methods appropriate for judging the quality of digital learning resources (Means & Harris, 2013). The backend data available from digital systems provide a window into an individual user's pattern of interaction and can be analyzed to reveal learning over time (U.S. Department of Education, 2013). Advances in analyzing log file data will make it easier to obtain longitudinal measures of learning on much larger samples of learners than it has been feasible to study through qualitative case study work of the sort described by Barron (2006) and Ito and her colleagues (2010).

Because informal learning situations are not subject to the mandated curricula, accountability pressures, and strict time schedules that characterize schools, those who design online learning activities for these settings have greater degrees of freedom than those who design learning products for schools. We believe that this reduced set of constraints explains why some of the most innovative uses of technology for learning have come from the field of virtual gaming environments and other informal learning products. Because people are choosing to use or not use these products and there are no serious consequences for performing poorly or withdrawing from the activity, the stakes are low. A person can try one of these online resources, particularly the many free ones, and simply withdraw if it is not enjoyable or does not seem worthwhile.

Self-initiated learning is powered by affective as well as cognitive engagement. The element of choice and learner control is important for creating a sense of empowerment. As we have noted above, informal learning enthusiasts are promoting the idea that these elements can be brought into classrooms and other formal learning settings. Although we endorse the effort, we think it is important to point out that many things change once you make a learning experience mandatory. When it is not self-chosen it may not have the emotional appeal found in things we choose to do voluntarily. We may destroy the very features we so admire if we try to transplant them into classrooms. Moreover, learning environments that are effective for people who seek them out and choose to use them repeatedly over time may not have the same effects for "conscripted" learners who would not use them if left to their own devices. The third spaces, connected to school but based on informal learning principles, may offer a more viable alternative for capitalizing on informal learning mechanisms to enhance education outcomes.

Notes

1 We use the term "intentional" not to denote careful planning but rather in the psychological sense as the antonym for "implicit learning." Implicit learning occurs without any effort to try to learn something. Implicit learning, which happens throughout our waking hours as we read, hear, or observe, whether in the physical world or through electronic media, is a major subject in its own right, and is beyond the scope of this volume.

2 The play itself, full of outmoded social attitudes, is hardly impressive as literature.

3 *Duolingo* also crowd-sources language translation by combining translation activities with language learning. Although the language lessons are free and without advertising, Duolingo charges for language translation.

4 The top 50 include building a fire, driving a stick shift, performing cardio-pulmonary resuscitation, and—of course—conducting Google advanced search functions.

5 See http://www.cisco.com/web/learning/netacad/academy/index.html (accessed on July 5, 2013).

6 Although *Whyville* science activities are designed to enhance academic learning, the descriptions of how tweens spend their time in *Whyville* by Kafai and her colleagues suggest that the environment's appeal stems more from the opportunities it affords for social interactions and identity exploration than from a desire for academic learning. The researchers describe how *Whyville* users (70 percent of whom are girls) establish an online presence, play with others by tossing projectiles back and forth, exclude someone from some portion of the *Whyville* world by throwing many projectiles at him, and flirt by throwing a heart or a kiss.

Chapter 5

Blending Teacher and Online Instruction in K-12 Schools

K-12 classrooms at all grade levels are incorporating online instruction into the school day. With increased access to high-speed bandwidth, low-cost devices, and a flood of new educational apps and open educational resources, schools and teachers are looking for ways to leverage and integrate the best online activities in their instruction. Over the last decade, districts and schools have made significant investments in learning management systems to streamline administrative functions, and many states and districts have set up online virtual schools. Only recently have we seen signs of similar levels of investment directed toward the use of online resources to augment classroom instruction within traditional brick-and-mortar schools. The Web-enhanced learning environments of charter schools such as Rocketship Education and Carpe Diem, and being used in clusters of innovation in public schools such as New York City's iZone schools and the League of Innovative Schools, are receiving tremendous media coverage. They have become the new poster children for the promise of technology in the classroom and, arguably, represent the future of K-12 education.

In this chapter we explore prevalent and emerging models of the use of online learning in K-12 classrooms, the role these models play in teaching and learning, and practices that support more effective adoption of these models.

The Emergence of Blended Instruction

Along with the increase in access and supply of digital content and tools, several additional factors are currently motivating districts, schools and teachers to consider blended learning models. Some school districts are using online courses provided by a third-party provider to expand their course offerings, particularly advanced courses and electives within disadvantaged rural and urban schools. Some are using blended models to extend instructional time without adding major costs by using online resources to deliver instruction during an extra instructional block while paraprofessionals monitor the classroom or lab. Others are introducing blended learning as a way to give students opportunities to develop life-long learning skills such as digital literacy and self-directed learning. Some teachers are using blended models to add variety to their instruction, freeing them up to spend more time working with individual students and facilitating instructional activities that allow students to apply their new knowledge to complex real-world problems. And some are turning to online learning to help them teach some of the most conceptually challenging content.

Schools are also using the adaptive and self-paced nature of some online systems to re-engage unmotivated students, particularly those with the most pressing academic needs, by offering students the opportunity to learn at the their own pace and at the appropriate level of challenge while monitoring student progress using data captured by the online programs. This may mean that students with remedial needs use their time on the online programs filling in foundational skills and catching up to their peers, while more advanced students can use online resources to gain exposure to new material that goes well beyond the curriculum and the content studied by the rest of the classroom.

Defining Blended Learning and Instruction

There are many different ways in which online and classroom-based, teacher-led instruction can be combined. In their report *The Rise of Blended Learning*, Horn and Staker (2011) offered a definition of blended learning:

> Blended learning is any time a student learns at least in part at a supervised brick-and-mortar location away from home and at least in part through online delivery with some element of student control over time, place, path, and/or pace.
>
> (p. 3)

For our purposes, a simpler definition of blended learning will suffice: "the use of online learning in conjunction with traditional teacher-led forms of instruction" (if for no other reason than that we can remember it without writing it down). All of the models and examples described in this chapter qualify as "blended learning," using our definition.

Horn and Staker's blended learning report also defines six different blended learning models, later consolidated into four models with four different variations on one of them—the "rotation model" (Staker & Horn, 2012). One kind of rotation blended learning model has students moving across multiple activity stations, at least one of which involves online learning, in their regular classroom. In the lab rotation model, online instruction occurs in a computer or learning lab, separate from the classroom where core, teacher-led instruction occurs. The students' regular teacher may lead lab activities or students may be under the supervision of a lab monitor or education technology specialist. In some blended learning models, students spend their lab time participating in a fully online course offered by a virtual school (see Chapter 6).

Five Purposes for Blending Instruction

This chapter will provide examples of the kinds of K-12 blended learning models we have observed in our research. Rather than defining models based on the physical location, decision maker, and timing of learning, as Staker and Horn (2012) do, we present a discussion organized around the goals that schools and teachers have for adding online elements into their instruction. These include:

- broadening access to instruction
- facilitating small-group and one-to-one teacher-led instruction
- serving students with very diverse needs
- providing more opportunity for productive practice
- adding variety to instruction and enhancing student engagement
- supporting learning of complex, abstract concepts.

Like any set of categories used to describe educational practice, these are imperfect, and it is easy to come up with examples addressing more than one of these goals, as will be illustrated by the examples we use below.

Broadening Access to Instruction

Many rural and small middle and high schools cannot provide their students with the same range of course offerings available in larger and wealthier districts because of the limited resources associated with their small size. In response to this limitation, some rural and small schools have included online courses in their course offerings to provide their students with access to courses they would not be able to take without online learning. Among the most prevalent examples of this practice are rural school districts' use of online AP and language courses. The relatively small number of students interested in these classes in small rural schools and the distance between schools in rural areas make it impractical for these schools to invest in their own certified teachers to teach such courses. In some states, like Florida and North Carolina, state-run virtual schools were created with the explicit mission of filling this need for their rural counties. Third-party course providers, such as K12 Inc. and Apex Learning, are also active in this area, providing courses to tens of thousands of students who take them as part of their regular school day. (See Chapter 6 for an extended discussion of virtual schools of different types.)

With increasing emphasis on completion of a rigorous, "college ready" secondary curriculum, advanced course taking is not a luxury; it is associated strongly with better options for post-high-school college and careers. Results from a recent experimental study of a pilot online algebra program in Maine and Vermont suggest that using online learning to provide access to advanced courses can have impacts that go beyond the course itself to influence a students' later academic trajectory.

Prior to the 2008–9 school year, many middle schools in these two New England states did not offer Algebra I in eighth grade, an opportunity that has become increasingly common as states and districts strive to make sure their students have enough mathematics preparation in secondary school to succeed in a science, technology, engineering, or mathematics (STEM) major in college. Nationally, 75 percent of students who finish grade 7 with a level of mathematics achievement suggesting they are ready for algebra do enroll in Algebra I in eighth grade (Walston & Carlivati McCarroll, 2010). Successful completion of Algebra I in middle school is an important predictor of, and gatekeeper for, taking more advanced math courses throughout high school (Spielhagen, 2006).

The researchers recruited 68 mostly rural middle schools to participate in the online algebra experiment. The schools agreed to identify those of their students ready for Algebra I at the end of seventh grade and to be assigned at random to either the treatment group, for which an online Algebra I course would be made available to the school at no cost, or the control group, which would continue placing all eighth graders into general mathematics as usual. During the 2008–9 school year, algebra-ready students in the schools assigned to the treatment condition were given the opportunity to enroll in an online algebra course. Students with similar academic abilities in the control schools were enrolled in the traditional eighth-grade general mathematics course. All students took assessments of general grade 8 mathematics and of algebra at the end of the year.

Researchers analyzed the students' spring test scores at the end of grade 8 and later examined their high-school transcripts to see what mathematics courses they took (Heppen et al., 2012). They found that the students who had exposure to the online Algebra I course learned more algebra in grade 8 (not a terribly surprising result, given that the general math course covered less algebra content) while performing equivalently on the general mathematics test. More importantly, compared to algebra-ready students who took general math in grade 8, the students who took Algebra I online went on to take more advanced math courses in high school. Algebra-ready students who took the online Algebra I course in eighth grade were more than twice as likely as their counterparts in control schools to be taking a course above Algebra I in grade 9.

Facilitating Cost-Effective Small-Group and One-on-One Instruction

Under the direction of talented teachers, one-on-one tutoring and small-group instruction (typically two to six students) are considered more effective than conventional whole-class instruction (Hattie, 2009). However, in today's conventional classrooms of 30 or more students, a classroom teacher has little time to spend attending to the learning needs of individuals. And hiring extra teachers to reduce class size is prohibitively expensive for most school districts. While many advocate for the use of technology to individualize instruction through students' interaction with self-paced, adaptive online programs, others turn to technology primarily to facilitate teachers' ability to work with individual students and small groups while other students are learning online. This is being done within regular classrooms using station-rotation models, and in computer labs, with teachers pulling out students with the greatest needs for additional tutoring.

Enabling Small-Group Instruction at KIPP Empower Academy

Located in South Los Angeles, KIPP [Knowledge Is Power Program] Empower Academy is a member of the KIPP charter school network and serves 430 students from the surrounding low-income neighborhood. (Approximately 90 percent of the students qualify for the federal free or reduced-price lunch program.) When the school opened with its first kindergarten class in the summer of 2010, principal Mike Kerr was counting on a per-student subsidy from California's class-size reduction program to help offset the costs of implementing small-group instructional practices like those he had found effective in his previous position as principal of a New York City school.

When the state subsidy for class-size reduction was cut in response to California's worsening budget crisis, Kerr had to rethink his plans. Without the expected state subsidy, KIPP Empower Academy's classes would average 28 students in size. Kerr had to come up with an alternative approach to getting the small-group instruction he valued, and he turned to online learning for this purpose.

Believing that some online programs had matured sufficiently to be viable sources of instruction for young children, Kerr designed a station-rotation blended learning model for his school's literacy program. The design called for students as young as five years old to rotate between teacher-led instruction, activity stations for independent learning, and online instruction, all within their regular classrooms.

When not working with directly with their teachers, students at KIPP Empower Academy work independently with adaptive online software programs, progressing at their own pace with only occasional support from adults. For most of the class period, teachers lead small-group activities. At the same time, a technology specialist floats between classrooms, monitoring students while they work on the computers and helping students solve any technical problems that may arise.

For kindergartners, instruction is organized into three stations, two led by teachers and one targeting skill building where students receive instruction through an adaptive software program. Two teachers work with the kindergartners: an experienced lead teacher who conducts lessons in phonics and fluency and a less-experienced ("intervention") teacher who leads a guided reading and vocabulary station. Each station has a group of 6–14 students working there at any one time, and students with similar levels of proficiency are grouped together so teachers can tailor their lessons to the level of the group. Each kindergartner spends about 30 minutes a week working with the online learning program.

In first grade, a single teacher oversees students rotating through four stations—online instruction, teacher-led guided reading, independent reading, and independent work in workbooks. Each station activity consumes 20–30 minutes, and students rotate through all stations in a 90-minute block. Every week, first graders engage in approximately 90 to 120 minutes of online English language arts instruction.

KIPP Empower Academy took several steps to prepare for implementing this blended learning model with such young children. The school used its two-week summer session to prepare students for the in-class rotations. Students practiced the ritual of transitioning from station to station, following the rotation schedule they were going to experience in their English language arts and math classrooms. Students practiced these transitions until, as a class, they could move from one station to the next in under 60 seconds. Then during the first weeks of the school year, teachers devoted time to modeling the behaviors they expected when students are at the online instruction station, including refraining from talking, procedures for logging in and out of the software programs, and what to do when technical problems occur.

The process of efficiently logging in and out of the various adaptive software programs, a potential time sink, was made more efficient through the development of a single sign-on portal (or "launch pad") that allowed even these very young children to enter each of the cloud-based programs quickly and securely. The students' computer desktops display a set of icons representing the various software programs, and students can enter a particular program by clicking on the appropriate icon. The students then log on to the program by clicking on the appropriate series of images (a picture of the teacher, the student, and the student's picture password) rather than entering complex alphanumeric usernames and passwords.

Principal Kerr reports encouraging student outcomes at his school. At the start of the school's first year of operation, just 9 percent of the kindergarten students had proficient literacy skills, as measured by a standardized assessment.

By the end of the year, more than 96 percent of these students displayed proficient or advanced literacy skills for students their age. Certainly multiple factors within this KIPP school are likely to be contributing to this academic success, but the school regards its blended instructional model and the small-group instruction it makes possible as important factors.

Enabling teachers to spend more time interacting with individual students and with small groups is also one of the ideas behind the notion of the "flipped classroom." Sal Khan made this concept popular by presenting it in a TED talk. In the flipped classroom model, instead of focusing their classroom time on lecturing or other forms of content presentation, teachers assign Web-based videos to introduce new concepts or background knowledge as homework—sometimes videos of themselves lecturing and sometimes videos from third-party providers such as the Khan Academy. Teachers can then use class time to work on deepening students' understanding of the ideas and procedures in the video lectures. The original concept was to have students practice applying the concepts presented by the video in class, working on what traditionally might have been homework, so that the teacher can observe where students struggle and offer just-in-time individual assistance.

As the flipped classroom concept has spread and evolved, some teachers prefer to use the class time freed up by having students view content presentations at home on follow-up discussions or on interactive activities or projects. Attempts at flipping the classroom are still at the exploratory stage. But there is a growing community of like-minded teachers teaching a wide range of subject areas and grade levels who are experimenting with different ways to organize their instruction by sending students to the Web for a good portion of their learning and focusing their own interactions with students on the development of deeper learning skills.

Serving Students with Very Diverse Needs

For many districts and schools, the motive behind turning to blended models of instruction is the need to serve students with a very broad range of prior knowledge and skill. Many online learning systems provide self-paced, mastery-based learning, and these can be used to extend the time spent learning in key subject areas, and at the same time help students develop skills as independent learners.

In the self-paced portion of these models, students progress through the curriculum at their own rate, moving to a new skill or concept only after demonstrating mastery of the current one (although teachers may have the option of relaxing this requirement to varying degrees, depending on the specific implementation model).

The teacher's role in such blended classrooms typically includes teaching conceptual content that is not well covered in the online learning system, regular monitoring of student progress on the online system, and offering mini-lessons or tutorials to small groups of students struggling with the same concepts.

For the past two years, we have been studying the use of the Khan Academy online learning system in 21 schools in the San Francisco Bay Area. The Khan Academy started as a collection of a few hundred YouTube videos on a range of math problem types created by Sal Khan himself. Over time, with extensive philanthropic funding, it has developed into to a free online digital learning system incorporating more than 3,000 videos and hundreds of problem sets covering the majority of K-12 mathematics topics.

As students work on Khan Academy problem sets, they receive immediate feedback on the correctness of their answers and embedded supports, including links to related videos and the ability to view the steps in the correct solution path, to help them learn from their mistakes. While students are using Khan Academy, teachers can monitor their progress online, seeing for each student and each skill area the problem sets the student has attempted, the amount of time spent on each, and whether or not each skill has been mastered.

Meeting Students Where They Are at a Diverse Urban School

One of the schools in our Khan Academy research is a charter high school in a densely urban neighborhood. The school's students are 85 percent Latino and 13 percent African American; over 80 percent qualify for the federal subsidized lunch program; and over 75 percent come from immigrant families whose home language is not English. The ninth-grade classes, where Khan Academy is used most intensely in this school, have at least 26 students each, packed into long rows in extremely compact classrooms. Generally, poverty, unsafe neighborhoods, and a lack of familiarity with American public schools and college entrance requirements are some of the barriers these students face.

The school has adopted Khan Academy as the core of its mathematics instruction for grade 9. This urban charter school finds that using a blended model with mastery-based learning helps it deal with the wide disparities in its ninth graders' entering math skills and reinforces the school's mission of building character and personal responsibility.

Incoming ninth graders at this school tend to be years behind grade level in their mathematics achievement. Many students have critical gaps in their basic mathematics skills, gaps that make learning grade-level content extremely difficult. Khan Academy has made it much easier to access and practice appropriate content from any grade level, particularly the skills of prior grade levels that were never learned and that hold back new learning.

The school uses Khan Academy in three different freshman classes—an Algebra Readiness class for students with the greatest needs, the regular Algebra I class, and a mathematics learning lab.

In Algebra Readiness, the class designed for the students entering ninth grade with the least math preparation, the first semester is geared toward making up all of the math learning that should have happened between kindergarten and grade 8. The teacher relies on students' performance on Khan Academy problem sets to identify which skills each student does and does not possess. Reports generated by the Khan Academy system identified those students lacking the most basic skills, such as dividing double-digit numbers. The teacher creates small groups to teach these very basic math skills while other students work on Khan Academy exercises dealing with the more advanced skills they are ready to master.

In the Algebra class, the teacher gives a daily lesson and then has students work on Khan Academy problems sets related to the lesson's topic. After giving the lesson, the teacher distributes mini tablet computers, and students work on the relevant Khan Academy exercises for the remainder of the period. Students know that any unfinished exercises in the Khan Academy unit will have to be done as homework to avoid detention.

Generally, teacher-led instruction lasts for about 20 minutes and practice on Khan Academy consumes the other 20 minutes of the class period. These time allocations, along with the structure of class, are highly consistent throughout the school year, and have proved to be an efficient means to work through the course content. The algebra teacher informed us that his two Algebra I classes using this blended learning model moved through the content so efficiently that they were able to advance far beyond the point reached by his previous algebra classes, enabling him to spend significant time on later material, like geometry.

The third context for using Khan Academy at this school is the learning lab, a mandatory second period of mathematics for all freshmen at this school. The entire 40 minutes in learning lab are spent on computers. Students are given a list of Khan Academy goals to complete for the week. When they enter the lab space, their small laptops are already set up at their desks and they simply check their "playlists" and begin independent work.

The advantage of mastery-based learning is that students work at their own place in the curriculum and move at their own pace. Although it is theoretically possible to implement mastery-based models without technology, advances in online instructional programs and Web-based learning management tools make it much easier to manage. It is also possible to incorporate other information about students, such as their preferences for different instructional formats, into blended learning models with mastery-based learning, as described below.

Matching Student Needs at the School of One

A well-known example of a blended learning model incorporating mastery-based learning is the School of One in New York City. Starting in 2009 the

School of One model has been piloted in a number of New York middle schools as a strategy for helping teachers differentiate instruction for students with a range of achievement levels and different learning preferences.

During two back-to-back math periods each day, School of One students are exposed to a variety of different instructional modes, including online learning, guided by a "playlist" that is customized for each child. The playlists, accessed by students when they log in to their assigned computer stations, shows the child the skill he or she will be working on that day and the type of instructional activities he or she will engage in. The activities include a mix of teacher-led, online, independent, and collaborative learning. Instruction takes place in a large, open classroom with a student–teacher ratio of 10:1.

As students enter the room, large monitors around the classroom display the opening activities and skills each student will work on to begin the day. For the first 10 minutes of class, students check in with their homeroom math teacher who is responsible for monitoring individual student progress in the program. On any given day, a student may participate in a teacher-led large or small group, an online live-tutorial, collaborative project work with other students, and independent online or workbook practice. At the end of each daily instructional block, students take an online assessment on the day's skill; if they pass, they move to the next skill in the sequence on the next day of class. If they do not pass, the next day they receive a different mix of instructional activities on their playlist to help them master the skill, sometimes including live one-on-one online tutoring.

The School of One model requires teachers to change their role in the classroom and the way they plan lessons. Teachers need to be able to provide instruction across a variety of modalities and to learn to use technologies that allow them to monitor and grade their students and help prepare their lessons. School of One teachers are expected to deliver instruction to large and small groups, facilitate peer learning activities, and support students as needed when they are working independently. Each evening, teachers receive their assignments for the following day, including the skills they will teach, the students they will be teaching, whether students have been exposed to the content before, and links to lesson plans from a variety of textbooks. Teachers then modify their lessons based on the needs of the students. At any time, teachers can log in to a portal to see which skills they will likely be teaching over the next several days.

At the core of the School of One model is a computer-based learning algorithm that creates each student's daily playlist. The algorithm takes into account the student's prior academic performance and diagnostic assessment scores, and the school's available resources, including classroom space, teacher time, and technology. Teachers can modify the playlists for individual students based on their knowledge of the student and the instructional modes they believe will be most effective for that student.

A study published in June 2012 by the Research Alliance for New York City Schools based at New York University examined the impacts of the adoption of the School of One model in three middle schools during 2010–11, its first year of implementation as a schoolwide math program (Cole, Kemple, & Segeritz, 2012). The study found that overall there were no differences in math achievement on state assessments between students experiencing the School of One program and similar students attending other New York City public middle schools. However, the study reports that effects varied by school, with one school showing a positive effect, one no difference from math achievement in other middle schools, and one a negative effect. We second the report authors' caution against drawing any firm conclusions about the potential effectiveness of the School of One model, given the early stage of its development and implementation within these schools, and their recommendation that the project increase its focus on implementation research to better understand the sources of the variation in effectiveness across different schools.

Using Mastery-Based Learning at Summit Public Schools

Another example of a blended mastery-based model that places high demands on students' ability to direct their learning is being developed by Summit Public Schools, a charter management organization in the San Francisco Bay Area. Clearly influenced by the School of One model, the Summit model, which they call the Optimized Math Program, also uses playlists mapped to the state's math standards to guide students learning. During the 2012–13 school year, Summit piloted the blending of teacher-led instruction and online mastery-based learning in two of its small high schools, both located in San Jose, California. Both of these schools had opened in the fall of the prior year with a ninth-grade class and served ninth and tenth graders in 2012–13. These schools are both small (fewer than 100 students per grade) and occupy the same campus so that they can share space and teachers and combine students from the two schools for math instruction.

Summit's aim for their blended learning math program is to provide a supportive, self-directed learning environment that prepares students for college. One way Summit tries to support students' preparation for college is to create opportunities for students to assume more responsibility for their own learning. Summit's teachers and administrators firmly believe that non-cognitive factors, such as grit, perseverance, and tenacity, are critical to students' eventual college success. Thus, their blended learning model is meant to support not only growth in mathematical competencies but also the development of these non-cognitive skills.

To a first-time observer, math instruction in Summit's San Jose schools can seem confusing, chaotic, and perhaps even unproductive, as students slowly enter the room, open their laptops, and get to work with little or no direction from teachers. The level of conversation among students is high, more akin to what one would expect in a high-school cafeteria than in a classroom. But if you listen carefully, most of the conversation is about math or involves one student helping another navigate the learning management system or use a particular digital resource.

None of the usual markers of the conventional classroom are present in Summit's personalized learning space. Each day, in two different shifts, 200 students from mixed grade levels assemble for their math instruction during a two-hour instructional block. At least one hour of this instruction is student-directed "personalized learning time" guided by playlists created by teachers and accessed by students through the school's learning management system.

Students are at different points in the curriculum from the very start of the school year, based on their results on a diagnostic assessment administered at the beginning of the year. At any one time, half of the students, 100 or so, are working on their playlists, arranged in small groups of four to six students, each with his own laptop and working at his own pace.

The playlists are comprised of multiple digital resources, among which Khan Academy content is prominent, and cover specific skills such as calculating the circumference and area of a circle or factoring polynomials. At the end of each playlist, the student takes an assessment on the targeted skill that must be passed before starting the next playlist in the curriculum sequence. In addition to Khan Academy videos and problem sets, the playlists include both free open educational resources and subscription-based digital resources from other sources as well as teacher-developed worksheets.

During personalized learning time, Summit students who are struggling to learn a new concept or skill have several options for getting support. The teachers and learning coaches encourage students to seek help from their peers, and most of them do so. The din of students talking to each other about math is the result. In addition, two "tutoring bars" are set up in the center of the large personalized learning time space, and teachers and adult volunteers are there to answer student questions.

Students' progress within the self-directed curriculum is closely monitored by learning coaches who receive nightly reports, generated by the learning management system, showing the number of assessments each student has successfully passed. Teachers work with any student who falls behind to create a "back-on-track" plan that outlines the steps that she will take to catch up. Teachers and learning coaches regularly monitor the progress of students with back-on-track plans, using the nightly reports and, if necessary, scheduling daily check-ins.

At any one time, half of the students are working through their playlists in the personalized learning time space, the other half are in adjoining rooms experiencing teacher-facilitated instruction. This classroom-based instruction focuses on higher-order mathematical skills and concepts in the Common Core State Standards for Mathematics and includes assignment of complex, multi-step problems that require students to apply the procedural skills they have learned during personalized learning time while simultaneously developing competency in higher-order skills and qualities of perseverance.

Providing More Opportunity for Productive Practice

Skill acquisition requires practice, and lots of it. In addition, receipt of immediate, informative feedback during practice is, under most circumstances, particularly conducive to improving competence (Bransford, Brown, & Cocking, 2000; Kluger & DeNisi, 1996). Practice and immediate feedback on closed-ended problems (those with one right answer) are readily enabled by online learning systems, and many schools are turning to these systems to provide their students with extended practice in mathematics and reading skills.

Widely used online programs providing extended practice opportunities include both open educational resources (e.g., Khan Academy, ASSISTments) and subscription-based products (e.g., iXL, TenMarks, Mathalicious).

Supplementing Core Instruction With Online Practice

Like most of the schools where we have studied the Khan Academy in action, Eastside College Preparatory Academy uses Khan Academy resources to supplement its core mathematics instruction with extended, self-paced practice. All the students at this school are students of color (95 percent Latino or African American), and the majority are low income. Students enter in grade 6 with very different educational backgrounds and proficiency levels. The school's mission is to prepare every single one of them for admission to a four-year college with a learning plan that includes successful completion of calculus or pre-calculus.

The school's mathematics teachers for grades 6 through 8 spent the summer of 2012 preparing for the integration of Khan Academy into their mathematics curricula. They developed lesson plans weaving Khan Academy content, mostly the practice problem sets, into each lesson. Then, throughout the school year, their students spent a portion of their extended-period mathematics class in teacher-led, whole-class instruction and another portion—half or more—in self-directed, mastery-based learning guided by playlists developed by their teachers.

After a whole-class lecture on a particular topic, students would refer to the playlist for the topic, which included the related Khan Academy content, worksheets procured by the teacher, homework problems from the textbook, and the teacher-developed assessment that students would need to pass before moving on to the next topic and its associated playlist. Students moved through the material within a curriculum module at their own pace, practicing what they had learned from their teacher by working through the Khan Academy problem sets on notebook computers, relying on the Khan Academy videos for review if needed, completing the worksheets and homework assignments, and, then when ready, attempting the unit assessment in the presence of the teacher.

Although all students in a grade level started the year in the same place in the curriculum, soon students began to diverge and ended up spending their self-directed time working on different topics. While the middle school math teachers faced the new demands of monitoring and supporting students at a variety of places in the curriculum, they seemed to enjoy it. They reported preferring it to the alternative of being solely responsible for the majority of instruction and moving students through the curriculum all at the same pace, which was too fast for some students and held others back.

With their new instructional model in place, the teachers said they found themselves spending less time in the front of the classroom providing whole-group instruction and more time working with individual students while others were engaged in skill practice with the Khan Academy content. The teachers also reported that they were able to move through the curriculum more quickly than in previous school years.

These middle school teachers used the teacher dashboards provided by Khan Academy to identify concepts that were proving difficult for most of their students. They used this information to modify their plans for whole-class instruction so that they could target or reteach those topics.

The teachers believe that using Khan Academy in this way increases students' sense of responsibility and ownership for their learning. Through the direct feedback students receive on every problem and the student dashboards that show students what they have mastered and where they need more work, the students are now more aware of both their strengths and their weaknesses and are making their own decisions on where they need to spend more time practicing, rather than relying on the teacher for direction. As the sixth-grade mathematics teacher told us, "Students are working for their own learning. They know what they know and don't know, and it's up to them to check their problems and take responsibility for their learning."

Although blending mastery-based online learning with teacher-led instruction is a common model, as illustrated above, we do not want to leave the impression that this is the only form of K-12 blended learning. Quite the contrary. Many teachers are integrating online instructional resources into their practice for very different reasons. They see online learning resources as a way to keep students actively engaged in learning and to support students in learning abstract concepts and advanced skills that are difficult to master without technology.

Adding Variety to Instruction and Enhancing Student Engagement

As K-12 schools have moved to increase their focus on increasing achievement in core curriculum areas, many have turned to the use of longer instructional periods for these subjects, as in several of the examples above. One of the challenges facing the teacher when periods are 90 or 120 minutes long is how to hold the attention and interest of their students from beginning to end.

A number of educational researchers have suggested that schools should look to non-school settings where young people spend hours voluntarily engaging in learning activities for insights into how to address this challenge (Gee, 2013). These scholars stress the importance of giving students agency in selecting or shaping their own learning activities and the advantages of maintaining an ideal, challenging but not frustrating, level of difficulty in the way that well-designed games do. This thinking has led some educators to bring online games and other tools that students use in their free time into the classroom.

Whyville is a multi-user virtual environment game designed for players between 8 and 15. *Whyville* players are represented by avatars and move through the *Whyville* spaces interacting with the virtual objects there and with each other. *Whyville* was designed to be entertaining enough that young people would use it on their own time but also to include experiences of educational value, specifically the solving of science-related challenges. (See the more extended description of *Whyville* in Chapter 4.) Over time, more and more schools have brought *Whyville* into the classroom as a strategy for engaging students in science practices (http://jamesmbower.com/blog/?p=64).

Another online activity that has migrated from free time to classroom use is *Scratch*, a visual programming environment created to allow young people to build working programs for projects like interactive games, simulations, or animations by "snapping together program blocks" (Resnick et al., 2009). Originally designed for use in afterschool clubs, *Scratch* is being used in a growing number of classrooms as a way to introduce programming and computational thinking skills in elementary or middle school (Resnick et al., 2009).

Brennan (2012) interviewed 12-year-old students and teachers using *Scratch* in their classrooms. Students said they enjoyed using *Scratch* because it gave them a means of self-expression, while teachers cited their reasons for introducing *Scratch* as the desire to promote students' creativity and problem solving skills. Brennan cites students' descriptions of their process of multiple cycles of trying *Scratch* programs out, seeing them fail to achieve the desired effects, and then revising them as evidence that experience working with this programming language builds persistence. She also notes that students remix programming segments created by others, and much of their learning occurs through this remixing process.

Some developers and companies are designing online learning games specifically for use in classroom settings. Digital learning games for classrooms are not new; we have seen them all the way back to *Math Blaster* and *Oregon Trail*. What is new, besides the migration of games from technologies such as CDs to the Internet, is the emergence of games that are much more closely aligned with the curriculum standards for which teachers are responsible and vastly increased capabilities to adapt to the individual student based on analysis of past interactions with the game and comparisons to game play of others with similar profiles (Richards, Stebbins, & Moellering, 2013; U.S. Department of Education, 2012).

Barab et al. (2007) describe their work developing the online computer game *Quest Atlantis* to "satisfy teachers and parents, appeal to girls as well as boys, support academic learning, and engage users in real-world issues" (p. 154). Designed for children ages 9 to 12, *Quest Atlantis* is a three-dimensional multi-user environment representing the mythical world of Atlantis. The game's storyline concerns threats to the ecological sustainability of Atlantis and the decision processes of that world's misguided leaders. To use *Quest Atlantis*, children must be enrolled through an adult-supervised program, either a school or an afterschool program. Each player is represented as an avatar and moves through different Atlantis villages, each of which offers a challenge engaging users in scientific inquiry. Some of the activities are performed online within the virtual environment while others (such as measuring local rainfall) are performed offline. Students submit their responses to a quest and also a reflection on their experience with their quest online. *Quest Atlantis* has been used by over 65,000 children in more than 1,000 classrooms in countries around the world.

Similarly, *River City* is a multi-user virtual environment designed for use in classrooms. Developed with funding from the National Science Foundation, *River City* provides engaging online experiences intended to help students acquire skills of scientific inquiry and learn concepts concerning infectious diseases (Dede, 2009). Working in teams of four or so, students move their avatar through the simulated nineteenth-century industrial town, trying to figure out what has made so many of the inhabitants fall ill.

One of the best-known commercial providers of games targeted to the school market is BrainPOP, a privately held company, started in 1999, that offers online movies, animated games, mobile apps, quizzes, experiments and other activities. With a target audience of grade 3 and up, BrainPOP applications make heavy use of humor and feature an animated robot named Moby. School subjects covered by the BrainPOP materials are mathematics, science, social studies, English technology, health, arts, and music. The company supports teachers' use of BrainPOP materials by tagging them to the Common Core State Standards and providing an online search tool. In 2013, BrainPOP said that their products were used in almost 20 percent of U.S. schools and that they had millions of users a month.

Supporting Learning of Complex, Abstract Concepts

Finally, for many teachers and curriculum directors, the rationale for blended learning is that it enables bringing the affordances of technology to bear in teaching conceptually challenging abstract and complex content. Some of the most difficult key ideas in mathematics and science have been the focus of research and development efforts in learning technology. Resources to support students' developing understanding of these ideas are now available online, not only from the original developers but also through portals acting as aggregators, such as Explore Learning, PBS LearningMedia, PowerMyLearning, and Gooru.

An example of the kinds of resources being blended with classroom instruction to address challenging concepts is the modules from Technology-Enhanced Learning in Science (TELS), a center at the University of California, Berkeley, funded by the National Science Foundation. TELS modules offer online interactive visualizations of scientific phenomena, such as chemical reactions, which cannot be observed directly. Students explore these phenomena in the course of investigating current scientific issues, such as options for cancer treatment. The TELS software was designed to guide students through the processes of generating and testing predictions, explaining concepts and arguments in their own words, and engaging in discussions with peers.

In a five-day TELS unit called Chemical Reactions, for example, students conduct a series of activities about chemical processes related to the greenhouse effect (Chiu & Linn, 2012). They work with an interactive visualization of hydrocarbon combustion reactions, manipulating variables to look at the relationship between ratios of reactant molecules and products, and they consider the implications of their variable manipulations for carbon dioxide levels in the air. Students are prompted to conduct investigations and explain their understanding of related scientific processes. After completing these activities, they use what they have learned to write a letter to their congressperson about climate change and alternative fuels.

In a study involving 26 teachers incorporating TELS modules into their science instruction for 4,328 students, students experiencing this blended model of science instruction significantly outperformed their counterparts experiencing traditional curricula in their understanding of scientific phenomena (Linn et al., 2006).

The Diversity of Blended Learning

The above descriptions should convey a sense of the vast array of blended learning purposes and practices in K-12 schools. Blended learning may be fundamental to the school's design and organization for instruction (as in the cases of School of One and Summit Schools), an expedient for providing a class not otherwise available (as in the grade 8 Algebra I example), or a set of resources that individual teachers decide how to integrate into their practice (as in the games and TELS examples).

Blended Learning as Disruptive and Hybrid Innovations

In a recent publication, Christensen, Horn, and Staker (2013) address the question of the extent to which different forms of blended instruction will transform the nature of schooling as we know it. They add a new concept to their disruptive innovation theory—that of a "hybrid" solution that attempts to get "the best of both worlds," by combining the strengths of a new innovation with those of the traditional approach as in a hybrid car that runs on both electric power and gasoline. Many practitioners describe blended learning in these terms, as the best of technology and the best of human teachers, a notion that is compatible with our own concept of augmenting teacher intelligence and capabilities with technology tools (see Chapter 9).

Christensen and his colleagues would consider most of the blended learning models described in this chapter to be hybrid innovations, which they identify by using four criteria:

- a combination of old and new approaches that requires no more than tweaking the facilities, staffing, and operations models of schools
- designed principally for existing students taking core subjects in school classrooms
- requires students to be in their seats for a prescribed number of minutes
- not fundamentally simpler than the traditional system and in fact requires all the expertise needed by traditional approaches plus new skills in using and integrating digital resources (Christensen, Horn, & Staker, 2013, p. 30).

From the perspective of disruptive innovation theory, Christensen and his colleagues consider hybrid innovations a form of sustaining innovation because they do not fundamentally conflict with the established way of doing things. Christensen, Horn, and Staker (2013) predict that in the long run, fully online learning models and more disruptive forms of blended learning, like those that do away with grades and allow students to begin and end learning when they are individually ready, will change K-12 education fundamentally. But they acknowledge that this transformation is far in the future and predict that sustaining, hybrid blended learning models will dominate elementary and secondary school instruction for some time, a prediction with which we concur.

Improving the Design and Implementation of K-12 Blended Learning

Use of blended learning in K-12 classrooms is very much in an exploratory and experimental phase. Districts, schools, and teachers continue to experiment with ways of using online learning resources to make classroom instruction more tailored and responsive to students' needs. Schools and teachers are using blended learning models to provide better access to courses, facilitate small-group instruction, help students acquire complex skills and concepts, sustain student engagement, and provide opportunities for self-directed learning and more productive practice.

Given the great diversity of purposes for implementing blended learning, the many different instructional elements that might be blended, and vast differences in learners and contexts, it makes no more sense to try to make a blanket statement about blended learning "working" or "not working" than it does to make such pronouncements about online learning. Even when the same blended learning model is implemented in different schools (Cole, Kemple, & Segeritz, 2012) or when very similar models are implemented in the same schools (Wang & Woodworth, 2011a, 2011b), impacts may vary. Prior effectiveness research can help educators make wise choices about online learning resources to try, but there is no escaping the need to evaluate the effectiveness of the particular blended model as implemented in the set of schools and classrooms for which an educator is responsible.

Prior research can also help educators anticipate the kinds of implementation challenges that are likely to arise, and some of the strategies that can be used to mitigate them. Based on our years of research in the field and the insights shared with us by administrators, teachers, students, and their parents in schools adopting a variety of different blended models, recommendations for technology developers and those who implement blended learning models are starting to emerge.

Online Learning Resources Should Be Designed to Support Integration into the Teacher's Instructional Plan

For schools and teachers to make more use of online learning resources, the resources should be designed and organized so that they can be flexibly integrated with regular teacher-led instruction. At a minimum, the content needs to be aligned with the school's curriculum standards and searchable by grade-level standards. In addition, since many schools would like to use online content as a supplement to teacher-led instruction, teachers need to be able to assign the content and tasks they would like students to complete on a unit-by-unit basis. Currently, many adaptive online learning programs are closed systems that do not allow teachers to intervene to override decisions being made by the system's adaptive algorithms. While teachers generally like the adaptive nature of these programs that allow students to proceed at their own pace, they still want greater control of the content presented to their students so that they can integrate the use of the online resources with their classroom lessons.

Reports of Student Progress Within Online Programs Should Be Easy for Administrators and Teachers to Access and Interpret

Online learning systems log student performance and progress data that can be presented in an individual student or class view. At present, teachers and administrators at most schools fail to capitalize on the full potential of these data for diagnostic and formative purposes. Administrators and teachers use student data from online learning systems primarily to monitor the progress of students' engagement and productivity. In general, the reports are not used as a source of information about what students do and do not understand.

Developers and system integrators need to address several challenges to realize the promise of online instruction as a tool to collect and report near-real-time learning data that can be acted on by students and teachers. First, administrators and teachers must be able to trust that the online program's measures of content mastery are valid and provide a solid basis for instructional decisions and for identifying students who are struggling and need more support. For the majority of sites participating in our studies of blended learning, this trust has not been present. Developers can address this issue by validating their mastery algorithms and making the supporting research data available to educators.

Second, the student data need to be not only easy to find and understand but also easy to combine with other student information. We have found that the underutilization of online student learning data is particularly likely when a school is using multiple online programs, each with its own way of measuring and communicating student performance and progress. The burden for administrators and teachers in interpreting and making sense of multiple data streams for instructional purposes is too great, so potentially valuable learning data are not being used.

The hope in the field is that adoption of interoperability standards by publishers and developers will one day make it easier for schools to integrate data from multiple online learning programs with their learning management systems; but until there is standardization of what constitutes mastery across online programs providing instruction in the same subject area, the potential benefits of having ready access to real-time learning data will most likely go largely untapped.

Lab Rotation Models Need to Foster Strong Linkages Between Learning Labs and Classrooms

Typically, the online instruction that students receive in a learning lab is intended to supplement classroom instruction by providing students with opportunities to practice skills and fill in gaps in their prerequisite knowledge. Often the programs used are designed to be adaptive (for example, *STMath* and *DreamBox Learning Math*), allowing students to work at their own level and pace. In addition, in many schools, non-certified teaching staff are used to monitor students' use of these programs in the learning lab. In this kind of implementation model, with students working at their own pace in a separate room under the guidance of someone other than the classroom teacher, the instruction and content that students receive in the learning lab can quickly get out of synch with what teachers are covering in the classroom.

In some cases, this kind of disconnect is by design because schools want to use time in the learning lab for getting students with the greatest skill gaps caught up, letting teachers focus on the teaching of grade-level content. However, one of the consequences of this separation of the learning lab and the classroom is that classroom teachers may not be invested in what students are doing in the lab or in the online programs used, and in such circumstances they often do not consider how the online system or the data it is generating on student progress can support what they are doing with students in their classrooms. Another consequence of separation between the classroom and learning lab instruction is that students may not invest as much effort in their learning lab work, knowing that their teachers are not watching over them.

Charter management organizations that place great reliance on learning labs in their elementary schools, such as Rocketship Education and FirstLine Schools in New Orleans, are taking steps to ensure greater linkages between what happens in the classroom and what happens in the lab. Both organizations have refined their implementation model to include bringing teachers into the lab to support students' efforts there and to work with students who are struggling. Almost all teachers in FirstLine's Arthur Ashe Elementary Charter School, for example, spend some time each week monitoring students in the learning lab. Some teachers are also assigned to work one-on-one or with small groups in a pull-out classroom where students work on a different set of online programs than their peers do in the larger lab.

In response to these challenges Rocketship Education is modifying its lab rotation model to better integrate teacher-led and online instruction. Beginning in the 2013–14 school year in fourth and fifth grades, Rocketship will have students engage in their online learning in a large, open classroom with as many as 115 students. Three credentialed teachers and a full-time support staff member will be in the room to work with students. Students will spend time in both teacher-led (small-group and teacher-facilitated project-based learning) and online instruction in this setting.

Students Need Support for Learning to Manage Their Own Learning

There is little in the prior schooling experiences of today's K-12 students preparing them for self-directed learning as required in many of the blended learning models. A majority of students have been schooled in conventional classrooms where teachers are the primary source of instruction and where the teacher, guided by curriculum pacing guides, determines what to study and when and how to study it. In most classrooms, when students have questions or are struggling to understand new concepts, they seek out the teacher as their primary source of help. A large percentage of the current cohort of students now being exposed to more self-directed digital learning environments will need to be taught how to manage their own learning, how to persist in the face of failure, and how to seek help from resources other than the teacher, including online resources.

Schools Should Plan Their Implementations of Blended Learning Carefully, with Attention to Needed Changes in Teaching Practices and Supports as Well as Curriculum and Assessment

The descriptions of blended learning above should make it clear that online learning is no magic pill being added to the daily diet of schooling. Blending online instruction with teacher-led activities can enable better learning when it provides a unique, new capability that supports the processes of learning, and when it increases the amount of time during which students are actively engaged in learning. But to capture these benefits, schools need to carefully plan and execute the incorporation of online learning so that the necessary supports are in place and aligned with each other. These include:

- the allocation of time for different learning activities
- physical arrangements of the environment
- a well-crafted curriculum specifying students' learning progressions
- strong pedagogy with coaching and mentoring for teachers being asked to change their practices
- assessment and ways to use assessment data to adapt instruction
- support from the school's leadership.

In years of study of the incorporation of technology into K-12 instruction, we have found repeatedly that the most successful uses of blended learning occur in schools where all of these components are present and internally consistent with each other.

Chapter 6

Online Schools and Universities

In this chapter we describe institutions established to offer fully online courses and the controversies surrounding them. These organizations, whether public or private, for-profit or nonprofit, provide learning management systems, course content, and sometimes online instructors not as a sideline for their brick-and-mortar operation but as their primary delivery mechanism.

Called variously online universities, virtual schools, e-schools, or cyberschools, these organizations are active in higher education and K-12. They may offer complete programs leading to a high-school diploma or a postsecondary degree or credential that they award, or they may provide online courses that are taken by students who are also enrolled in brick-and-mortar schools from which they will receive their diplomas.

Online Institutions of Higher Education

Universities began enhancing some of their courses by using email and computer conferencing as early as the 1970s. Individual courses were offered over the Internet in the 1980s, before the advent of the World Wide Web, by institutions such as the New Jersey Institute of Technology and Nova Southeastern University. In 1986, the New School for Social Research launched an Internet-based degree program. In 1989 the for-profit, open admission University of Phoenix began offering an online master's in business administration program (Hanford, 2013).

Today, the University of Phoenix is the largest online higher education institution in the U.S. with an enrollment of 320,000 students (Fain, 2013b). Other large for-profit online higher education institutions include Capella, Full Sail, Kaplan University, Strayer University, and Walden University. In the U.S., for-profit online universities account for about 10 percent of all college enrollments and grew rapidly in the first decade of this century (Christensen et al., 2011; Cummings, 2011).

The fact that low-income students in the U.S. can obtain federal Pell grants to underwrite their tuition at an online university, if it is accredited by either the

Distance Education and Training Council or the regional accrediting authorities that accredit most colleges and universities, has led many new companies to establish online degree programs. Anyone who has ever entered an education-related search term into Google has been instantly bombarded with ads for online degree programs. Some of these are offered by traditional brick-and-mortar colleges with regional accreditation, but many are offered by institutions established explicitly for the purpose of offering online degree programs. There are now so many of these programs in the U.S. that the *U.S. News & World Report* began ranking online college degree programs in 2012.

Some newer online providers are trying out innovative approaches to appeal to more potential students. To take one example, New Charter University opened in 2013 with a business model based on charging students $199 a month, during which they can take up to three courses toward a degree. New Charter describes its courses as self-paced and outcomes-based so that a student finishing all course material in less than a traditional academic term can start additional coursework. Other distinctive features are making their educational materials available to anyone over the Internet and extensive use of social media to foster peer-to-peer interaction.

In the public education sector, Western Governors University (WGU), an entirely online education institution, was founded in 1997 with support from the governors of 19 states in the western U.S. WGU offers competency-based online courses and degree programs. Although enrollment numbers were modest in WGU's early years, in 2010 WGU began establishing state-affiliated online colleges, the first of which was WGU Indiana, and its enrollment across states rose to 20,000. Since then, in some cases with private foundation funding, additional state WGU affiliate online universities have been set up in Texas, Washington, Tennessee, and Missouri. In 2012 WGU's total enrollment figure was over 38,000.

In recent years, several new nonprofit organizations have entered the online university space as well. University of the People describes itself as a tuition-free online academic institution with the mission of providing global access to higher education. University of the People uses open educational resources, open-source technology, and peer-to-peer learning. It offers associate and bachelor's degrees in business administration and computer science. Founded in 2009, the University of the People had served students from 130 different countries by the end of 2012.

MyCollege is a new nonprofit opening its virtual doors to students in fall 2013. MyCollege seeks to enroll low-income, young adult students from across the U.S. in its associate degree programs. MyCollege stresses the use of adaptive learning and student support services as well as low tuition (just slightly above the size of the federal Pell grants available to low-income students).

Advantages of Online Universities

For students, the major appeal of online universities is the flexibility they offer with respect to the time and place for learning. Rather than having to go to the campus where the degree program of interest is located, the (virtual) campus will come to you. For those who live in remote areas or desire a kind of postsecondary program not offered locally, an online program is often the only alternative short of physical relocation.

Of interest to even more learners, the timing of online course activities can be tailored to avoid conflicts with a job, child rearing, or other important activities. However, we note that the same competing priorities that lead people to seek out the flexibility of an online program may also work against their ability to actually complete it. Course and program completion rates for fully online college programs run well below those of traditional programs, as will be discussed below.

Some commentators argue that online courses can be more rigorous and more engaging than traditional classroom-based instruction, especially the large lecture halls that are prevalent in lower-division university courses. Terry Anderson (2004), the director of the Canadian Institute of Distance Education Research, describes the congruence between Web-based learning and principles of how people learn. Anderson suggests that the hyperlinked organization of material online fits with psychologists' understanding of knowledge construction. Communication and interaction can be greatly enhanced relative to the average classroom-based course in which a teacher lectures and asks questions to which only a single student replies.

Harvard professor Clay Christensen and his colleagues (2011) assert that traditional colleges were not built to provide higher education to all students, meeting their individual needs and preparing them for all kinds of jobs outside of academia, regardless of their level of achievement on college entry. Christensen et al view the self-pacing and competency-based programs made possible by online learning as a strategy for meeting these unmet demands.

Controversies Over Online Universities

Online universities have had to face a significant degree of skepticism on the part of regulators, employers, potential students, and the general public. Some critics regard virtual universities as just the newest form of diploma mill. Writing in the *Chronicle of Higher Education*, Kelderman (2011) characterized critics' view of online programs, especially those of for-profit institutions, as "the dark underbelly of higher education."

Because there have been so many large, very visible for-profit providers of online degree programs, attitudes toward online education get mixed up with feelings about for-profit companies providing publicly funded education services. In the U.S., federal student aid is vital to the companies providing online degree programs: almost 90 percent of the revenues of the hundreds of for-profit colleges providing all or most of their instruction online comes from federal student aid (Kelderman, 2011). Although only about one in ten U.S. postsecondary students is enrolled in a for-profit institution, 25 percent of federal financial aid ends up going to these colleges (Cummings, 2011). More troubling, 44 percent of the student loan defaults are associated with students who attended for-profit colleges.

In addition to uneasiness about the amount of federal financial aid going to for-profit online universities and the failure of many of their students to repay their loans, there are concerns about the aggressive recruiting practices of some of these for-profit universities, as highlighted in print and television news stories. It is not unusual for online universities to have recruiters, who may receive a "bounty" for each student enrolled, pursuing low-income young adults and veterans who qualify for financial aid. Some institutions have been portrayed as enrolling students in online degree programs that are unlikely to lead students to a job with enough income to pay off their student loans. Charges have been made that many students enroll in these online degree programs and receive federal financial aid, but relatively few actually finish degree programs. Some enrolled students purportedly never even logged on to the university's system.

In 2009 the Inspector General of the U.S. Department of Education recommended limiting or revoking the accrediting authority of the regional accrediting association that had accredited most of the for-profit online colleges. In 2010 a series of congressional hearings were held on the practices of for-profit and online colleges. Congressmen expressed concern about for-profit online colleges with high dropout rates, low per-student spending, and high executive salaries (Kelderman, 2011). Two investigations by the General Accounting Office, instigated at the request of Senator Tom Harkin, chairman of the Senate Education Committee, reported on recruiting and online course practices of for-profit, online colleges.

In 2011 the U.S. Department of Education released new regulatory restrictions with the goal of clamping down on some of the perceived abuses. The new regulations required online colleges to be accredited in the state in which the student receiving a federal loan resides, a requirement that would be cumbersome and expensive for online institutions to adhere to and that was subsequently struck down by a federal judge. The regulations also redefined what it means to be enrolled or not enrolled in an online course, requiring active participation in an "academically meaningful class or faculty discussion" for an online contact to count as enrollment (and hence eligibility for financial aid). In addition, higher education degree programs aimed at preparation for a specific occupation offered by for-profit institutions were required to show that their graduates were attaining "gainful employment" in that field.

In response to new regulations and increased scrutiny, two of the largest online degree providers, University of Phoenix and Kaplan, instituted practices to increase their course and program completion rates. University of Phoenix instituted a free, three-week student orientation to online learning. Kaplan began offering a five-week trial period during its courses, allowing students to drop the course without any financial obligation. It found that about 25 percent of its course enrollees would leave the course during these five weeks, with about half of those counseled out by Kaplan because they were not making progress (Fain, 2013a). In addition, both companies began focusing their recruiting on students who had reasonable chances for success, a move that caused a sharp drop in their enrollment figures. The University of Phoenix, for example, went from an enrollment of 600,000 in 2010 to 320,000 in 2013 (Fain, 2013b).

For-profit online universities argue that they should not be held to higher standards than their competitors from the nonprofit sector or than online divisions of traditional colleges and universities. Although this position sounds reasonable on its face, there are significant differences in how these different types of institutions operate. Whether because of antiquated attitudes or appropriate caution, accrediting bodies and government regulators are likely to impose a higher level of scrutiny on for-profit education providers for some time.

Ultimately, the public will be best served by having access to data about degree completion rates and subsequent employment and salary levels for all higher education programs, not just those of for-profit institutions and not just those offered online. Given apples-to-apples comparative data concerning outcomes and costs, higher education consumers can decide for themselves.

At present, however, all online degree programs and online learning in general continue to suffer by association with some of the more egregious practices in the for-profit sector. Only 30 percent of the chief academic officers responding to the Babson Survey Group's online education survey in 2011 said that their faculty accepted the "value and legitimacy of online education"—the lowest response to this question since 2005 (Allen & Seaman, 2013). Online enrollments have continued to grow year-to-year overall, but the rate of growth has slowed. It is difficult to tell how much of this can be attributed to the much larger base of students taking online courses (thus requiring more enrollments to achieve a given percentage of growth) and how much stems from the negative publicity around for-profit online universities' aggressive recruiting practices and low rates of course completion.

As for the students themselves, a survey of current and prospective online education students showed that they are more concerned with employer acceptance of online degrees and credentials than with what faculty at traditional universities think (Sheehy, 2013). A report published by Cleveland State University in 2009 documented the low regard that corporate human resources officers had for degrees earned online at that time (Columbaro & Monaghan, 2009). More recently there are anecdotal reports that this viewpoint is starting to soften, however (Haynie, 2013). Some employers reportedly appreciate the persistence shown by someone who completes a degree online while juggling other commitments.

Online K-12 Virtual Schools

Within a decade of their debut in higher education, fully online schools began to emerge at the K-12 level. In the early years of K-12 virtual schools, the major players came from the public and private nonprofit sectors. Canada was a pioneer in virtual schooling, which was used to serve rural students in a number of provinces starting in the mid-1990s. The first fully online schools in Alberta, Canada, appeared around 1995. A few years later, a research project was providing online learning to rural secondary students in the provinces of Newfoundland and Labrador. This project evolved to become the Centre for Distance Learning and Innovation (CDLI), a virtual school operated by the Newfoundland Labrador Department of Education (Barbour & Reeves, 2009). Later the province of British Columbia established LearnNow, a province-wide virtual school to serve its rural students in 2006.

The first two virtual schools in the U.S., the Virtual High School (VHS) and the Florida Virtual School (FLVS), began in 1997. The contrasting origins and relationship to traditional brick-and-mortar schools of these two virtual schools is interesting. FLVS was established by the state legislature as an independent state-funded organization making online courses available to Florida students either directly or through their school districts. In its first year, it had just 77 students in five fully online classes. In 2009–10, FLVS served an estimated 97,183 students whose participation resulted in 213,926 course enrollments (Watson et al., 2010). In 2012 it was serving roughly 150,000 students and offering some 120 different courses in core subject areas and electives (such as visual arts, world languages, and even drivers' education). Public, private and homeschooled students may enroll in FLVS courses with approval from parents and school representatives. Florida Virtual School (n.d.) reports that in 2011–12 about two-thirds of FLVS students were enrolled in regular public or charter schools, and 25 percent were homeschoolers (with the remaining 7 percent enrolled in private schools or declining to provide a school affiliation).

In contrast, VHS began operating with funding from a federal grant to the Hudson School District for technology innovation and used a non-monetary sharing arrangement in which schools from many different districts provided a teacher for an online course in exchange for being able to enroll a classroom-sized group of students in any of the courses offered by teachers from the other participating schools. After just a few years of operation, VHS included 200 high schools in 24 states and operated in ten other countries as well (Zucker & Kozma, 2003). In 2012 VHS became the VHS Collaborative, and it now supplements the courses offered by the teachers it has trained with courses offered by Connections Inc.

There is considerable variation from course to course within a virtual school, but each of these three well-established virtual schools—CDLI, FLVS, and VHS—has its own characteristic approach to instruction that shapes the online student's course experience. The vignettes in Figures 6.1 through 6.3 provide portraits of the self-paced, asynchronous communication typical of FLVS, the active role of the teacher in synchronous and asynchronous online activities in VHS, and the synchronous instruction that typifies CDLI.

As the vignettes in Figures 6.1 and 6.2 illustrate, VHS and FLVS represent very different instructional models. In designing their courses and training their online instructors, FLVS started with a model with its roots in traditional correspondence courses, while VHS sought to create online equivalents to traditional classroom practices. FLVS uses a mastery learning approach, with students advancing to the next module of a course only after demonstrating mastery of the content of the current module, and allows students to start a course at any time and finish it whenever all course objectives have been mastered. In contrast, VHS is cohort-based, with the class of online students progressing together and a focus on synchronous and asynchronous discussion and peer interaction.

Until very recently, neither FLVS nor VHS offered high-school diplomas. Students got credit for completing their online courses from their homeschool

---

Working at home, the student dons her headphones, logs onto the system, and finds her place in her self-paced Algebra I course. A dashboard shows her which modules she has completed and which she still has to do. The modules are aligned with Florida's curriculum standards and include problem solving as well as learning concepts and procedures. Lessons include slideshow presentations with associated audio, opportunities to practice, and formative and summative assessments. The student views material in her current module, using the headphones for audio content. After completing an assessment that demonstrates her knowledge of the content, she then calls up the next assignment, Quadratic Equations, and begins viewing introductory multi-media materials. Finding part of the assignment difficult to understand, the student sends a message to the course instructor requesting a phone call for the next day. The teacher, who is responsible for about 165 students taking the course, sends an email reply accepting the suggested time for the call. The teacher plans to use the opportunity not just to respond to the student's questions about the assignment, but also to perform one of the FLVS-required check-ins, discussing some of the content the student has recently completed to make sure she really understands it.

Figure 6.1 An FLVS Course Experience

Source: Bakia et al. (2013)

The VHS Bioethics course uses elements of self-pacing and classroom pacing. The student logging on to the system clicks his online course and finds a photo of the teacher and other students as well as the course syllabus, assignments, and assignment due dates. Using online content and a textbook, the student reads and works on the week's assignment. This week the student is required to select a recent news article about bioethics, write a synopsis of the article, and post the synopsis online for other students and the teacher to see. For next week, the student needs to review the synopses of articles posted by other students and make comments on those articles. The teacher reviews the students' online discussion, once in a while making a comment to correct a factual error or to press for deeper thinking. The teacher also provides written feedback on each of the 20 students' synopses.

Figure 6.2 A Virtual High School Course Experience

Source: Based on descriptions in Zucker and Kozma (2003).

Students sitting in a classroom log into the various online courses they are taking. Several students taking French for English speakers enter their virtual classroom where they have direct messaging and virtual hand-raising capabilities. The other classmates and the teacher are online, working from their own physical schools located throughout the province. The online French teacher starts the class by asking, "Quel temps fait-il chez toi?" Some students respond orally using their microphones. Others type in their answers using the direct messaging tool. The teacher then presents slides about different kinds of weather using the online whiteboard. She asks questions and presents new vocabulary. Later, she divides her class of 25 into smaller groups, sending each group to a different virtual room where they can interact with each other, practicing their French discussion skills using the system's audio capabilities and giving each other feedback.

Figure 6.3 A Centre for Distance Learning and Innovation Course Experience

Source: Based on descriptions in Murphy and Coffin (2003).

or district. In 2012, however, FLVS started a full online high-school program that students without affiliation to a traditional school district could complete to earn a diploma, in co-operation with the education and publishing corporation Pearson. The VHS Collaborative now offers a full-time high-school program as an alternative for students who do not do well in a traditional high-school environment, through arrangements with the traditional high schools that will award the diploma on completion.

From the mid-1990s to today, the phenomenon of fully online K-12 schools has grown rapidly. The supply side now has a large number and diversity of online course providers, and there is rapid growth in enrollments on the demand side. Watson et al. (2012) estimate that 275,000 U.S. K-12 students were attending fully online schools in school year 2011–12. Others put the enrollment figure somewhat lower, at 200,000 (Miron, Horvitz, & Gulosino, 2013). Twenty-seven states have sponsored their own virtual schools, with active programs including those of Alabama, Georgia, Michigan, and Montana in addition to Florida's FLVS described above.

The trend for states to set up their own virtual schools appears to have lost steam in recent years, however. One explanation is the growing number of private providers of K-12 online courses and high-school programs with a national reach coupled with a growing number of programs offered by individual school districts and consortia (Watson et al., 2012).

An example of the latter is the Riverside Unified School District, which began offering online courses to increase access to courses required to qualify for admission to California's universities (the "A-G requirements"). Many students, particularly from rural, low-income or immigrant backgrounds, find that they have no chance for admission to a state university because they have not taken required courses that were not even offered at their high schools. This concern led the district to start offering selected online courses in 2005. The success of these courses led the district to create the Riverside Virtual School in collaboration with Riverside's neighboring districts in 2008. In addition to making online courses available to their own students, the Riverside Virtual School cooperating districts now make complete curricula for grades 3–12 available to homeschoolers.

A second explanation for the declining role of state virtual schools is the severe cuts to state education budgets experienced after the end of the federal stimulus package that followed the 2008 economic crisis. A number of states lost funding or were severely underfunded for their virtual schools during this period. For example, FLVS recently cut about a third of its workforce, mostly teaching adjuncts, to accommodate a decline in year-to-year enrollments and a state-legislated reduction in per-pupil expenditures for students enrolled part-time in FLVS (Herald, 2013).

Another common strategy is for entities other than states and districts to establish virtual schools as charter schools (Miron & Urschell, 2012; Watson et al., 2012). State laws regarding charter schools vary markedly; some states do not permit charter schools and some cap the number of charter schools or the total charter school enrollment. These state regulations affect the level of opportunity for online schools as well. States also regulate virtual schools explicitly and may disallow them or cap the number of students who may participate. By 2012, 31 states plus the District of Columbia permitted the operation of fully online schools within their jurisdictions. However, a number of states considering legislation to permit the operation of charter schools in recent years decided to postpone any action until more information concerning the effectiveness of these schools becomes available.

Virtual charter schools typically provide instruction at all elementary and secondary grade levels (Bakia et al., 2013; Watson et al., 2012). Some charter schools are nonprofit organizations, but others are run by for-profit education management organizations. Miron, Horvitz, and Gulosino (2013) reported that of the 311 full-time virtual schools in the U.S., two-thirds are operated by education management organizations. The largest single for-profit online education provider, K12 Inc., served 77,000 students in 2011–12.

It is also common for a state or district to set up its own virtual school but turn to one of the major for-profit online providers (such as K12 Inc., Apex, or Classroom.com) or to a nonprofit virtual school (most often FLVS) to actually provide their school's courses.

Universities have provided online learning opportunities for talented secondary schools students (e.g., Stanford's Education Program for Gifted Youth, Johns Hopkins Center for Talented Youth's CTYOnline) for many years, but a newer development is a university setting up a separate organization to run a virtual high school. Recently, George Washington University entered a partnership with K12 Inc. to establish the George Washington University Online High School, offering a college preparatory education (Watson et al., 2012).

Because online schools promote students to higher grade levels and grant diplomas, they are subject to the same state accountability standards that guide brick-and-mortar public and other charter schools in the U.S.

Using data from the National Center for Education Statistics, Miron, Horvitz, and Gulosino (2013) report that virtual schools run by for-profit entities serve more students in the middle school grades than in high school while virtual schools operated by districts and states serve more students in grades 9–12. They interpret this difference as possibly stemming from for-profit providers' interest in serving homeschoolers (K12 Inc. was founded with this mission) while school systems look to online learning to serve students who need an alternative education approach or who seek specialty or advanced offerings not available in their districts. Table 6.1 shows the distribution of U.S. virtual school enrollments by type of provider.

The data show that although about two-thirds of U.S. virtual schools are public, their enrollments are smaller than those of the for-profit providers, and public virtual schools account for only a third of virtual school enrollments.

Reasons for Offering Online Courses and Programs

Initially K-12 online schools filled three distinct niches by providing:

- courses not available in a student's physical school, such as AP courses or a specific world language, or some of the mathematics and science courses required for university admission
- options for families preferring to homeschool their students

Table 6.1 U.S. Virtual School Student Enrollment in School Year 2010–11, by Provider Type

	Number of providers	Number of students	All enrollment	Average enrollment per school
For-profit	95	133,128	66.7%	1,401
Nonprofit	9	2,156	1.1%	240
Public	207	64,309	32.2%	311
Total	311	199,593	100.0%	642

Source: Miron, Horvitz, & Gulosino (2013) using data from the National Center for Education Statistics.

- credit recovery and alternative education programs for students at risk or seeking to return to school after dropping out.

Many programs of the latter type are run by school districts. In states where districts receive per-student funding for online enrollments, retaining students or luring back those who have dropped out with an online option is a way to increase enrollment and hence funding. The National Center for Education Statistics reports that 62 percent of U.S. school districts offer online courses for credit recovery (Queen & Lewis, 2011). In addition, more and more school districts have turned to online courses as a strategy for saving money by replacing traditional summer school courses.

While it is very likely that students enroll in virtual schools with multiple and distinct motivations, getting a clear handle on the proportion of students with particular goals and intentions is not easy. Kim, Kim, and Karimi (2012) assert that students "who choose online learning do so because they do not like traditional schools' structure and conventional learning materials." In their study of students' experiences in FLVS Algebra I and English I, Bakia et al. (2011) found another reason that students choose online courses—a significant portion had failed the course previously and were taking it again to qualify for graduation. In responding to criticism concerning their low graduation rates, representatives of virtual schools in Colorado reported that in the early days of these schools most enrollees "tended to have at least one involved parent and homeschooling experience" but that their recent school populations included more students turning to online schools as a last resort.

Barriers Faced by K-12 Virtual Schools

The challenge that higher education accrediting practices, most of which emphasize inputs such as facilities, number of faculty, and class contact hours, pose for online universities was described above. If anything, the regulatory obstacles that online K-12 schools face are even more challenging. Every state has its own set of laws and regulations concerning the conduct and funding of education. In some states, students may be taught only by a teacher with a credential from that state, undermining the potential economies of scale that a national or regional online school could have. Some states limit the number of students per course, and impose the same limits on online courses as for face-to-face courses. In California, concern about online schools "poaching" students (and hence the per-pupil aid that follows them) from school districts led to a regulation allowing an online school to serve students only from its own district and those districts geographically contiguous, a requirement that has limited the growth of the Riverside Virtual School.

Teachers' unions, while not opposed to blended learning approaches, have voiced their disapproval of virtual schools. The California Federation of Teachers, for example, has stated that online learning should be used only in cases where attending a brick-and-mortar school is not feasible. Further, it has developed language around provisions to prevent a district from using online learning to eliminate or consolidate faculty positions for use by its local affiliates when they are negotiating their contracts with districts.

Effectiveness of Fully Online Courses and Programs

To bowdlerize a Woody Allen line, the quality of the research on the effectiveness of virtual schools is generally poor, and "there's so little of it!" In general, organizations that advocate for technology-based learning or charter schools produce reports showing that virtual schools perform as well or better than brick-and-mortar schools while those who oppose charter schools and the involvement of for-profit players in public education write reports showing abysmal performance, with neither camp doing much to control for pre-existing differences between students in virtual and brick-and-mortar schools.

On the positive side, a study of advanced placement (AP) examination results for students who took their AP courses through Apex Learning, VHS, or FLVS found them to have higher-than-average examination scores (Smith, Clark, & Blomeyer, 2005). Unfortunately, this analysis did not control for differences in the characteristics of students taking online and classroom-based AP courses or for differences in the percentage of students starting an AP course who actually finished it and took the examination.

Another favorable report was published by the Florida Tax Watch (2007), a conservative group that analyzed costs and student outcomes for FLVS and compared them to those for regular Florida schools. Analyzing data from students who took FLVS courses in 2005 or 2006, the Florida Tax Watch found that FLVS students earned higher grades than students taking the same courses in traditional classes for all the subjects they analyzed except visual arts.

Students who took FLVS courses in mathematics or English also earned higher scores on the corresponding portions of the state test than did students taking these classes in the traditional format. Unfortunately, these analyses did not control for pre-existing differences between the two sets of students or for the higher rate of course withdrawal for FLVS.

A subsequent study by Bakia et al. (2011) attempted to address these deficiencies in an examination of the performance of FLVS students in English I and Algebra I (two of FLVS's highest enrollment courses) relative to students taking the same courses in traditional classrooms. Bakia et al. found that students taking English and algebra through FLVS were as likely as those taking these courses in regular classrooms to pass the course and that they achieved higher scores on the corresponding portion of the state test. This same pattern was found after controlling for student differences in prior achievement and ethnicity.

On the negative side, a study of Colorado virtual schools by Hubbard and Mitchell (2011) and a series of reports from the University of Colorado's National Education Policy Center (NEPC) raise concerns about the outcomes students of virtual schools achieve. Reports on virtual schools produced by NEPC include a study of schools operated by K12 Inc. (Miron & Urschel, 2012), a 2013 report on U.S. virtual schools in general (Miron, Horvitz, & Gulosino, 2013), and several earlier think pieces (Glass, 2009; Glass & Wellner, 2011).

Glass and Welner (2011) expressed alarm at policies made to accommodate online schools at a time when "Little or no research is yet available on the outcomes of such full-time schooling" (p. i). Hubbard and Mitchell (2011) examined records for 2,400 online Colorado students who had taken the state achievement test the prior year. They reported that the likelihood of scoring proficient for these students actually went down. (They do not explain that the state's test changes from grade to grade, so "proficiency" is not necessarily equivalent in the two years.) Hubbard and Mitchell point out also that online schools had among the weakest state rankings on graduation and dropout rates—with a virtual school student being three times more likely than a regular school student to drop out.

Defenders of Colorado's virtual schools have argued that their institutions were the last chance for many at-risk students, an assertion that may be true but that state data on student poverty rates and achievement prior to entering virtual schooling suggest cannot explain the entire graduation gap (Hubbard & Mitchell, 2011). Another argument is that virtual schools are less likely than brick-and-mortar schools to know when a student has switched to another school and hence can be counted as a transfer rather than a dropout. The extent of this problem is not known.

Another NEPC study looked at the 48 full-time virtual schools operated by K12 Inc. in 2010–11. Miron and Urschel (2012) found that students in K12 Inc.

virtual schools had average test scores lower than the averages in the states where they operate. The gap ranged from 2 to 11 percentage points in reading and from 14 to 36 in mathematics. The NEPC analyses used school-level data rather than analyzing effects for individual students and controlling for differences in the prior achievement and educational histories of the students being compared.

Similarly, an NEPC analysis of all U.S. virtual schools by Miron, Horvitz, and Gulosino (2013) compared three years of data for virtual schools with data for all U.S. public schools on whether or not the school made adequate yearly progress, whether or not the school was deemed "academically acceptable" by its state, and the school's on-time graduation rate. The researchers compared data for the two types of schools without considering differences in the types of students served or the very large state differences in adequate yearly progress criteria, the rigor of their assessments of proficiency, or their graduation requirements. Nevertheless, the differences between the rates for virtual schools and those for traditional brick-and-mortar schools, all favoring the latter, are so large (for example, an on-time graduation rate of 38 percent in virtual schools versus 79 percent in U.S. high schools overall) that it is unlikely that rigorous controls for state practices and assessments and student characteristics would eliminate the gaps completely.

Miron, Horvitz, and Gulosino (2013) did not disaggregate their data by the nature of the virtual school operator, making it difficult to say anything about the relative effectiveness of virtual schools run by nonprofit organizations or public agencies (such as states and districts). One thing we know from our own experience is that virtual schooling providers often maintain very little data about the prior educational experiences of the students who enroll in their courses. This practice makes student-level longitudinal analyses for students moving into and out of virtual schools of the sort conducted by Bakia et al. (2011) very resource-intensive to conduct, as student data must be obtained from both state education agencies and virtual school providers and then linked through student-level matching that usually requires hand-checking to get an acceptable match rate. Even when school districts or states offer virtual school options, their student data systems may not distinguish between courses taken online and those taken in regular classrooms, making comparative analyses impossible. Under these circumstances, it is not surprising that *Education Week* reports that only 16 percent of school districts have compared student outcomes for their online courses to those for their conventional courses (Ash, 2012).

The controversy over the effectiveness of virtual schools underscores the need for better data systems that would permit tracking individual students longitudinally and identifying the portions of their education program taken online.

Criticisms of K-12 Virtual Schools

Like online universities, K-12 virtual schools, particularly the complete high-school programs offered by for-profit companies, have engendered extensive suspicion and criticism. We review the four major critiques, which concern whether these schools are educating their share of hard-to-serve students, the effectiveness of the educational experiences they provide, and concern about profiteering at the public expense, and the ease of online cheating.

Full-time Virtual Schools Enroll Fewer Hard-to-Serve Students

Ethnicity appears to be associated with the likelihood of a student enrolling in an online course. Molnar (2013) compared the demographic characteristics of students in virtual schools to national student data and concluded that the former are more likely to be non-Hispanic Whites (75 percent versus 54 percent). Hispanic students are particularly under-represented in virtual schools, comprising only 11 percent of that population compared with 23.7 percent in the public school population as a whole (Molnar 2013). In the same vein, the report *Keeping Pace* by the Evergreen Education Group (2012) notes that online learners are less likely to be special education students, English language learners, or eligible for free or reduced-price lunch than are students in traditional schools.

Virtual Schools Have Low Achievement and Low Graduation Rates

The low average test scores and on-time graduation rates for virtual schools compared with traditional schools and U.S. public schools as a whole were described above. Critics like the NEPC contend that virtual schools, especially those run by for-profit companies, have poor student outcomes and that accountability and oversight for these schools have been lax (Brown, 2011; Glass, 2009; Glass & Welner 2011; Hubbard & Mitchell, 2011). In their review of the literature, Barbour and Reeves (2009) conclude that

> the only students that are typically successful in online learning environments are those who have independent orientations towards learning, who are highly motivated by intrinsic sources, and who have strong time management, literacy, and technology skills.

These authors note that the characteristics associated with success in an online program are those that distinguish the adult learner from the less-mature learner, and that online learning technologies and practices have their roots in higher education, where learners are adults. They note the need for more research on how to design online learning practices for younger students (Barbour & Reeves, 2009). We believe the problem is more extensive and complex than that of learner age per se (see Chapter 7) but second the call for research and design activities focused on different kinds of learners looking to online opportunities to meet different learning goals.

Virtual Schools are Profiting at the Expense of Taxpayers

Although funding mechanisms for K-12 and higher education are quite different, in both sectors we see significant concern that virtual schools run by corporations are seeking profits at public expense (Glass, 2009; Glass & Welner, 2011). In elementary and secondary schools, most funding comes from state allocations based on the number of enrolled students (average daily attendance) supplemented in some cases by local property or parcel taxes and by federal funds for special purposes and needs. In states permitting the operation of online schools, the schools receive their share of average daily attendance funds based on student enrollments (or in the case of Florida and Texas, on the basis of the number of online courses completed successfully). In an era when enrollments in many school districts are falling and traditional public schools are competing already with brick-and-mortar charter schools, many districts do not like the idea of having virtual schools drain off some of their students.

Online Courses Cannot Prevent Students From Cheating

Another concern about online education is the ease with which students can cheat, either by using disallowed resources while taking tests or by having someone else complete required work and examinations in their place. Virtual schools use a number of different strategies to keep such cheating in check. For example, FLVS trains its teachers to give each student a number of spontaneous assessments during phone calls to make sure that the student really does understand the material. They believe that they can identify flagrant cheating through this mechanism because students who have not done the work will not be able to give reasonable answers. Some other providers are experimenting with technological solutions. Some virtual schools have students use a Webcam so that a proctor located anywhere can detect suspicious eye movements or the vocal suggestions of anyone trying to assist. Another technological solution is software that detects a student's distinctive pattern of keyboarding and issues an alert if a person with a different pattern starts using the course software. A low-tech solution is the use of physical testing centers with on-site proctors for high-stakes examinations. Pearson has set up a network of such testing centers, which are being used by companies like Udacity.

Online Schools from the Perspective of Innovation Theory

Notwithstanding all of the criticisms and controversies that have arisen around online universities and K-12 virtual schools, there are those who believe that history and market forces are on their side. In their book *Disrupting Class*, Harvard professor Clay Christensen and his colleagues (2011) view the rise of online learning through the perspective of the disruptive innovation theory that they developed through their experience with other market sectors, such as the computer, airline, and steel industries.

They define a disruptive innovation as one that transforms a sector by making its products and services more simple, affordable, and convenient. They note that disruptive innovations do not succeed by competing with the well-established way of doing things head on. Rather, disruptive innovations first seek to serve those who were not served by the well-established product or service, and they succeed with those who were non-consumers in the past by redefining quality and offering a simpler product without incurring the cost structure of the traditional product. Technology and new business models are key components of disruptive innovations according to Christensen et al.

Online schools and universities fit this conceptual model quite well. In K-12 education, they got their start by serving students who could not get the educational experiences they sought in a regular school—rural students who had access to a limited range of courses, homeschooled students, gifted students who needed more challenge than their local high-school classes could provide, and so on. Apex got its start by offering online AP courses to students whose schools did not offer them, for example. The original market targeted by K12 Inc. was that of homeschoolers.

In higher education, WGU was concerned with citizens who had developed considerable competence through life experiences and could not easily take the time or travel the distance to undertake a traditional college program. Other than WGU, the biggest online university players have been for-profit companies that have targeted lower-income and working individuals who are looking for ways to earn a degree while continuing to hold a job. Christensen et al. (2011) explain that these online programs can dispense with the coupling of research, campus lifestyle, and instruction found in traditional universities and instead can be "laser focused on preparing students for a career . . . [thus] mitigating costs and improving student outcomes for those historically poorly served by college" (p. 4).

Christensen's theory predicts that a disruptive innovation like online schools and universities will initially be disparaged as being of poor quality, but that as its providers gain experience with their niche markets they will be able to improve their products so that they become more and more powerful and can begin to compete with traditional products and services for the core market.

Because the disruptive innovation can offer a lower price point, Christensen et al. argue that inevitably it will win the lion's share of a transformed market. Based on the quantitative model they developed studying disruptive innovation in other industries, Christensen and his colleagues predicted in 2008 that 50 percent of all high-school courses in the U.S. would be taken online by the year 2019 (Christensen, Horn, & Johnson, 2008). In 2011 they predicted that half of all higher education course enrollments would be online by 2014 (Christensen et al., 2011).

Another tenet of Christensen's theory is that disruptive innovations are never led by a mainstream organization offering the traditional product or service:

> There is no instance in the history of the hundreds of industries where disruption has occurred in which a significant company in one of the inner circles becomes a leader in a subsequent disruptive circle if it attempted to navigate that transition from within its mainstream business.
>
> (Christensen et al., 2011, p. 19)

In this analysis, the independent virtual schools and online universities, many of which are for-profit companies, are the potentially disruptive force in education. Christensen et al. acknowledge the significant barriers that regulatory restrictions can pose for disruptive innovations, but they argue that innovators find ways to work around those barriers.

In higher education, accrediting agencies, which base their judgments of quality largely on measures like the faculty-student ratio that are linked to the amount spent per student, have posed challenges for online universities. The fact that higher education funding in the U.S. is largely in the form of Pell grants that are given to students who can use them at any accredited institution means that online universities need accreditation to survive, but that once they attain that accreditation, they can compete with traditional colleges and universities for these students.

In K-12 education, state and district laws and regulations pose different barriers and complexities in different states. Online providers and political proponents of school choice have been lobbying for changes that will make it easier for virtual schools to operate. And they have had some success. For example, a number of states have passed legislation allowing students to take online courses from a combination of different providers, making it easier for a student to receive a high-school diploma on the basis of courses taken online (Evergreen Education Group, 2013).

To make smart policies about virtual schools, education systems should have good longitudinal data about their students' achievement outcomes and subsequent education. Unfortunately, the data systems in most states and districts have not been structured in a way that permits rigorous analyses that can disentangle the effects of online schooling relative to traditional schooling from differences in the nature of the students served by the two kinds of institutions. Many state and district data systems have no data element indicating whether a particular course was taken online or in a regular classroom. Virtual schools have data on which courses a student took from them, but typically lack information about the student's prior achievement and educational history and if a student leaves their school, they have no information about whether the student has moved to another online school, to a brick-and-mortar school, or has dropped out of education altogether.

Until data systems are improved in ways that support longitudinal analyses of student outcomes, online education consumers and the taxpayers who underwrite these experiences will be flying blind.

Online schools and degree programs do operate at lower costs (see Chapter 8) and they are experimenting with new models and new technology supports for learning and assessment. Regardless of their fates as institutions, they are pointing the way toward efficiencies and improvements that more traditional institutions are likely to adopt.

Chapter 7

Online Learning for Less-Prepared Students

As described in earlier chapters, online learning started out in higher education and homeschooling. Online pedagogies assumed a level of independence, motivation, and self-regulation on the part of learners, or the presence of parental guidance for younger students working at home. As the fields in which online learning is applied have expanded, education systems are using online learning to serve new purposes for younger students and for those with less motivation and poorer preparation for independent learning. This chapter describes such applications, the state of available research on their effectiveness, and current thinking on how to adapt online learning for less-prepared learner groups.

Programs for Secondary Students at Risk of School Failure

High-school graduation rates have remained unacceptably low for the U.S. as a whole and alarmingly low for some student subgroups and some types of schools. Almost a third of public school students fail to earn a high-school diploma; and among African Americans, Hispanics, and students in the country's 50 largest cities, the on-time graduation rate is in the area of just 50 percent (Dessoff, 2009).

In trying to prevent these students from leaving school or helping them to return and earn a diploma if they have dropped out, many school districts have turned to online learning as part of their approach.

Two distinct but related kinds of programs are referred to generally as "credit recovery" and "alternative education."

Credit Recovery

Credit recovery programs give students the opportunity to pass and receive credit for a course they attempted previously without performing well enough to earn credit toward graduation (Watson & Gemin, 2008). Most students who drop out of high school failed one or more of the courses they attempted in grade 9; most credit recovery efforts are aimed at helping students recoup their lost credits and stay with their high-school class (Watson & Gemin, 2008).

Many districts are turning to online courses to support their credit recovery efforts. Blackboard (2009) reports that more than 60 percent of the 4,000 district technology directors responding to a survey said they use a learning management system for credit recovery. FLVS, highlighted in Chapter 6, reports that a third of its course enrollments are for students who previously attempted but failed the course they are taking online (Dessoff, 2009).

An example of a large-scale credit recovery program using online learning is the Online Learning Program of the Los Angeles Unified School District. The courses offered for credit recovery use an active online instructor and course content segmented into chunks, permitting the differentiation of instruction. Students can test out of portions of the course they have already mastered from their first experience with it, and focus entirely on those chunks they still need to work on. The district works with individual schools to set up a course management system and Web conferencing so that courses can use both synchronous and asynchronous communication. Online teachers often start a unit with a diagnostic test followed by flexible combinations of group work and individual tutoring for different students.

Oliver et al. (2009) surveyed students taking courses through the North Carolina virtual schools and found some interesting differences between responses of credit recovery students and students in general, honors, or AP online courses. The credit recovery students were more likely than all the others to express the opinion that they learned more online than in classroom-based courses. They were also more positive about the instructional skills of their online teachers. One the other hand, they were more likely to express a lack of confidence that they were technically prepared to take a course online (60 percent) and to report limitations in their access to Internet connectivity at home and at school and to a computer at school (Oliver et al., 2009).

Alternative Education

While credit recovery programs are typically structured around specific courses and may be of relatively short duration, alternative education programs focus on taking the student all the way through to the diploma with a different learning environment, and typically a greater network of support, than is found in conventional classrooms and schools.

An example of a model for using blended learning in alternative education is the Performance Learning Center program developed by Communities in Schools, a nonprofit dropout prevention organization that first implemented the program in Georgia in 2002 (Kronholtz, 2011). Communities in Schools promotes this program for students who have performed poorly in regular schools, and have poor attendance, low motivation, and challenges such as poverty or pregnancy. The four performance learning centers operated in Virginia reported that in 2009–10 a third of the students at these centers were two or more years behind their grade level in terms of academic credits earned (Kronholtz, 2011). Performance learning centers operate as small schools with four or five teachers for fewer than 100 students, who work in four or five classrooms, depending on the number of teachers. Most of the instruction is carried out through online courses, but a teacher is present in each classroom to act as a coach and answer questions.

The Bridge Program of the Salem-Keizer school district in Oregon is another alternative school model combining online and classroom-based instruction. Bridge Program students take one course at a time and attendance is mandatory for the two hours a day they work in a computer classroom. Students are expected to undertake additional work online from home or other offsite locations, but program hours are flexible so students can stay in school while also working. The Bridge Program staff consists of two online teachers and two assistants who work in the computer lab to provide on-site help and keep students on track.

Student Outcomes

The research literature lacks rigorous experimental tests comparing student outcomes for credit recovery and alternative education programs with and without an online component, but districts are reporting numbers of students recovering credits and receiving diplomas after participating in these programs (Archambault et al., 2010; Kronholtz, 2011; Watson & Gemin, 2008). In many cases, it is likely that districts would not be able to offer such programs at all if they did not have the option of using online learning.

Recommended Practices

Based on their experience trying out and refining these programs, practitioners have started to develop a consensus around important elements of programs for students who have fallen behind grade-level expectations or for other reasons are at risk of not completing their high-school program. These include:

- use of mastery-based learning organized around competencies, which allows students to test out of portions of a course's content that they have already mastered and to proceed through each course as quickly as they are able, while preventing them from moving to new content before they have mastered the prerequisites (Archambault et al., 2010; Watson & Gemin, 2008)

- blended learning programs in which students can work on well-structured course modules at their own pace but also have interaction with a teacher or teaching assistant who is physically present to provide encouragement and answer questions (Dessoff, 2009; Watson & Gemin, 2008)
- an online orientation to accustom students to the mechanics of the course management system and the requirements for keeping track of their own progress (Archambault et al., 2010; Kronholtz, 2011)
- training for online teachers in how to engage students online, differentiate instruction, and use multiple instructional strategies in that medium (Watson & Gemin, 2008)
- training for facilitators or teaching assistants working with students on-site in how to manage the classroom, find additional learning resources for students who need help, and draw on other services such as those of a reading specialist if appropriate (Archambault et al., 2010)
- intensive contact between instructors, mentors, and students and between program staff and students' families (Archambault et al., 2010; Trautman & Lawrence, n.d.).

Less-Prepared Students in College Programs

As pressure to obtain a college degree has increased, larger and larger numbers of students enter college without the level of academic preparation needed to carry out college-level work. Students' language and mathematics skills are assessed at college entry, and those who lack college-level competencies are required to complete remedial coursework—usually called "developmental" coursework—for which they do not earn credit toward their degree.

An estimated 20 percent of entrants into public four-year colleges need developmental education, but in two-year community and technical colleges the problem is much more widespread. Estimates of the proportion of first-time community college entrants who need to take one or more developmental courses range from 42 percent to 75 percent (Attewell et al., 2006; Bailey, 2009; National Center for Public Policy in Higher Education and Southern Regional Education Board, 2010; Russell, 2008). In some California community colleges, the proportion of entering students requiring remedial coursework is as high as 95 percent according to Grubb et al. (2011a).

In the U.S., two-year community and technical colleges are the most common path to postsecondary education for low-income students and those from immigrant families and under-represented minorities (Hachey, Conway, & Wladis, 2013). Many of these students need to take developmental courses, and at the same time deal with other life stresses and family issues.

In Chapter 3 we described the rapid growth of online learning in higher education generally, with roughly one out of every three college students taking an online course. Online learning has grown even more rapidly in community colleges: in those settings about two out of three students are taking an online course in any given academic term (Pearson Foundation, 2011).

Online instruction is attractive to community colleges for multiple reasons. The motivation cited most often by academic officers is online learning's capability to make courses available to people with work or family responsibilities that make attending scheduled sessions on campus difficult (Parsad & Lewis, 2008). Other attractions of online courses are the potential for saving costs and for obtaining greater consistency across different sections of a course.

Completion Rates in Online Community College Courses

The rapid growth of online course enrollments in two-year colleges, like that in credit recovery programs discussed above, suggests that online learning is becoming prominent in education programs for the most vulnerable students. In an extensive analysis of data from Virginia's community colleges, for example, Xu and Jaggers (2011a) found that the likelihood that a student's first English or mathematics course would be taken online was highest at those community colleges spending the least money on instruction and serving the highest proportion of students on financial aid (p. 368).

In general, the proportion of students completing a course with a grade of C or better (the "course completion rate") has been in the range of 60–70 percent for online community college courses (Tyler-Smith, 2006). Such data have led some to question whether online learning is a good option for community college students or, more generally, for students in need of basic skills remediation (Jaggers & Bailey, 2010).

A review of studies comparing online and classroom-based course success rates by Jaggers (2011) put the average difference between community college online and classroom-based course attrition rates at 10–15 percent. Some observers are optimistic that this "completion gap" is narrowing. Among 142 community colleges responding to the 2012 annual survey conducted by the Instructional Technology Council, 47 percent said that completion rates for their online courses were as good as, or better than, their completion rates for classroom-based courses (Mullins, 2013). The report authors note that this finding contrasts sharply with the early days of online learning when it was not unusual to find a distance education course completion rate below 50 percent (Mullins, 2013).

Institutional administrators may not have the most rigorous perspective on relative course completion rates, however. One issue is that within community colleges (as in other institutions), students choosing to take courses online differ substantially from those choosing to take the same courses in a traditional classroom-based format. Students taking courses online tend to have higher GPAs, higher entering skill levels, more hours of weekly work, and a higher likelihood of being white, female, English fluent, on financial aid, and older than their counterparts taking classroom-based courses (Carpenter, Brown, & Hickman, 2004; Xu & Jaggers, 2011a, 2011b). In traditional classroom-based courses, some of these student characteristics are associated with a higher likelihood of dropping a course (e.g., number of hours of weekly employment), but many others are associated with higher likelihood of completion (e.g., higher entering skills, grade point average, and age). To get a fair comparison of online and classroom-based course completion rates, an analyst needs to compare similar students in the two kinds of courses, a kind of analysis that few higher education institutions ever make. Moreover, several researchers have noted that community colleges tend to lack awareness of the characteristics of the students taking their online courses (Hachey, Conway, & Wladis, 2013; Maxwell et al., 2003).

Xu and Jaggers, two researchers at the Community College Research Center (CCRC) at Teachers College, Columbia University, compared online and conventional course completion rates within two state community college systems, using student records data to control for differences in the characteristics of students taking the two types of courses. Among students entering one of the 23 colleges in Virginia's community college system, 8 percent took their first English course online and 7 percent took their first math course online (Xu & Jaggers, 2011a). Because students choosing online versions of these courses were more likely to be older, white, and female than the students taking their first English and math courses in the classroom, Xu and Jaggers restricted the sample of students in classroom-based courses for their analysis to those with entering characteristics like the students who enrolled in online courses at the same school. This restriction meant reducing the analysis sample from 12,417 to 1,513 in English and from 7,243 to 844 students in math. Xu and Jaggers' analyses of the resulting data set found that students who took their first English course online had a lower probability of completing the course with a grade of C or better (74 percent versus 77 percent), a "completion gap" of 3 percent. The completion gap using the same methodology for mathematics was 6 percent, with 67 percent of online course takers earning a C or better compared with 73 percent of students in classroom-based mathematics (Xu & Jaggers, 2011a).

Xu and Jaggers (2011b) also looked at outcomes for online and classroom-based courses in Washington State's 34-campus community and technical college system. They used a different strategy for dealing with dissimilarities between students electing to take online and face-to-face versions of courses in this piece of research. They restricted their analytic sample to students who took at least one online course between 2004 and 2008 and compared course attrition and success rates for online and face-to-face courses taken by these students. With this design plus statistical control for student characteristics such as age, gender, and enrollment in developmental education, they found that Washington community college students were more likely to drop out or fail to earn a C or better in their online courses than in their classroom-based courses.

Student Outcomes in Developmental Courses

Within the community college student population, the most vulnerable students are those entering the college without the skills needed for college-level work—those who are required to take developmental education courses.

Many of the students in the Virginia community college data set analyzed by Xu and Jaggers (2011a) were taking developmental mathematics or English language arts, but their data were combined with those for students taking a first college-level course in one of these subjects for purposes of the analysis. To examine outcomes for community college students in developmental courses—those students most in need of high-quality instruction—we turn to several other studies.

Summerlin (2003) examined outcomes for students taking developmental mathematics either online or in the classroom. Summerlin's analysis controlled for a number of student characteristics, including reading ability, age, gender, and ethnicity. Among students who completed their developmental math course, performance on a state test of mathematics was similar for those who took the course online and those who too it in the classroom. However, the rate of withdrawal prior to completion was roughly 20 percent higher for students in the online version of developmental mathematics, so the odds of completing the course successfully were significantly lower for those enrolling in an online section than for those enrolling in a section meeting face to face.

A study of outcomes in a developmental writing course by Carpenter, Brown, and Hickman (2004) provides some insight into the differential nature of attrition in online and classroom-based courses. In this study, students who completed the developmental writing course online were more likely to earn a good grade than those taking the classroom-based course, but as in the Summerlin study, withdrawal rates were significantly higher for online students. When Carpenter et al. examined the characteristics of students withdrawing from the course, they found that in the online sections, students with lower writing skills at entry (as measured by the college's placement test) were more likely than other students to withdraw, while in the classroom-based sections, the students with higher placement scores were more likely to withdraw. This study's findings underscore once again the need to take differential attrition rates into account when comparing outcomes for students in online and face-to-face courses.

Recently, the spectacular failure of the developmental mathematics MOOC at SJSU has sparked public debate about the use of fully online instruction with lower-achieving students. With encouragement from the California governor,

SJSU formed a partnership with xMOOC provider Udacity to offer a set of MOOCs to SJSU students for credit (and others on a non-credit basis) in the spring of 2013. One of the courses selected for the pilot program was developmental mathematics, a course that California State University students placed into developmental math must pass within the first 12 months of initial enrollment or face expulsion from the system. SJSU students taking developmental mathematics in the spring were all students who had already attempted the classroom-based developmental mathematics course in the fall but failed to pass it.

Udacity worked with SJSU's director of developmental education and with the developmental mathematics instructor to create a MOOC with the course's content chunked into small pieces, short video segments of an instructor teaching those segments, animations of key procedures, and online exercises. Because students would be receiving SJSU credit for taking the course, midterm and final examinations were taken in person with a proctor present. In an interview with one of us, the director of developmental education revealed that SJSU did not receive any information about the progress of individual students' specific skills until the midterm examination, at which time she learned that students' performance was "abominable." Usually SJSU teaches developmental mathematics in classrooms using a mastery learning pedagogy that allows students to retake assessments of each skill until it is mastered. In the end, only 29 percent of students taking the developmental mathematics MOOC for credit passed the course, an outcome that created considerable uproar when it was leaked to the press (Kamenetz, 2013). The outcomes and attendant press coverage were so negative, in fact, that Udacity's founder, Sebastian Thrun, stated publicly that MOOCs are often a "lousy product" inappropriate for low-income, vulnerable students: "These were students from difficult neighborhoods, without good access to computers, and with all kinds of challenges in their lives . . . It's a group for which this medium is not a good fit" (as quoted in Chafkin, 2013).

While Udacity has pivoted to focus on education for employment, the embrace of online learning by community colleges is unabated. Serious consideration should be given to the warning of Jaggers and Bailey (2010): "For low-income and underprepared students . . . an expansion of online education may not substantially improve access and may undercut academic success and progression through school" (p. 11).

Potential Contributors to Poor Outcomes When Less-Prepared Students Take Courses Online

The preponderance of research evidence described above suggests that when differential attrition rates are taken into account, community college students who take developmental education, or fully online courses generally, have a lower likelihood of successful completion than those taking the same courses in a conventional classroom-based format. Researchers have considered alternative sources for this poor performance in online courses: It may have something to do with the characteristics or life circumstances of that portion of the community college student population electing to take coursework online, or it may stem from weaknesses in the online courses themselves.

Starting with the second of these, there is some indication that the typical community college online courses, if those studied by the CCRC are representative, were far from exemplary in the years before and shortly after 2005. Researchers at the CCRC conducted qualitative studies of 23 online introductory academic courses at two of the Virginia community colleges that were part of the analyses conducted by Xu and Jaggers (2011b), interviewing students and course instructors as well as reviewing course materials. They found that some of the so-called online courses consisted solely of posting a course syllabus online and collecting assignments through the course management system (Bork & Rucks-Ahidiana, 2012). Many of the courses were primarily textbook driven and contained no multimedia elements. In the language of academic understatement, Jaggers and Xu (2012) sum up these qualitative data by stating that "many online courses in the community college setting are not thoughtfully designed" (p. 1). Such findings suggest that the research comparing outcomes for students in online and classroom-based community college courses, while providing sobering insights into what has been done in the past, tells us little about what *could* be done with well-designed online or blended courses, a topic we will take up later in this chapter.

Whether or not community colleges are offering high-quality online courses, the characteristics and life circumstances of students enrolling in these courses may undermine odds for success. In the opinion of experienced online instructors, key factors in online learning success are time management skills, facility with technology, initiative, and communication competency (Mandernach, Donnelli, & Dailey-Hebert, 2005). Data-based inquiries using higher education student data systems show that prior grade point average, number of online courses taken previously, and successful prior completion of an online course all predict successful online course completion (Bernard et al., 2004; Cheung & Kan, 2002; Dupin-Bryant, 2004; Xu & Jaggers, 2011a).

The literature generally points to four categories of student characteristics potentially accounting for community college students' weak performance in online courses:

- weak academic preparation
- competing workplace and family priorities
- lack of technology skills and needed technology infrastructure
- underdeveloped skills for learning independently.

Weak Academic Preparation

As noted above, multiple studies have found a relationship between prior grade point average or class rank and likelihood of success in an online course (Bernard et al., 2004; Cheung & Kan, 2002; Dupin-Bryant, 2004; Xu & Jaggers, 2011a). Many online courses make extensive use of text and, not surprisingly, students placed into developmental reading programs have a lower likelihood of completing an online course (Wojciechowski & Palmer, 2005).

Competing Priorities

The community college students who opt for online options are more likely than their same-college peers in all classroom-based courses to have extensive weekly work hours, family responsibilities, and financial aid (Hachey, Conway, & Wladis, 2013; Hagedorn, 2010). Community colleges want to serve such students—doing so, they say, is their primary motivation for offering online course options—but these life circumstances also increase the risk of non-completion (Conklin, 1997; Grimes & Antworth, 1996; Hachey, Conway, & Wladis, 2013).

Several of the studies described above attempted to control for such life circumstances in their analyses and still found poorer performance in online courses (Carpenter, Brown, & Hickman, 2004; Xu & Jaggers, 2011a, 2011b). Xu and Jaggers (2011b), for example, limited their study sample to students who had enrolled in at least one online course between 2004 and 2008 and compared their course completion rates for their online and classroom-based courses. This strategy assures that we are looking at the same kinds of students in the online and comparison courses—in fact, we are looking at the very same students. Xu and Jaggers found that students had a higher completion rate for their classroom-based courses than for their online courses. It could still be argued, however, that even though Xu and Jaggers examined the results for the same people in the two types of courses, personal circumstances may not have been stable over a four-year period. Taking on a new job or care of a sick family member is the kind of event that could lead a student to choose an online course option and at the same time create a level of demand and stress that would work against course completion.

Lack of Technology and Technology Skills

Lack of access to technology—or inability to use it with facility—can make online learning much more difficult than it has to be. To participate effectively in an online course, a student needs reliable broadband access to the Internet, a laptop or desktop computer, and facility working with email, attachments, chat rooms, search engines, and discussion threads. Inability to access course materials at home, protracted download times, difficulty completing assignments or online tests, and so on can leave a student frustrated and angry about an online course. These problems are more likely to affect the lower-income, immigrant, and minority populations seeking higher education through community colleges than the students enrolling in four-year colleges and universities. Rainie (2010) reports that the high-speed Internet access that is needed to participate effectively in online learning is available at home for less than half of Hispanics and of adults with a high-school diploma or less education, and household incomes under $30,000.

Even if low-income students do have access to the necessary technology infrastructure, they may not have developed fluency in the skills that Internet-based learning systems assume learners bring with them. Survey responses from 96 faculty teaching online courses identified lack of technological fluency as one of the top three barriers to success in an online course (Mandernach, Donnelli, & Dailey-Hebert, 2005). Community college online instructors interviewed by Bork and Rucks-Ahidiana (2012) reported concern that students were registering for their courses without reliable home Internet access, and that a surprising number of students had difficulty with very basic technology skills such as copy and paste or file attachment. Some instructors reported having to spend time working with students on technology skills, taking away from the time they had to devote to course content.

Underdeveloped Skills for Learning Independently

When asked what kinds of students do well in online courses, most online instructors will say "self-disciplined, independent learners." Many online courses, particularly those that use a mastery learning, self-paced approach, give students flexibility about when they do their coursework. That very flexibility makes it possible for a student to do too little in the early stages of a course and to find later that the work to be done is overwhelming. Successful online students are described as starting their active participation and work early, scheduling regular work periods, asking questions when they need help, and having the metacognitive awareness to realize what they do and do not understand (Mandernach, Donnelli, & Dailey-Hebert, 2005). Conversely, student failure in an online course is often attributed to procrastination (Figlio, Rush, & Yin, 2010).

In a study examining student outcomes in an online psychology course, Waschull (2005) found measures of motivation, self discipline, and willingness to commit time to be related to online course success. Several studies have found that having an internal locus of control (sense of responsibility for the outcomes one achieves) is positively associated with success in online learning (Parker, 2003; Wang & Newlin, 2000). All of these characteristics are areas where low-achieving students and students in developmental courses tend to be weak (Silva & White, 2013).

In their interviews with students and instructors in online courses at two Virginia community colleges, Bork and Rucks-Ahidiana (2012) found that instructors believed that online students needed the discipline to log on and work with the course materials independently at least three times a week while students harbored the expectation that teachers would lead them through the material. For the most part, neither expectation was satisfied.

Strategies for Improving the Online Course Success Rate of Under-Prepared Students

These insights into the multiple sources of students' difficulties in completing online courses lead naturally to alternative (but not mutually exclusive) strategies for increasing course success rates. Essentially, online course providers can seek to limit online enrollments to students with good prospects for success or redesign their online courses and associated support systems to foster learner behaviors that lead to successful learning. Ways in which these strategies might be put into practice are summarized in Figure 7.1 and discussed below.

Setting prerequisites for taking online courses:
- Administer an assessment of "readiness for online learning."
- Restrict enrollment to students with a qualifying grade point average or age.
- Require successful completion of an online orientation prior to course enrollment.

Improvements to the pedagogy of online courses:
- Ground teaching of a new concept or skill in a concrete context.
- Ask learners to apply key skills in multiple contexts.
- Use spaced, quick assessments of learning and cumulative, comprehensive examinations.
- Represent concepts in multiple media but avoid overloading the learner's cognitive capacity.
- Include practice and assessment items that require students to generate answers and provide feedback as quickly as possible.
- Provide feedback that addresses the nature of a student's misunderstanding and includes tips for remediation.
- Apply the Goldilocks principle in selecting problem difficulty.
- Build in scaffold for developing self explanations and self-assessment routines.
- Harness the power of peer-to-peer collaboration.
- Create a sense of instructor presence and responsiveness.

Improvements to the support systems for online students:
- Counsel students individually to clarify course expectations and set up needed arrangements before the course starts.
- Provide mentors for online learners.
- Institute "early alert" systems based on learner analytics and course progress measures.

Figure 7.1 Strategies for Increasing Success Rates in Online Courses

Set Prerequisites for Taking Courses Online

There have been a number of efforts to create a self-assessment instrument that prospective online students can use to ascertain whether they are "ready for online learning." These instruments typically contain items such as "I am good at setting goals and deadlines for myself" and "I am willing to send emails to or have discussions with people I might never see." Many colleges ask students to take one of these assessments before registering for their first online course, but evidence that the instruments really predict whether or not a student will succeed in an online course is largely lacking (Aragon & Johnson, 2008). A general problem with such self-assessment inventories is that the answer indicative of readiness to take an online course is obvious, and students seeking to take their course online may well give this "correct" response regardless of their true state of affairs.

A study of predictors of success in K-12 virtual schools by Roblyer and Davis (2008) did find evidence that a self-assessment inventory focused on learning-to-learn skills and attitudes taken at the beginning of an online course can help predict course success. Several other student characteristics were more strongly correlated with success in the online course, however. These were prior grade point average, having a home computer, having a class period at school set aside to work on the online course, and age (with older students having a higher likelihood of success).

Although taking a self-assessment on readiness for online learning may be useful in helping to set course expectations, it is unlikely that such instruments will be used by many schools and colleges to restrict the population of students allowed to enroll in online courses. One reason is that the validity of the instruments is not well established, as noted above, and hence their use as a gatekeeper could be challenged on legal grounds. More fundamentally, use of such instruments to restrict enrollment would fly in the face of the inclusion agenda of public school systems and community colleges.

An alternative to trying to limit access to online courses to those with a reasonable probability of success is to try to design preparatory experiences that increase the likelihood that less-prepared students will succeed.

A fairly common practice is to encourage or require students to attend an orientation session describing how to use the relevant course management system and, less frequently, discussing productive behaviors in an online course. Wojciechowski and Palmer (2005) found that attending a face-to-face orientation session does predict success in a subsequent online course, but this finding relates to a voluntary orientation and making it mandatory might reduce its predictive power. At present, orientation sessions are typically brief and lack opportunities to practice online learning skills, one of which is time management, that can only be exercised over time, not in a one-hour session. An alternative to a single-shot orientation session is a course in learning how to learn online. An example of such a course is Bridge to Success, a joint effort of the Open University, Anne Arundel Community College, and the University of Maryland University College. Bridge to Success is designed for students beginning their college experience with concerns about their ability to succeed, particularly in mathematics. Bridge to Success includes two open (freely available online) courses, Learn to Learn and Succeed with Math. The latter course integrates critical thinking with basic and developmental math content.

A potential problem with requiring an orientation course before students attempt online courses for their degree program is that such courses extend the amount of time required to complete the degree program, and each transition between courses in a sequence is a juncture where some students are lost.

A more promising strategy may be designing scaffolds for effective learning online into every online course and using learning analytics from the digital learning system to identify students with problematic course behavioral patterns (e.g., failure to log on or to complete online assignments) early on for proactive intervention by the system, the instructor, or an advisor. Both of these strategies will be discussed in more detail as aspects of improving online pedagogy and student supports.

Improve Online Pedagogy

In observing classes at 13 California community colleges, Grubb et al. (2011b) found a preponderance of what they call "remedial pedagogy,"—"drill and practice on sub-skills, usually devoid of any references to how these skills are used in subsequent courses or in adult roles" (p. 1). They point out that this approach, which they observed to be dominant in community college classes in California, flies in the face of instructional design principles based on learning research.

The work of Grubb and his colleagues reminds us that classroom-based learning is oftentimes far from ideal. Moving a course online can be an opportunity to move toward a much more learner-centered, research-based pedagogy. Because online instruction is new to most college faculty, there is no shame in admitting you do not know how to do it well. For some faculty, such as those described in the last chapter as appreciating their experience with MOOCs, serious engagement in course design or redesign for online delivery can be a professionally rewarding experience. Other faculty, however, attempt either to recreate what they do in class or to meet the requirements for online delivery with the least possible effort (Jaggers, 2011). Institutional change initiatives providing incentives and supports for faculty to engage with instructional designers in the development of high-quality online courses are needed.

Two sources of guidance for designing online instruction are the learning science research literature and empirical studies contrasting digital learning systems with different features.

There are many syntheses of learning research developed as guidance for instructional design (Graesser, 2009; Kali & Linn, 2010; Koedinger, Corbett, and Perfetti, 2012), and a full discussion of all of this guidance is beyond the scope of this volume. Below we present some of the principles that we see as most germane to designing online instruction (or selecting among available online courses) for students with relatively weak academic and learning-to-learn skills.

Introduce a New Concept or Skill by Grounding it in a Concrete Context

Stories or narratives and concrete perceptual and motor experiences are highly memorable to human learners and can provide motivation for learning. Instructors often fail to follow this principle when introducing mathematical ideas purely as symbols or formulae. Where possible, providing a concrete context related to students' occupational interests is a good instructional strategy provided that the context is relevant to the learner's needs and interests rather than "window dressing" for the content.

Teach for Transfer by Asking Learners to Apply Key Skills in Multiple Contexts

The purpose of education is to support learning concepts and skills that can be applied in new situations outside the classroom. Unfortunately, some instruction deals with a concept or skill in only a single narrow context, for example, presenting all linear equation problems in exactly the same format. When this is done, learning may be so tied to the particular context in which it took place that the learner does not transfer the skill to new situations where it is relevant. This situation is so common that it has earned the nickname the "inert knowledge" problem. To avoid this problem, online courses should provide students with practice applying skills or concepts with a range of different content or problem types. Online simulations make it possible to present students with realistic occupation-related scenarios like the real-world circumstances in which it is hoped they will apply the course content.

Use Spaced Quick Assessments of Learning and Cumulative, Comprehensive Examinations

People learn more with many, spaced practice trials (learning scientist-speak for a quiz or set of practice items) than with a single longer practice session. One of the virtues of online learning systems is that it is easy to create short assessments and distribute them throughout the course. But it is also important to have longer, cumulative assessments because learners tend to forget what they have learned if they know they will not be assessed on it again. This is one of the flaws of some mastery learning systems that assume that once a student has earned a passing score on an assessment of some piece of content that that learning will be retained and does not need to be reinforced or re-assessed.

Represent Concepts in Multiple Media but Avoid Overloading the Learner's Cognitive Capacity

Learners have systems for processing auditory and visual information, and representing to-be-learned information in both systems can enhance memory. However, designers should be careful not to overwhelm the cognitive system by presenting too much information at once, for example, by presenting a complex animation and an extensive text explanation (both of which must be processed by the visual system) together. Graphic elements and details that are not relevant to the content to be learned can impede rather than enhance learning.

Include Practice and Assessment Items that Require Students to Generate Answers and Provide Feedback as Quickly as Possible

There are two principles around designing assessments to promote learning that are in some degree of tension. Generally, learning is enhanced when feedback is provided very close to the time the student makes a response. Immediate feedback can help insure that the student thinks about the correct answer and does not spend excessive time learning the incorrect answer. At the same time, people learn more when they generate an answer than when they select an answer from multiple options (a multiple-choice item). But learning systems can generate immediate responses to multiple-choice items while open-ended items often require human scoring, which entails delays. Some designers are working on ways to get the best of both worlds, for example, by requiring students to work mathematics problems on a digital whiteboard and then after submitting their work to select an answer from an array of options. Students can receive immediate feedback on the correctness of the latter, and the system can store the student's work for later inspection by an instructor or teaching assistant. Advances in machine learning are also making it feasible for more sophisticated learning platforms to recognize correct handwritten answers to mathematics problems, but there is more work to be done to enable immediate feedback to a wider range of student-generated responses.

Provide Feedback that Addresses the Nature of a Student's Misunderstanding and Includes Tips for Remediation

Most online courses provide feedback concerning whether a learner got an assessment item right or wrong, but they could do much more. Feedback can be made more useful by including an example of how to work the problem correctly, a diagnosis of the likely source of the error, and recommendations of resources or additional practice items that can be used to address the misunderstanding or lack of skill fluency (Bakia et al., 2013; U.S. Department of Education, 2013).

Build in Scaffolds for Students to Develop Self-Explanations and Their Own Self-Assessment Routines

The ultimate goal is for students to learn how to be active learners and assess their own understanding so that they realize when they need to do further studying or seek help. Explanations get at causes, relationships between ideas or events, and the justifications for claims. Incorporating explanations into the instruction and then prompting students to provide their own explanations as they work with online material is one way to encourage an active approach to learning. Students can also be prompted to ask themselves how well they understand the material they have been learning. Some of the courses developed by the Open Learning Initiative at CMU employ this technique, providing prompts for the student to reflect on his own understanding in order to fill in a textbox describing "What was the muddiest point?" A simple checklist of things a student should have learned from an online module can be used to prompt self-assessment and can be accompanied by a help function linking the student to an on-call teaching assistant or referral to faculty office hours.

Apply the Goldilocks Principle in Selecting Problem Difficulty

Content that is too hard for an individual learner can lead to discouragement and quitting. Content that is too easy does not help the learner progress and may result in boredom. Some adaptive learning systems use banks of practice items at different levels of difficulty and use artificial intelligence techniques to identify those problems that an individual learner has a reasonable, but not too high, probability of getting correct (U.S. Department of Education, 2013). This is the same principle that digital game designers use in setting player levels to maintain arousal and engagement.

Harness the Power of Peer-to-Peer Collaboration

In addition to being visual and narrative learners, humans are also social learners (Meltzoff et al., 2009). Collaborative learning is an effective technique in classrooms, and it appears to be similarly positive in learning online (Bernard et al., 2009). Working in groups, students are called on to explain their ideas to others and get exposure to other students' ideas about how to approach problems. Several studies show that online students report greater enjoyment and better learning in courses in which they feel they are interacting with "real people" (Akyol et al., 2009; Swan & Shih, 2005). Liu, Gomez, and Yen (2009) found that the more students sense "social presence" in their online course, the more likely they are to finish the course and the higher their final grade.

Create a Sense of Instructor Presence and Responsiveness

Research on online community college courses suggests that the sense that the instructor is present online and interacting with students is even more important than interactions with peers. In analyzing 23 high-enrollment introductory academic courses, Jaggers and Xu (2012) found that students earned higher grades in courses in which they had more interaction with the instructor. Aspects of instructor actions promoting interaction included frequent posting of reminders, inviting questions through different modalities, responding promptly to student questions, and soliciting and using student feedback to shape the course. In talking about online courses they like, students described these interactions as evidence that the instructor cares about their performance. Similarly, Boston et al. (2009) analyzed data from almost 29,000 students who took an online course from the American Online University System (a for-profit, online provider) and completed the community of inquiry survey at the end of the course. They found that the survey items on the inventory most predictive of remaining in their course of online study concerned instructor behaviors such as clear communication of course goals, objectives, and instructions; guiding the class toward understanding; and helping to keep participants engaged and on task.

Enhanced Student Support Systems

Given online community college students' greater risk of failing a course and the greater likelihood that they are working long hours and juggling family responsibilities along with their course demands, improving completion rates is likely to require attending to non-academic as well as academic support needs. A number of colleges are developing more intensive support programs for their online students.

Integrating online learning readiness assessments into a more comprehensive process of counseling and support seems more promising than relying on the assessment taker to take appropriate actions. Discussing results of such a self-assessment with the individual student and devising strategies for dealing with potential issues (e.g., arranging childcare for a set period of time each week when the student can work online or identifying a "study partner" to work with regularly) are strategies for individualized student support being tried at some institutions.

Matching online students with a coach or mentor to work with them throughout their degree program is a practice at WGU (Jaggers, 2011). The University of Phoenix Online makes supporting students a team endeavor, providing each student with a "graduation team" comprised of an enrollment advisor, a finance advisor, and an academic advisor.

Increasingly, mentoring and support programs are starting to take advantage of automated "early alert systems" using learning analytics. An early adopter of this approach was Sinclair Community College in Dayton, Ohio. Sinclair developed its Web-based student success plan system in 2004. This system combines information on courses and grades from the college's student information system with faculty-generated alerts regarding course activities and demographic and admissions information from the college's data warehouse. The system generates an alert for a student's advisor and triggers development of an individual learning plan if the student appears to be at risk of dropping out (Campbell, DeBlois, & Oblinger, 2007). The Sinclair campus research office reports that 76 percent of fall 2006 first-time students actively working with an individual learning plan persisted to the next semester, compared with 66 percent of students who were not using an individual learning plan. Sinclair Community College has won multiple national awards for its innovative use of student data to improve student support services. Sinclair is now making its software available in open-source form so that many more colleges can use it.

Another community college actively using learning analytics to improve student retention rates is Rio Salado, a pioneer in online community college degree programs. Rio Salado is participating in the Predictive Analytics Reporting (PAR) Framework project, a collaboration of multiple colleges working under the leadership of the Western Interstate Commission for Higher Education Cooperative for Educational Technologies. (The Western Interstate Commission for Higher Education is a nonprofit organization promoting higher education in its 15 member states.) Together these colleges are building a database of more than a million student records (with identifying information removed), which can be explored to identify clusters of student actions and characteristics associated with dropping a course. Rio Salado has built the Progress and Course Engagement (PACE) system, which is integrated with its learning management system. When a student logs on to the learning management system, she sees an indicator (red, yellow, or green) of how well she is doing in the course compared with other students who have completed it successfully in the past. RioPACE uses information about how many times the student logged on to the learning system, how long she spent on it, and how much course material she completed to generate this indicator. This kind of interim feedback supports students who may not have an accurate perception of their degree of effort relative to a course's demands. The course instructor sees the red, yellow and green indicators for all students in the class. The goal is to identify any difficulties in time to help students recover and earn course credit.

During the 2013–14 academic year, Rio Salado College began to pilot new support services for students in its associate of arts and associate of general studies degree programs. An entering student will be paired with a personal advisor, who will work with her using the RioPACE analytics that track the completion of course work and performance on assessments for all her courses.

Using Blended Learning as Part of a Systemic Approach to Improving Developmental Education

For many low-income, immigrant, and minority students, developmental courses, and especially developmental mathematics courses, are a major barrier to degree completion. Helping students who did not acquire the basic skills covered in these courses through 12 years of elementary and secondary school do so in a semester or an academic year is a huge challenge. Colleges that fail to meet this challenge end up as a revolving door, with students entering and starting developmental education courses, failing or dropping out, and being replaced by new students with the same issues and the same low prospects for success.

Although not focused on online learning in particular, the work of Grubb and his colleagues (2011b) looking at instruction in developmental courses provides a vivid picture of instruction in community college remedial classes. They describe classes devoid of student–student interaction, in which teachers look for correct answers and do not seek to diagnose what students do and do not understand, where content is presented as a sequence of sub-skills without explanation of why these skills might be useful in some real-world context, and material is covered quickly without a check for understanding (Grubb et al., 2011b).

Grubb and colleagues recommend a multipronged, systemic approach to improving developmental education courses including:

- incorporating online practice and assessment systems
- connecting basic skills content to students' occupational interests and courses
- dealing with non-cognitive aspects of success in the developmental course
- adding flexibility and lowering institutional barriers.

To Grubb's quartet of recommendations we would add:

- using small-group collaborative learning techniques.

Recently, we undertook a serious of interviews of instructors and developmental education directors for 17 developmental mathematics courses that had been nominated as innovative (six of them were participants in the first wave of Next Generation Learning Challenge grants). The interviews were used to make ratings of various aspects of the intended course design, including features relevant to the five practices highlighted above (Means, Shear et al., 2013).

Although the courses are not a representative sample and in fact were selected to represent more innovative practice, the ratings suggest that at least some developmental mathematics courses are moving beyond the dismal remedial pedagogy described by Grubb and colleagues.

The use of online practice and assessment systems, for example, is typical of these courses. Over 80 percent of these courses were using frequent online assessment to provide ongoing information about each student's developing mathematics competency in each of the course's target skills. Over three-quarters used online practice as part of the course.

It should be noted, however, that online learning experiences are part of these courses and not their entirety.

There is a widespread belief among much of the developmental mathematics community that offering all instruction online is not an effective approach for the kinds of students taking developmental courses. Most of the course designers and instructors we interviewed emphasized the importance of small-group, collaborative learning activities, which were cited as a feature of 75 percent of the courses. One developmental education department head explained,

> Small group work helps because one student knows what to do and reinforces their own learning as he or she explains to other group members. It's good for the others to see that a peer has gotten it, and they feel comfortable asking a fellow student to repeat and explain.

In our interviews and ratings, we decomposed the category of dealing with non-cognitive barriers to course success into four more specific practices:

- teaching of learning habits and success strategies within the course
- addressing math anxiety or mind set within the course
- emphasis on reflection and communication of math reasoning
- integration with college support programs.

A majority of course designers and instructors reported dealing with math anxiety or learning mindset and learning habits within the developmental math course. And indeed, we saw some evidence of this in observed classrooms. One teacher made comments emphasizing that mastering mathematics is a matter of time spent working on it: "For somebody who does not see the numbers, you need to practice until you do. There is no magic; you just need to practice." An emphasis on the important learning skill of reflecting on your learning and being able to express it verbally was cited by seven interviewees. The same teacher described above exhorted her students, "You have to [be able to] explain what prompted you to do what you did. You need to talk to yourself when you solve the problem." Later, one of us watched students in her class work on problems in small groups. Four young women moved to the whiteboard to begin working on the algebra problem they had been assigned. One student did the writing, but others gave input. When they had finished, one of the young women asked, "Can we explain it in case she chooses one of us to explain?" Clearly these students were accustomed to the expectation that they show how they arrived at an answer and explain the reasoning behind each step.

A developmental course improvement practice recommended by Jaggers (2011) is integration with the college's general support programs. This practice appeared to be relatively uncommon among the blended learning courses covered by our interviews; only four interviewees cited any such integration.

We heard more about flexibility than about lowered institutional barriers. It was not uncommon for courses to have policies of letting students take assessments when they were ready or retake assessments with only the higher grade counting. Many of the developmental programs also had intensification strategies allowing students to complete two semesters of work in a single term or to take a brief, intense course in preparation for the college's math placement exam. But strategies requiring change on a larger scale, such as changes to course sequences, pairing courses, or allowing partial credit, were less common.

Applying Continuous Improvement Processes to the Design of Blended Learning for Less-Prepared Students

Designing interventions that are effective for less-prepared students is a major challenge, and one with which many schools and colleges are struggling. We believe that education institutions grappling with this complex problem would do well to apply continuous improvement processes informed by data to guide iterative cycles of refinement. Such practices are the exception, rather than the rule within education. But as pressure is increasing on education institutions to justify their costs on the basis of outcomes (course completions and earned degrees) rather than enrollment, the incentives for instituting such practices are increasing as well.

We will close this chapter with a description of continuous improvement processes used in the Pathways Project, a collaboration of 28 community colleges working with the Carnegie Foundation for the Advancement of Teaching and the Charles A. Dana Center of the University of Texas. The Pathways Project was designed to address the problem of the low proportion of students needing developmental mathematics who complete their developmental requirements and go on to earn credit in a college-level math course, a requirement for graduation.

The Carnegie team defined its goal as doubling the number of students who earn college math credit within one year of continuous enrollment at a participating institution. They recognized that such an effort would require a collaborative community and an infrastructure to support its success. The colleges that Carnegie convened agreed to collaborate with other colleges and with researchers and developers to analyze their developmental mathematics failure rates and then redesign their approach to developmental mathematics through collaborative development of new courses and associated policies, followed by analyzing system data and feedback from early implementations and subsequent refinement of the courses and practices.

The developmental mathematics practices that the Pathways Project designed through this process embody many of the features recommended by Gruber et al. cited earlier. From the beginning, the collaborators sought to lower institutional barriers. The collaborators found that many students were "lost" in the transition between multiple courses in a developmental mathematics sequence, and that existing courses often failed to engage students. As a recent report put it, "Faced with a long sequence of pre-college-level, non-credit courses, often repeating math material they've failed before, half of them quit within the first few weeks of enrolling in the courses" (Silva & White, 2013, p. 3). The Pathways Project designed an alternative, intensified approach that would minimize the number of transitions. It called for a two-semester course that would cover the basic skills content of developmental math and college-level mathematics. By completing the one two-semester course, students could satisfy their developmental math requirement and earn a college math credit.

Two different Pathways courses were designed, one emphasizing statistics (*Statway*) and one emphasizing quantitative reasoning (*Quantway*). Both connect to students' occupational interests through extensive use of real-world problems.

Statway and *Quantway* include courseware built on the platform developed by the Open Learning Initiative, and hence include opportunities for online practice and assessment.

But like the developmental math instructors we interviewed, the Pathways instructors do not rely on courseware alone. They make extensive use of classroom-based collaborative learning. Students in "learning teams" tackle math problems together, questioning each other, sharing strategies, and justifying their answers to each other. Analyses of Pathways student survey data show that a student's sense of "social belonging" within the course is the strongest survey-based predictor of course completion (Silva & White, 2013).

Finally, the Pathways Project has made a major effort to deal with the non-cognitive aspects of success. Drawing on research by psychologists such as Carol Dweck and James Stigler, Pathways researchers and instructors have designed and tried out a number of techniques for dealing with the need to change self perceptions around mathematics and develop academic persistence. Over 70 percent of students entering a Pathways course come in with doubts about their ability to succeed in math. The Pathways courses commence with three weeks of "starting strong" activities, which include reading and writing a response to an article based on Carol Dweck's "growth mindset" work about how the brain changes in response to mental effort and practice. Carnegie researchers worked with the instructor at one community college to assign students randomly to either read this article or to read another article about the structure of the brain. They found a major effect of this simple manipulation: students who read the growth mindset article were twice as likely as those who read the parts of the brain article to finish their developmental mathematics course—and they earned significantly higher grades (Silva & White, 2013).

Pathways instructors and researchers try out innovations such as these, collecting data on the results and sharing findings with other members of the collaboration. Carnegie's term for this data-based continuous improvement approach is "improvement science." The idea is that researchers and practitioners work together, developing a testable hypothesis about what might improve student success rates, trying it out, and collecting the data that will help them determine whether or not their approach was an improvement. Data about successes and failures are shared across the network so that effective practices can spread rapidly.

The same process was used in developing the course software. A number of two-year college faculty tried out some of the original *Statway* modules with their classes in fall 2010. Based on this experience, the project team realized that the materials needed a major revision before being implemented on a wider scale. A team of mathematics faculty from multiple colleges came to Carnegie to work together on redesigning the course, and the result was *Statway* Version 1.5, which was tried out by 21 colleges in school year 2011–12. Prior to implementing the Pathways approach, the collaborating colleges saw just 6 percent of their entering students requiring developmental mathematics earn a college-level math credit within 12 months of continuous enrollment. Among colleges using *Statway* in 2011–12, 51 percent of Pathway students met this goal (Strother, Van Campen & Grunow, 2013). Early results for *Quantway* appear even more impressive—56 percent of *Quantway* students completed their developmental mathematics requirement in a single semester (Silva & White, 2013).

The Case for Blended Learning

This chapter has focused on the use of online and blended learning with less well-prepared students. The challenges of finding instructional designs and student support practices that are effective in these settings are considerable, and the ability of online courses to deliver effective instruction to these students has been questioned. Technically, it is possible for online systems to include collaboration tools that can be used by a skilled online teacher to foster a sense of social presence and meaningful peer-to-peer collaboration rivaling those found in the classrooms of effective teachers. But documented examples of such successes in courses for under-prepared students are hard to come by. In the interim, we believe that blended learning approaches, leveraging the data collection and individualized practice capabilities of learning software in combination with classroom instruction emphasizing small-group collaboration and the development of productive mindsets and learning habits, will be the preferred strategy for developmental and alternative education.

Developmental and credit recovery courses are among the most difficult to teach well. If we can apply data-based continuous improvement processes to figuring out blended learning approaches that work well in these contexts, there will be far-reaching benefits not only for high school and college completion rates but also for our ability to design effective and engaging online courses. We will have developed a set of insights and practices that are likely to benefit all kinds of students in all kinds of courses.

Chapter 8

Online Learning and Educational Productivity

A case can be made that the productivity of the K-12 education system in the U.S. has been declining for decades. Government and student spending on K-12 education has increased by 70 percent over the last 30 years with very little improvement in outcomes (U.S. Department of Education, 2010b). In higher education, the costs of tuition and fees have increased an astonishing 274.7 percent between 1990 and 2009 (Christensen et al., 2011).

Economists describe this situation as the "Cost Disease," a dilemma endemic to service industries that depend on highly skilled labor. Like a symphony orchestra, a university cannot escape the need to have skilled employees in a range of different areas by substituting equipment or other capital outlays. They must pay increasing wages for skilled labor, and cannot cut costs without cutting the number of employees, which would bring associated declines in output (Bowen et al., 2012; Hill & Roza, 2010).

The most common purposes for adopting online learning have been expanding access, improving quality, and reducing costs. These three factors— cost, quality, and access—are often referred to as the "iron triangle" of education, suggesting that a positive change in any one is achieved at the expense of a negative impact on the others. In other industries, technology has been the key to raising productivity, and a number of policy makers are making the argument that the state of the art in online learning has now risen to a level where it can do so in education (U.S. Department of Education, 2010b; Wise & Rothman, 2010).

The Concept of Educational Productivity

In economics, "productivity" is defined as a measure of output per unit of input. Program inputs are typically measured according to financial value or time, and program outputs can be either quantitative or qualitative. In times of economic challenge, policy makers look for productivity improvements to allow them to maintain the same level of service with declining dollars.

U.S. Secretary of Education Arne Duncan has been a major proponent of the concept of measuring and improving educational productivity, asserting in a 2010 speech at the American Enterprise Institute that in what he called "the New Normal" K-12 and postsecondary educators were going to face the challenge of "doing more with less." Duncan urged educators to see this challenge as an opportunity for innovation and highlighted the role of technology:

> Technology can play a huge role in increasing educational productivity, but not just as an add-on or for a high-tech reproduction of current practice. Again, we need to change the underlying processes to leverage the capabilities of technology. The military calls it a force multiplier. Better use of online learning, virtual schools, and other smart uses of technology is not so much about replacing educational roles as it is about giving each person the tools they need to be more successful—reducing wasted time, energy, and money.
>
> (Duncan, 2010)

Economists note that productivity can be increased in either of two ways, specifically by:

- reducing costs while maintaining (or improving) outcomes relative to other alternatives
- improving outcomes while maintaining (or reducing) costs.

They refer to the first of these as increasing efficiency and to the second as increasing effectiveness. It is important to note that measures of productivity can be estimated only if data on both costs and outcomes are available and can be used only when two or more alternatives are being compared to each other (Levin & McEwan, 2001).

We have discussed online and blended learning outcomes at some length in previous chapters. In this chapter, we turn to the topic of reducing costs with online technology and the relationship between costs and student outcomes.

Does Online Learning Reduce Costs in K-12 Education?

Comparative Costs of Fully Online Virtual Schools

It is widely assumed that the use of online learning as a substitute for classroom-based instruction in programs such as those described in Chapter 6 will lower costs. Obtaining objective, systematic data to substantiate this premise and estimate the magnitude of the cost savings is surprisingly difficult, however.

The cost estimates for K-12 full-time virtual high-school degree programs provided in the literature vary considerably from program to program and study to study as shown in Figure 8.1, which contains estimates from seven different reports (none of which appeared in a peer-reviewed journal).

There are many possible sources for the variations in estimates of face-to-face and online per-pupil costs. As Watson (2004) notes, studies of public virtual school costs tend to use district and state budgets as their source. An exception is Watson's (2004) Colorado estimate, which was based on the estimated value of a set of resources that teachers and administrators identified as essential to the program, an approach more closely aligned with standard education cost estimation procedures (Levin & McEwan, 2001). The data presented by Cavanaugh (2009) are 2008 cost per full-time online student estimates obtained from a survey by the Center for American Progress of 20 virtual school directors in 14 different states.

More recently, as part of a project sponsored by the Thomas B. Fordham Foundation, Battaglino, Haldeman, and Laurans (2012) investigated the costs of K-12 online learning. They interviewed 50 entrepreneurs, policy experts, and school leaders to obtain information on costs in the categories of labor, content acquisition, technology, operations, and student support services. They estimated the average annual cost for a student in a full-time virtual high school to be $6,400 (with a range of $5,100 to $7,700). With the average cost of educating a student in a brick-and-mortar school (after removing administrative costs) estimated at around $10,000 a year, the virtual school costs do indeed

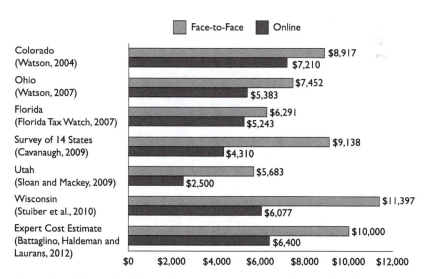

Figure 8.1 Published Comparisons of Per-Pupil Costs for Virtual and Conventional Schools

Source: Bakia, Shear et al. (2012) and Battaglino, Haldeman, and Laurans (2012).

appear lower. Unfortunately Battaglino et al. do not provide details concerning their methodology.

The work of Battaglino, Haldeman, and Laurans contains useful guidance concerning the different components of traditional and online education costs, but like many reports in this field, it leaves the reader wondering about the extent to which vendors and service providers are giving accurate information, untainted by a desire to make the economic case for online learning.

An earlier study conducted for the Bell South Foundation by Anderson et al. (2006) estimated that if transportation and capital costs are excluded, the costs of K-12 virtual schooling are about the same as those of regular brick-and-mortar schools when similar services are provided.

The uncertainties regarding what is included in particular estimates and whether alternatives are treated similarly within particular analyses plague cost studies of online learning. Studies vary in how infrastructure, capital, and "start-up" costs are included. Often these elements are omitted from the analysis. Similarly, several studies compare the costs of online learning programs (either actual costs or allocated funding) with per-pupil allocations in the state, even though the latter cover a broader array of services provided by traditional public schools, including transportation and nutrition services, school counselors and nurses, libraries, media specialists and resources, clubs, activities, and professional development services (Cavanaugh, 2009).

Critics of studies like the ones described here are concerned about potential biases (Hollands, 2012). First, these studies use cost data based on self-report, and respondents are being asked to generalize across experiences, something that is mentally challenging. In addition, respondents likely underestimate the value of the technical and capital infrastructure on which education relies (since expenses for these items are often found in different budgets). Finally, these reports' lack of transparency about the researchers' data collection and estimation approaches makes it difficult to know whether capital costs such as facilities are being included. Without a more rigorous cost accounting, there is not really a way to know whether reported figures tell the full story. Later in this chapter, we describe what it would take to conduct a thorough analysis of the costs and productivity of online learning. In the interim, the studies summarized here are among the best (and just about the only) estimates currently available. We recommend that readers take the nature of the organization sponsoring a cost study into consideration.

Comparative Costs of Blended and Conventional Instruction

In addition to estimating costs for virtual schools, Battaglino, Haldeman, and Laurans (2012) also offered calculations of the average costs of blended instruction, which they estimate as $8,900, plus or minus 15 percent, thus overlapping the $10,000 national average per-pupil cost of instruction. It is difficult to interpret the estimate provided by Battaglino et al., however, in the absence of detailed information about the particular blended learning models included in their research.

As described in Chapter 5, there are many different objectives for, and models of, blended instruction. Some produce cost savings by using technology to reduce the number or skill level of staff (for example, having students spend a class period taking an online course instead of receiving instruction from a local teacher) or by increasing student–teacher ratios (as in the example of Summit schools' personalized learning time described in Chapter 5). In such cases, the blended learning option need be only "as good as" its face-to-face alternative when considering student outcomes to increase productivity.

Other blended learning models involve supplementing face-to-face courses with technology-rich experiences, either by adding instructional time or by having the instructor present while students use the technology. In such cases there are usually added costs, and to increase productivity, the blended learning approach needs to improve outcomes sufficiently to offset the additional expenditures.

Several of the charter schools implementing the blended learning models described in Chapter 5 report associated cost savings. The principal of KIPP Empower Academy, for example, describes the use of a blended learning rotation model within larger classes as the academy's solution to dealing with a projected $200,000 budget shortfall in its first year of operation. The two Summit schools in San Jose were able to open with one fewer math teacher than the other high schools in the Summit network because of their heavy use of Khan Academy and other online resources (Bernatek et al., 2012). Both obtained strong learning outcomes for their students, providing at least some evidence that they were able to obtain above-average educational productivity through their blended learning implementation models.

There have been very few rigorous, independent analyses of the costs of implementing blended learning models. An exception is an analysis of the costs of the pilot implementation of the School of One (described in Chapter 5) conducted by Fiona Hollands (2012), a researcher at Teachers College, Columbia University.

Hollands estimates the total development cost for School of One as almost $8 million over two years. This total included technology development costs for the learning algorithm and the costs of obtaining the capacity to house 5,000 math lessons that could be completed and assessed online, estimated at $5 million. Another $2.4 million was spent over two years to pay for a team working on system and interface design. The School of One was implemented with approximately 1,500 students in three middle schools in school year 2010–11. If all of the development costs were assigned to just this one year of implementation, they would be over $5,000 per child. But the

School of One and New York City planned to reach much greater scale over time.

Hollands calculated the ongoing costs of implementing School of One at a hypothetical middle school with 480 students. Hollands's estimate included the costs of renovating a school space to provide the large room needed for the School of One model, an in-house digital content manager, professional development for staff, hardware, expected licensing fees for School of One content, and the costs of the online tutors that are part of the model. Her estimate excluded development costs, which the school would not be expected to pay. By her calculations, replicating School of One would add $1,352 per student over and above the normal per-pupil expenditures. By performing a break-even analysis, Hollands calculated that School of One would need to produce a mathematics achievement gain almost twice as large as that produced by the average school program to be cost effective. As noted in discussing School of One in Chapter 5, this kind of impact has not been demonstrated thus far.

Online Learning and Cost Reduction in Higher Education

In higher education, Bacow et al. (2012) report that the most common rationale for developing online degree programs is revenue growth. The purpose of these programs is generally to reach new students who might not otherwise enroll. Administration of online programs takes a variety of forms, but Bacow et al. (2012) find that universities usually create a separate cost center with a different mix of staff and facilities that allow the programs to contain costs. There may be attendant savings in facilities costs as well, but no serious efforts to fully cost online degree programs within traditional colleges are readily available, so findings remain somewhat speculative. Ironically, although the working assumption is that fully online courses save universities money, students may be charged more for the "convenience" of taking a course online (Bacow et al., 2012).

The leader in using blended learning to control or reduce costs in higher education in the U.S. has been the National Center for Academic Transformation (NCAT). With support from the Pew Charitable Trusts, NCAT has developed six proof-of-concept alternatives to large lecture courses that use technology and other methods to reduce costs and, it is hoped, improve quality at the same time (Twigg, 1999, 2005). Courses are redesigned to use teaching assistants and technology in place of more highly paid faculty for some portion of course contact hours. NCAT has reported an average cost savings of 37 percent with 25 percent improvement in learning outcomes for courses using their process.

Between 2011 and 2012, the Missouri Learning Commons, a consortium of the state's 13 public four-year colleges, worked with NCAT in a statewide course redesign initiative. Using various blended learning models, they redesigned 14 courses and piloted them in the spring or fall of 2012. In one example, the faculty member redesigned a mathematics course to be taught in a large computer lab space with 75 students working online with mastery learning software, with graduate students and adjunct faculty available to provide assistance. The Missouri Learning Commons reported that costs were reduced in ten of their 14 course redesign efforts, and that 12 of these courses produced the same or better student pass rates as prior versions of the courses.

While NCAT's work is very forward looking, it has some noteworthy limitations. The reported results are based on self-report data. The data are sometimes estimates, with a noted tendency to underestimate actual costs. For example, developing online learning resources tends to take longer and cost more than expected. Others have noted that the pre-post design used by NCAT to measure learning outcomes lacks any experimental or statistical control (Lack, 2013).

Despite these methodological weaknesses, the NCAT course redesign models demonstrate the potential of using blended learning models to improve institutional productivity by replacing staff time with a combination of technology and the labor of relatively less-expensive staff, such as teaching or graduate assistants. Bowen et al. (2012) reach the same conclusion on the basis of their work with the OLI statistics course implemented in blended learning models at six public universities. As described in earlier chapters, technology can reduce staff time in a variety of ways—through performing some of the functions related to content delivery, student assessment, feedback, and communication, or through automating administrative tasks such as attendance and other record keeping. As various tasks are shifted to technology, skilled staff can be redeployed for more complex tasks, such as facilitating students' work with complex concepts.

Major Factors Affecting the Costs of Online Education

As noted above, accounting for the costs of education, with or without technology, is a complex, labor-intensive undertaking. Putting aside the accuracy of estimates for total costs, we can be confident that three aspects of online learning have the potential to influence those costs in positive ways.

Use of Open Systems and Educational Resources

Content development and acquisition can be a significant driver of costs for online and blended programs (Battaglino, Haldemann, & Laurans, 2012). The increasing availability of open learning management systems, such as Moodle and Sakai, and open educational resources, as discussed in Chapter 3, makes online learning a more attractive financial proposition.

In the case of open educational resources like the Khan Academy, content acquisition is "free" in the sense that Khan Academy does not collect a fee for use of its materials. However, district technology officers are fond of pointing out that free digital learning resources are "free like a puppy." You may not have to pay a provider to use them, but you still need to pay for upkeep—the technology infrastructure to support their use and supports for teachers who need to learn how to use them well.

We examined the cost implications of one school district's use of Khan Academy resources. In this particular district, start-up costs were minimal because the district had a robust, technology infrastructure that could be deployed for using Khan Academy. This would not be the case in many schools districts, however. In addition, even though no direct cash outlays were required, the district did reallocate resources to implement Khan Academy systematically. Staff time was required to locate those Khan Academy resources that fit with the district's curriculum and its objectives for Khan Academy use. Teachers had to devote time to planning lessons that incorporated those Khan Academy resources. There were also opportunity costs associated with the use of the district's technology infrastructure, including technical support, and use of about 450 computers and schools' 100-megabit connections for this activity.

Process Redesign

Research across many industries suggests that the introduction of technology by itself will not increase productivity. Rather, to attain improvements in productivity, an institution needs to couple technology with organizational changes such as reengineering of key business processes and industry structures (Athey & Stern, 2002; Atkinson & McKay, 2007; Brynjolfsson & Hitt, 2000; McKinsey Global Institute, 2000, 2002).

An online course that involves teachers in replicating traditional lecture formats and delivering the bulk of instructional content verbally at the same teacher–student ratio—but doing so online—incurs additional costs and is unlikely to garner any compensating increases in student learning. Such applications may be justified on the basis of increasing access if they bring the course to learners who would not otherwise experience it, however.

Many have argued that the true productivity potential of educational technologies is in their ability to transform core instructional practices, including the use of student and teacher time. The availability of micro-data about student learning processes online can not only make the online system adaptive in ways that enhance learning but also inform teachers and counselors of the nature of needed corrective actions to avoid course failure (U.S. Department of Education, 2012).

Scale of Implementation

The term "economies of scale" captures the idea that per-unit costs are reduced as the scale of production increases. Conceptually, this is possible by leveraging high investment or "fixed" costs with low variable, recurrent costs. In the case of online learning, investment costs may be relatively big-ticket items related to infrastructure, including items like hardware, connectivity, and content development. Course development may constitute a large or small portion of fixed costs depending on the instructional model (Anderson et al., 2006). Recurrent costs represent annual ongoing expenses such as instructor salaries and technology maintenance.

One way to improve productivity is to increase the numbers of students whom high-skilled personnel can serve. Personnel (what economists call "labor") represent a significant proportion of ongoing cost in education. Personnel costs typically include the time of teachers, teaching assistants, developers, administrators, and any other staff involved in creating or running an educational program (online or otherwise). Per-student labor costs can be reduced if teachers and other staff can serve more students by changing what they do and how they do it. The NCAT work described above suggests several strategies for redeploying staff.

In cases with a high proportion of fixed costs, per-student costs go down as more students are served, since each student has to assume a smaller and smaller portion of the fixed costs. In the case of Hollands's examination of School of One costs described earlier, the project's ambitious software development goals combined with a need for a large bank of learning materials and assessments made the initial development costs fairly high (over $5,000 per child). If they were allocated to just the 1,500 pupils experiencing School of One in its pilot year, their impact on the cost of educating each student is substantial. If the software were used with 150,000 students, on the other hand, the per-pupil additional cost would be around $52.

Compared with conventional instruction, online learning usually incurs higher investment costs associated with designing a new program, developing new curriculum, and selecting or developing digital resources. A few studies in postsecondary education have found online learning to be an expensive alternative because of these initial development costs and the ongoing personnel costs for delivering instruction (Jones, 2001; Ramage, 2005; Smith & Mitry, 2008).

There are often-cited structural incentives of digital media that argue in favor of scale—once the investment in development has been made, why not get the course out to as many people as possible? Although online course content can be expensive to develop, once created it has the potential to be distributed to large numbers of students with relatively little additional expense (Adsit, 2003; Christensen, Horn, & Johnson, 2008; Watson, 2004). Once an online course is developed, digital resources can be reused at a relatively low marginal cost.

With the MOOC platforms it is clear that courses can be delivered not just to hundreds but to thousands and tens of thousands of students at a time. With these economies of scale, a greater investment in the design and development of high-quality online learning materials can be justified.

There are countervailing pressures. Higher education faculty and K-12 teachers entered their professions because they like the process of teaching and of creating their "own course." Although K-12 teachers have become more accustomed to the idea of mandated curricula than college faculty, they share the inclination to close the classroom door and teach it "their way." Developers of online courses and instructional resources face a tension between making their product so finished that instructors do not want to use it because they cannot make it their own, and making their product so open-ended that instructors feel they have to put too much advance work into setting it up for use with students.

One strategy for making inroads in the face of this kind of faculty resistance can be seen in the work of NCAT and a number of colleges, such as Rio Salado. A faculty member is responsible for a course and selects or develops the online and other curriculum materials but then has an adjunct instructor or graduate assistant actually teach the course using the online learning resources and other curriculum materials. This model appears to be gaining hold in college practice for lower-division mathematics courses and is starting to spread to other subjects as well.

Another important criticism is that large-scale delivery of courses reduces opportunities for the social and affective experiences that are important for developing life-long intellectual interests and learning habits (Bauman, 1997). Defenders of learning at scale note that the greater intimacy of small, in-person classes is great for those who are willing to pay for it. But many of the people enrolled in college courses just want to get the knowledge (or the course credit) at the lowest possible price.

Requirements for Measuring Educational Productivity

The question of whether online learning is more or less cost effective ("productive") than other alternatives does not lend itself to a simple yes or no answer. Comparison of relative productivity across alternatives requires attention to a host of factors, including the students served, the subject domain, scale, budget, and design factors such as the role of the teacher and the level of blending of online and face-to-face components. It is likely that different models of online learning use—and different implementation details—will impact cost and outcomes. Figure 8.2 illustrates the many components of an educational productivity analysis.

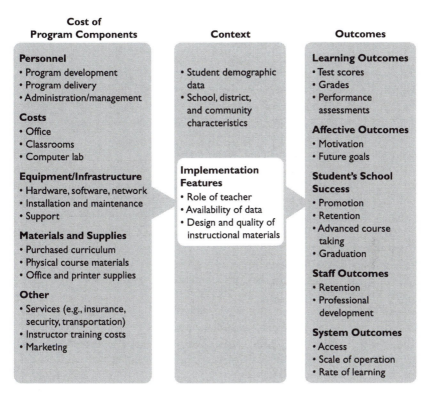

Figure 8.2 Components of Educational Productivity Analyses

Source: Bakia, Shear et al. (2012).

Although specific costs vary by program, the categories of costs that need to be considered are summarized in the figure:

- Personnel costs include the time of instructors, teaching assistants, developers, and anyone else involved in creating or running the educational activity.
- Facilities costs include those associated with buildings, remodeling, and furniture for administrative and instructional purposes as well as for housing and needed equipment.
- Equipment and infrastructure costs are those associated with hardware purchases and with supporting its operation as well as the costs of maintenance to keep the infrastructure in working order.
- Materials and supplies costs include purchased online curricula or learning management systems as well as textbooks and other physical goods or processes, such as the costs associated with printing and copying.

- Other costs include those needed for the successful and legal operation of a program that are not included in the categories above, including student support services.

An important feature of the model for educational productivity analysis in Figure 8.2 is its inclusion of the documentation of features of context and implementation. We have written elsewhere (Means & Harris, 2013) about the need to collect outcome data for the specific kinds of students, contexts, and implementation practices about which the researcher wants to generalize. The same admonition applies to cost estimates (Bakia, Shear et al., 2012). Multiple cost-effectiveness ratios will be needed to capture significant variation in implementation models. Policy makers and administrators should carefully consider the applicability of findings from particular studies to their own contexts. A study concluding that implementation of online learning was cost effective in a particular content should not be extrapolated to suggest that all forms of online learning are effective in all contexts for all students.

The "ingredients" approach to specifying costs, as described by Levin and McEwan (2001), sets forth a set of principles for identifying and comparing the costs of two educational alternatives. Cost analyses should include the costs or value of all resources essential to an intervention and its alternative, regardless of the source of funding. For example, this principle suggests that the labor of volunteers should be valued and included in cost estimates.

Another principle is that the same parameters should be used in estimating costs for the alternative interventions being compared. In comparing place-based programs with virtual schools, for example, if facilities costs are included for the brick-and-mortar schools, the physical plant used by the virtual school should be included as well. More details on the application of these principles to examining the educational productivity of online learning are available in Bakia, Shear et al. (2012).

Conclusion

Online and blended learning can be more or less cost effective than conventional classroom-based education, depending on the particular alternatives being compared. Costs vary dramatically depending on the implementation model, the number of students served, and the size of the investment in software development or subscription fees. We need to look at the particular online or blended learning model under consideration to assess whether or not it enhances educational productivity relative to a specific alternative, and unfortunately there are very few cases in which we have both good data about costs and good data about student outcomes.

Online and blended learning implementation costs are highly dependent on factors such as the number of students in a course or program and the way in which it is staffed—decisions that are typically made at higher levels of the education system, such as district superintendents or university department chairs, rather than by teachers or individual faculty members. At present, there is a web of regulations, union contracts, and accrediting criteria that limit schools' and universities' options in redesigning courses and programs to be more cost efficient. Charter school networks, which are freed from some of these restrictions in exchange for being accountable for student outcomes, appear to be leading the way among K-12 institutions in trying out new blended learning models and uses of school time and staff resources. At the same time, there is a concerted push on the part of a number of organizations to eliminate state, district, and accrediting agency restrictions on the organization of instruction and incorporation of online learning.

As the field moves toward use of these new models, it is vitally important that student outcomes are measured continuously and carefully to ensure that reductions in costs are not being obtained at students' expense. We believe that the road to greater educational productivity will be through investing more, not less, in the design and evaluation of online learning systems and implementation models, followed by widespread adoption of those that prove most effective.

Chapter 9

Conclusion

In this capstone chapter, we take a step back from the particulars of online learning in the different settings and applications discussed in chapters 3–8 to highlight some of the major themes running throughout the book. Building on these themes, we will conclude with a set of areas we judge ripe for research that could improve the design of online learning activities on the one hand and inform decisions about when and how to implement online and blended learning on the other.

Themes in Online Learning Research and Practice

Online Learning is a Broad, Complex Category

Because of the pervasiveness of the Internet and Internet access devices, online learning has become, like learning in general, life-long and life-wide. It is not only an expected part of formal schooling but also part of the fabric of our daily functioning and pursuit of enjoyment and professional advancement. As we have become accustomed to turning to online resources to learn things we need to know or are curious about, we have also learned to consult these resources for assistance when dealing with the demands of formal coursework.

The exceedingly wide range of different online learning experiences and the different blends of online and place-based learning described in this book attest to the fact that "online learning" is too broad a category to label as effective or ineffective. Not only the popular press but even much of the academic literature presents a one-dimensional portrayal of online learning as either the answer to all our education problems or a totally ineffective sham.

Clearly, there are forms of online learning that help some people achieve some types of learning goals under some conditions. But not every online learning experience is effective any more than is every classroom-based experience. The field needs a better understanding of the "active ingredients" of online learning and of the different aspects of context and implementation that influence online learning outcomes. We have offered a framework for describing particular types of online learning in hopes of fostering more precision in the description of online learning interventions and in the synthesis of research findings across studies.

Online Learning Experiences Could Be Improved with Greater Application of Learning Science

There is a huge gap between the kinds of learning environments we have the scientific and technological capabilities to design and what is typically provided in online courses (Bakia et al., 2013). The tradition of each instructor designing her/his own lesson plans and, at the college level, her/his own content coverage, has been carried over into the design of online and blended courses. Individual instructors are naturally limited in the time available for planning and development, and typically lack advanced expertise in learning research, user experience design, and assessment. Narrowing the gap between what is conceptually and technically possible and what schools are doing will require multiple kinds of expertise.

Applying the best of what we know to the design of online and blended learning activities and environments entails bringing together multiple people to work on design and development. No one person is likely to be a deep expert in learning research, user experience design, assessment, and the content to be taught. For most of history, the lesson a teacher would plan for the next day would be experienced by 20–35 students. At this scale, keeping the investment in designing that instruction small is a necessity.

As we move to online courses and learning resources that are going to be used by thousands and even hundreds of thousands of students, however, we can justify much larger investments in instructional design and development than we have made in the past.

Fully Online Experiences are Likely to Grow Outside of Mainstream Education Institutions While Blended Learning Becomes Pervasive Within Those Institutions

Making predictions about the future is always hazardous, but thus far at least developments in online and blended learning appear to be following Christensen et al.'s theory of disruptive innovation (Christensen, Horn, & Johnson, 2008) quite closely. As a potentially disruptive innovation, fully online learning got its start, and has been growing most rapidly, at the fringes of the core education system. It has been serving portions of the education market that were not being served before—rural students, homeschoolers, dropouts, working adults, and those who cannot afford tuition. Now well established in these niches, we see fully online education institutions trying to go mainstream with virtual schools, online degree programs, and MOOCs for college credit. These efforts are experiencing push back from policy makers, accrediting agencies, and some segments of the general public. Although there have been some individual successes for some of these endeavors, we do not foresee a "tipping point" any time in the next five years.

In contrast, blended learning, which Christensen calls a hybrid innovation, is being adopted by education systems on a broad scale. Blended instruction is not threatening to established teaching roles or to the authority of the classroom instructor. It can incorporate resources and practices that have proven effective in fully online applications while still leaving room for human instructors to do what they do best. We believe that blended learning is likely to become the most common modality, certainly for higher education and increasingly for secondary education as well within the next five years.

Use of Online Learning Can Be Justified on the Basis of Improved Access, Learning Outcomes, or Cost Effectiveness

Access, outcomes, and cost are sometimes characterized as the "iron triangle" of education. The challenge is to make improvements in one or more of these areas without causing poorer performance on the others. There are those who believe that online learning is the key to getting simultaneous improvements in all three areas, and we hope they are right but urge policy makers to consider the evidence.

The evidence is pretty good that online learning can improve access to learning without degrading student outcomes. For example, the online Algebra I experiment in New England demonstrated that eighth graders ready for this level of content could learn it online and then proceed with more advanced mathematics courses in high school (Heppen et al., 2012). Clearly online learning can work, making an a priori case for making it available when face-to-face instruction is not an option or where the learner prefers learning online.

The greatest potential, however, is in the use of online environments, resources, and activities to enhance important outcomes—to help people understand and do things that would otherwise be difficult or impossible to learn. Digital models, simulations, and animations can make abstract concepts visual, concrete, and manipulable. These resources can be explored individually or in collaboration with peers and mentors also working online. We have good evidence for many exemplars of this kind of technology-supported activity enhancing learning (Means, Shear, & Roschelle, in press), but no information on their cost effectiveness.

Given the Current State-of-the-Art, Blended Learning is the Preferred Approach for Less-mature, Under-prepared, and Less-confident Learners

Our optimism about the potential for enormously more powerful online learning experiences should not be construed as encouragement for educators to adopt fully online learning options in the absence of evidence that they are effective. There is considerable controversy around the use of fully online learning with some kinds of learners. Although disentangling the effects of learner characteristics from those of course modality has remained challenging, there is enough indication that less-prepared and less-mature learners have reduced success in fully online courses to suggest caution about imposing this form of instruction on them.

There is what seems to be a contradiction between the many studies of computer-assisted mastery learning, most of which found that younger and low-achieving learners benefited the most from this approach, and more recent analyses suggesting that these same kinds of learners are at greater disadvantage with online learning. This inconsistency points once again to the need to be more specific about what is being compared. The earlier computer-assisted instruction studies were often investigations of interventions of shorter duration and the computer-assisted instruction was part of a class, but not the whole thing—it was the equivalent of what we would call blended learning today. Most of the computer-assisted instruction interventions employed self-paced mastery learning, a pedagogy found in some online courses, but probably not in most of the instructor-developed courses studied by Xu and Jaggers (2011a, 2011b).

It is possible to blend extended practice and frequent assessment with feedback available from an online system with attention to conceptual understanding, peer learning, and modeling of productive habits of mind in the classroom, as illustrated by a number of the courses and programs described in Chapters 5 and 7. Such approaches appear to be as effective for less-prepared and low-income learners as for others.

Given the available evidence and the nature of present approaches to fully online instruction, we recommend a blended learning approach for younger, less-advanced, and less-confident learners. Although not impossible to provide online, work with peers and a personal connection to the instructor are easier to implement in a classroom setting. Absent a significant investment in online learning environments and instructor training to provide these qualities in an online system, a blended learning strategy is a less-risky option for younger and less-advanced learners.

The Rising Importance of Blended and Fully Online Learning Argues for Renewed Attention to Issues of the Digital Divide

Despite tremendous strides in mobile technology and Internet access, there is still a digital divide. Online learning conveys opportunities in both its self-initiated forms and as part of credit-bearing courses, and there is work to be done to make these opportunities equally available to people everywhere.

The problem is exemplified by what happened when SJSU and the MOOC provider Udacity teamed up in the spring of 2013 to offer online college-credit math courses to anyone, including high-school students, with a high-speed Internet connection. An Oakland charter high school had 45 of its students sign up. Several weeks into the course, the school found out that a number of its students had never once logged in to the course (Kolowich, 2013b). It turned out that their home computers and Internet connections were not up to the requirements for Udacity's online course. The school had to set up a class period when these students could use the school's computer lab in order to participate in the MOOC.

As in this example, school systems have been playing a role in reducing disparities in technology access. In the U.S., technology access within schools serving students from different backgrounds has been becoming more similar over time, and is less stark than the differences in home access (Warschauer & Matuchniak, 2010).

In June of 2013 President Obama unveiled a plan for a major reworking of the federal E-rate program that has underwritten connecting U.S. libraries and public schools serving low-income students to the Internet since 1996. The plan, called ConnectED, has the goal of giving 99 percent of U.S. public school students Internet access through libraries and schools at a speed of at least 100 megabits per second. For schools, the plan seeks to provide adequate bandwidth so that whole classes will be able to use next-generation learning applications at the same time, which is a major problem in many schools currently.

Even so, available evidence suggests that schools are not yet positioned to close the digital opportunity gap and that provision of adequate bandwidth needs to be accompanied by changes in the incentive structure and programs of professional support for teachers and leaders in schools serving low-income students. Researchers have found that the schools attended by children from homes of greater affluence, with more educated parents, are more likely to have students using advanced technologies, such as simulations, and to be creating products with technology, while schools attended by children from less-privileged homes experience school technology use in the form of drill-and-practice and online benchmark assessments (Warschauer & Matuchniak, 2010; Wenglinsky, 1998, 2005). This difference can be attributed at least in part to the accountability pressures these schools face. Feeling under the gun to avoid being labeled as in need of improvement, schools tend to respond with a relentless focus on language arts and mathematics test preparation, to the neglect of more advanced skills and other subjects.

Our Conceptual Framework Points to the Need for Online Learning Research to Take a Systemic Approach, Considering Implementation and Context As Well As Design and Outcomes

Even when online learning is designed carefully by expert teams, its effectiveness varies depending on implementation practices and contexts. One of the main ideas we hope to leave with readers is the understanding that effectiveness is a product not of a particular online learning environment or piece of courseware but rather of a system of variables including the way in which that online product is used, the context of use, and the nature of the learner. We cannot justify statements like "DreamBox works" any more than we can stand behind a claim like "online learning works." We do know, however, that when DreamBox was used to add extra mathematics learning time for low-income primary school students in a Rocketship charter school, that school's mathematics achievement gains were better than those of similar students without the extra online math instruction (Wang & Woodworth, 2011a).

Using all four dimensions in our conceptual framework—context, design features, implementation features, and outcomes—to describe online learning interventions and their effects generates a picture that may be more complicated than decision makers would like. But it is the only way we know to stay true to the evidence and avoid over-generalizations that lead to bad decisions. Outcomes vary depending on factors such as whether the online components serve as the complete course or as a complement to classroom-based instruction, whether the learners are self-confident students or plagued by math anxiety, the nature of other learning activities going on in the same class, and course grading practices and policies.

We believe that this level of complexity is unavoidable, but luckily we have technologies and analytic approaches to help us deal with it. Online learning systems have the potential to capture very fine-grained information about the learning behavior of every user. Potentially, these data are a tremendous resource for analyzing individual students' learning and the kinds of future learning experiences they need, and for testing instructional design principles and aspects of learning theories (U.S. Department of Education, 2013). Until fairly recently, the sheer amount of data generated by learning interactions overwhelmed our data storage and analysis capabilities. But that is no longer the case, and the nascent fields of educational data mining and learning analytics have the potential to provide us with a strong empirical base for making decisions about the design of future online learning activities and environments for different purposes and types of learners. Most providers of online learning have yet to figure out how to structure the clickstream data their systems generate in a way that is useful for analysis (Bakia et al., 2013), but work in this area is ongoing, and we expect major strides in the next five years.

The Greatest Payoff for Education Systems May Well Be Research-based Models for Productive Pairings of Human and Machine Capabilities for Supporting Learning

There are important niches for fully online learning in serving those who cannot be in the same place with qualified teachers at the same time. But we predict that the greater impact of online learning will be as an adjunct to classroom-based instruction in various forms of blending within courses and across courses within a degree program. We find it heartening that online learning options are stimulating instructors and school leaders, responsible for education ranging from kindergarten to graduate studies, to rethink how they are using the face-to-face time they have with students. Fifty years ago, SRI's Doug Engelbart, the inventor of the computer mouse, wrote about the concept of augmented human intelligence and its power to increase our capacity. He asserted that an artful blend of the capabilities of networked computing systems and human actors could enable "more rapid comprehension, better comprehension, the possibility of gaining a useful degree of comprehension in a situation that previously was too complex, speedier solutions, better solutions, and the possibility of finding solutions to problems that before seemed insoluble" (Engelbart, 1962).

Engelbart illustrates his concept with the vignette of an architect augmented by computing tools. Today we see school leaders and teachers trying to re-imagine the role of the classroom instructor with the capability to use online learning systems and resources when appropriate, examine detailed data on individual students' efforts and progress with these systems, and redeploy classroom time for things that are more difficult for an online system to do well—for engaging students in interactive discussions around complex ideas, involving them in collaborating with each other to jointly construct a shared understanding or develop a solution to complex problem, to convey the excitement of their field and their faith in their students' abilities and prospects for success.

Research Agenda

We will close with a consideration of future directions for research, taking into account gaps in our current knowledge and trends in the way online learning and blended learning are being used. Below we discuss seven topics, each of which could be the centerpiece for a whole program of research.

Exemplary Open Courseware for Critical High-enrollment Courses

Neither college faculty nor high-school teachers can be expected to have the time and expertise to develop learning technologies that represent the best of the breed in applying learning science principles, instructional design, and technology advances. The OLI at CMU, with its teams of faculty subject matter experts, learning scientists, and software developers working on course development, implementation, and refinement, provides a sense of the kind of work that can be done, given a significant investment and an iterative approach of design, development, implementation, and evaluation followed by course refinement. The Hewlett Foundation's investment in OLI has not been repeated, however, and technology has continued to advance. In K-12 education, there has not been an equivalent government or philanthropic investment in combining the best expertise in learning science, instructional design, content knowledge, and technology to produce exemplary open educational materials. Such an investment was hard to justify in the past when every state had its own grade-level standards and accountability tests. As the Common Core State Standards in English language arts and mathematics and the Next Generation Science Standards are implemented in large numbers of states, this impediment will be removed. Any major investment in developing online courseware should include specifying and testing models for how the courseware can be used, whether as a standalone fully online course or in a blended learning model. Practitioners will be important partners in developing and testing these implementation models. The R&D program should be designed with incentives for school districts and college systems that commit to try out multiple versions of the courseware or different implementation models and to provide the student outcome data needed to evaluate their effectiveness.

Designs and Implementation Practices That Support Lower-Achieving Students in Fully Online Programs

As described in Chapter 7, alternative education and credit recovery programs at the secondary level have been accumulating insights into design features associated with positive outcomes for at-risk students. Blended learning has been central to their designs, which appear to be having success through a combination of mastery-based online assessment and practice and a "high touch" approach with lots of in-person contact with a facilitator or mentor. At the same time, fully online programs and courses are experiencing high dropout rates, particularly among lower-achieving students at secondary and tertiary education levels. A research agenda investigating learning system design features and online instructor practices that can enhance student engagement, productive mindsets, and perseverance could have large payoffs for the field and for expanding the portion of the world's population able to benefit from fully online learning.

Models for Combining Instructor and Learning System Capabilities in Supporting Different Kinds of Learning

Learning research has provided general insights into factors that enhance different kinds of learning. Learning factual knowledge, for example, can be enhanced through helping students relate the new knowledge to what they already know, presentation in a variety of media, opportunities to use the information in performing more complex tasks, and repetition. The acquisition of skills is enhanced by extended practice with immediate feedback, observing models of skilled performance, and opportunities to engage as a member of a community practicing the skill over extended time periods. Motivational engagement is enhanced by having explicit goals; activities and materials with elements of challenge, surprise, and playfulness; the opportunity to make choices about learning tasks and content; records of personal progress; and connections to long-term goals and potential professions. All of these types of learning are important in education, and technology and human instructors can play a role in putting the supporting conditions in place. The design of effective learning activities and programs would be enhanced by use of a conceptual framework to guide decisions around the online learning system and the teacher's role.

Effective Techniques for Supporting Online Learning and Assessment in the Humanities and Other Loosely Structured Content Areas

Many of the examples of effective online learning in this volume come from subjects, such as mathematics, computer programming, and statistics, that have a significant procedural component where competence can be assessed by administering problems or tasks on which performance is either right or wrong. These fields appear to lend themselves to task decomposition, practice, and feedback—three things we know how to provide in digital learning environments. Online facilitation of intellectual debate and classroom discussions that build knowledge has been a focus of research and development, especially in Canada, but we see relatively little of this kind of interaction being provided by online systems at scale. Those designing MOOCs, for example, have had a much harder time figuring out how to provide meaningful interaction in courses in the humanities and other less-structured fields. There has been peer assessment of students' work in humanities courses, but the results have not always been satisfactory. Students do not necessarily value the feedback of peers assessing their products, and indeed not every student is equipped to provide good feedback in a field in which he himself is a novice. This area is ripe for further investigation and innovative design. The design of highly effective blended learning models for these subject areas appears rather elusive as well. The integration of online learning into blended courses in the NGLC initiative, for example, produced positive impacts on average for mathematics, social science, and business courses, but negative impacts for English and humanities classes (Means, Shear et al., 2013). Defining and testing design principles for effective learning of the important ideas and forms of argumentation in these fields would be a productive challenge spurring innovation.

Learning Analytics Around Processes Related to Different Kinds of Learning

Online learning systems can collect detailed information about each learner, such as the exact step in a complex problem where the student goes wrong, and provide feedback specific to that step. Aggregating this kind of data across problems and learners can reveal relationships between options in the learning process and increases in learning outcomes. Adaptations can also be based on motivational or affective factors. The major challenge in using detailed learning data for these purposes has been the difficulty finding robust interactions between patterns of use and alternative ways that learning resources can be adapted to produce learning gains. Although the idea that learning experiences can be made adaptive for the individual learner has intuitive appeal, it actually takes a fair amount of work to pin down solid evidence of combinations of user characteristics and specific adaptations that improve outcomes. A number of research groups are working actively in this area, and a research agenda that spurs the sharing of data across organizations could not only speed progress in the field but also ensure that resulting insights are used widely rather than in individual proprietary products.

Requirements for Making Learning Systems' Formative Feedback Usable in Teachers' Day-to-day Instructional Decision Making

The fact that learning systems are capable of keeping detailed records of every learner action opens up all kinds of new opportunities for assessing more complex learner performances and for doing so in the context of learning rather than stopping for "exam time." Unfortunately, the data that learning systems record for individual learners are underutilized as resources for improving education practice. The ability of online learning systems to collect and display information about each student's online work and proficiencies has outstripped educators' capacity, or inclination, to use the available data. In our research on the implementation of blended learning in K-12 schools, we are finding that many teachers and administrators are not using data available on their online systems to understand what students know and can do and where they need help.

There are many reasons for this and the problem can be addressed from multiple angles. Some teachers question the meaningfulness of system-generated data on skill mastery; some teachers believe that their own observations of students' performance in in-class activities or in conversations provide a better window into student competencies. Other teachers cite the time required to wade through the large amounts of data in the way it is formatted by the learning system they use. This problem is exacerbated in classes where multiple learning systems are in use, each with a different set of data and data displays. Administrators and teachers want to go to one place for all their learning information for a particular student. Finally, some teachers lack clear ideas about the instructional decisions they could make on the basis of student data, suggesting the need for teacher professional development or coaching around different instructional strategies appropriate for students with different patterns of assessment data. Design studies examining the instructional decisions teachers make day to day and testing the usability and utility of different kinds of, and formats for, student online learning data could help bridge this gap between potential and reality.

Kinds of Feedback that Produce the Most Constructive Responses on the Part of Students

Another application of learning analytics is the development of algorithms predicting the likelihood that a student will complete a course successfully, based on performance in past courses and other data from student information systems as well as data gathered by the learning management system as a course is under way. A number of programs, such as *Signals* at Purdue University, *UPace* at the University of Wisconsin, Milwaukee, and *E²Coach* at the University of Michigan are using predictive analytics and sending messages to students designed to increase their understanding of the gap between their performance in the course thus far and where they need to be to complete the course successfully, while also offering encouragement and specific forms of assistance. These efforts appear promising thus far, but there is much more to be learned about how to optimize feedback to students learning online and, more generally, how to design learning experiences and feedback to avoid discouraging students and instead help them develop perseverance and "grit" (Shectman et al., 2013).

Cost Effectiveness of Widely Used Online and Blended Learning Interventions

In Chapter 8 we noted how rare it is to have an independent, rigorous analysis of costs and benefits associated with an online or blended learning intervention. Obtaining good cost data and obtaining good outcomes data are labor- and resource-intensive. For ongoing monitoring of individual course redesign efforts, the kind of framework used by NCAT (Twigg, 2004) is generally sufficient, and certainly would be a major advance from where most education institutions are today. However, for online and blended learning interventions that are being used for large numbers of students for a high-stakes portion of their education (learning to read, for example, or Algebra I), we need rigorous, objective research studies that combine careful analyses of costs with controlled studies of learning impacts. We should not rely on private companies to perform this kind of research; we encourage government research funders and private philanthropy to develop agendae around the cost effectiveness of promising online and blended learning interventions.

Final Words

Finally, we close with the advice that development, implementation, and research on new online teaching and learning innovations need to go hand in hand to a much greater extent than they have in the past. Online learning effectiveness studies too often fail to specify the key features of the learning experience design, and treat the online aspects of a course or other learning experience as if they were self-contained, ignoring the broader context in which learning takes place and the relationship between online and offline learning activities. Bringing all of these features into a systems framework can help guide the design of new learning interventions and research on key design features and implementation factors. Only by undertaking careful work at this level of detail can we build an evidence-based understanding of how to design and implement online and blended learning for different purposes, kinds of learners, and settings.

References

Adsit, J. (2003). *Funding online education: A report to the Colorado Online Education Programs Study Committee.* Retrieved from http://www.cde.state.co.us/edtech/download/osc-VW.pdf.

Aiello, N. C. & Wolfle, L. M. (1980). *A meta-analysis of individualized instruction in science.* Paper presented at the annual meeting of the American Educational Research Association, Boston, MA.

Akyol, Z., Arbaugh, B., Cleveland-Innes, M., Garrison, R., Ice, P., Richardson, J., & Swan, K. (2009). A response to the review of the Community of Inquiry Framework. *Journal of Distance Education, 23*(2): 123–136. Retrieved from http://www.jofde.ca/index.php/jde/article/view/630/885.

Allen, I. E. & Seaman, J. (2008). *Staying the course: Online education in the United States.* Needham, MA: Sloan Consortium.

Allen, I. E. & Seaman, J. (2013) *Changing course: Ten years of tracking online education in the United States.* Babson College, MA: The Sloan Consortium. Retrieved from http://sloanconsortium.org/publications/survey/pdf/learningondemand.pdf.

American Society of Training Development (ASTD) (2010). *2009 State of the Industry Report.* Alexandria, VA.

Anderson, A. J., Augenblick, D., DeCesare, D., & Conrad, J. (2006). *Costs and funding of virtual schools: An examination of the costs to start, operate, and grow virtual schools and a discussion of funding options for states interested in supporting virtual school programs.* Report prepared for BellSouth Foundation. Denver, CO: Augenblick, Palaich, and Associates. Retrieved from http://www.inacol.org/research/docs/CostsandFunding.pdf.

Anderson, R. & Ainley, J. (2010). Technology and learning: Access in schools around the world. In P. Peterson, E. Baker, & B. McGaw (Eds.), *International encyclopedia of education.* 3rd edition. Amsterdam: Elsevier.

Anderson, T. (2004). Toward a theory of online learning. In T. Anderson & F. Elloumi, *The theory and practice of online learning.* Athabasca, Alberta: Athabasca University.

Aragon, S. R. & Johnson, E. S. (2008). Factors influencing completion and noncompletion of community college courses. *American Journal of Distance Education, 22*, 146–158.

Archambault, L., Diamon, D., Brown, R., Cavanaugh, C., Coffey, M., Foures-Aalbu, D., Richardson, J., & Zygouris-Coe, V. (2010). *An exploration of at-risk learners and online education.* Retrieved from http://files.eric.ed.gov/fulltext/ED509620.pdf.

Arnold, K. E. (2010). Signals: Applying academic analytics. *EDUCAUSE Quarterly, 33*(1). Retrieved from http://www.educause.edu/EDUCAUSE+Quarterly/EDUCA USEQuarterlyMagazine Volum/SignalsApplyingAcademicAnalyti/199385.

Ash, K. (2012). Single district virtual education seen growing fastest. *Education Week.* March 12.

Athey, S. & Stern, S. (2002). The impact of information technology on emergency health care outcomes. *RAND Journal of Economics, 33*(3), 399–432.

Atkins, D. E., Brown, J. S., & Hammond, A. L. (2007). A review of the Open Educational Resources (OER) Movement: Achievements, challenges, and new opportunities, report to the William and Flora Hewlett Foundation.

Atkinson, R. D. & McKay, A. (2007). *Digital prosperity: Understanding the economic benefits of the information technology revolution.* Washington, D.C.: Information Technology and Innovation Foundation.

Attewell, P., Lavin, D., Domina, T., & Levey, T. (2006). New evidence on remediation. *Journal of Higher Education, 77*(5), 886–924.

Bacow, L. S., Bowen, W. G., Guthrie, K. M., Lack, K. A., & Long, M. P. (2012). *Barrier to adoption of online learning systems in U.S. higher education*, May 1. Retrieved from http://www.sr.ithaka.org.

Bailey, T. (2009). Challenge and opportunity: Rethinking the role and function of developmental education in community colleges. *New Directions for Community Colleges, 145*, 11–30.

Bakia, M., Caspary, K., Wang, H., & Dieterle, E. (2011). *Estimating the effects of online learning for secondary school students: State and district case studies.* Menlo Park, CA: SRI International.

Bakia, M., Shear, L., Toyama, Y., & Lasseter, A. (2012). *Understanding the implications of online learning for educational productivity.* Washington, D.C.: U.S. Department of Education, Office of Educational Technology.

Bakia, M., Mislevy, J., Heying, E., Patton, C., Singleton, C., & Krumm, A. E. (2013). *Supporting K-12 students in online learning: A review of online Algebra I courses.* Menlo Park, CA: SRI International.

Barab, S., Dodge, T., Tuzun, H., Job-Sluder, K., Gilbertson, J., et al. (2007). The Quest Atlantis Project: A socially-responsive play space for learning. In B. E. Shelton & D. Wiley (Eds.), *The design and use of simulation computer games in education* (159–186). Rotterdam: Sense Publishers.

Barber, M., Donnelly, K., & Rizvi, S. (2013). *An avalanche is coming: Higher education and the revolution ahead.* London: Institute for Public Policy Research.

Barbour, M. K. & Reeves, T. C. (2009). The reality of virtual schools: A review of the literature. *Computers & Education, 52*, 402–16. doi: 10.1016/j.compedu.2008.09.009.

Barron, B. (2006). Interest and self-sustained learning as catalysts of development: A learning ecology perspective. *Human Development, 49*, 193–224. doi: 10.1159/000094368.

Barron, B., Gomez, K., Pinkard, N., & Martin, C. K. (in press). *The Digital Youth Network: Cultivating new media citizenship in urban communities.* Cambridge, MA: MIT Press.

Battaligno, T. B., Haldeman, M., & Laurans, E. (2012). *The costs of online learning.* Washington, D.C.: Thomas B. Fordham Institute.

Bauman, M. (1997). *Online learning communities*. Paper presented at the Community Colleges Online Conference. Retrieved from http://www.thencat.org/Newsletters/Jul07.htm.

Belanger, Y. & Thornton, J. (2013). Bioelectricity: A Quantitative Approach, Duke University's first MOOC. http://hdl.handle.net/10161/6216.

Bernard, R. M., Abrami, P. C., Lou, Y., Borokhovski, E., Wade, A., Wozney, L., Wallet, P. A., Fiset, M., & Huang, B. (2004). How does distance education compare with classroom instruction? A meta-analysis of the empirical literature. *Review of Educational Research, 74*(3), 379–439.

Bernard, R. M., Abrami, P. C., Borokhovski, E., Wade, A., Tamim, R., Surkes, M., & Bethel, E. C. (2009). A meta-analysis of three interaction treatments in distance education. *Review of Educational Research, 79*(3), 1243–1289.

Bernatek, B., Cohen, J., Hanlon, J., & Wilka, M. (2012). Blended learning in practice: Case students from leading schools. Michael & Susan Dell Foundation. Retrieved from http://www.msdf.org/blog/2012/09/blended-learning-we-need-evidence/.

Bienkowski, M., Feng, M., & Means, B. (2012). *Enhancing teaching and learning through educational data mining and learning analytics: An issue brief.* Washington, D.C.: U.S. Department of Education, Office of Educational Technology.

Blackboard. (2009). *Credit recovery: Exploring answers to a national priority.* Washington, DC: Blackboard. Retrieved from http://www.blackboard.com/resources/k12/Bb_K12_WP_CreditRecovery.pdf.

Bloom, B. S. (Ed.). (1956). *Taxonomy of educational objectives. Handbook 1: Cognitive domain.* New York: McKay.

Bork, R. H. & Rucks-Ahidiana, Z. (2012). Virtual courses and tangible expectations: An analysis of student and instructor opinions of online courses. Paper presented at the annual meeting of the American Educational Research Association.

Boston, W., Diaz, S. R., Gibson, A. M., Ice, P., Richardson, J., & Swan, K. (2009). An exploration of the relationship between indicators of the community of inquiry framework and retention in online programs. *Journal of Asynchronous Learning Networks, 1*(3), 67–83.

Bowen, W. G. & Lack, K. A. (2012). *Current status of research on online learning in postsecondary education.* Retrieved from http://www.sr.ithaka.org.

Bowen, W. G., Chingos, M. M., Lack, K. A., & Nygren, T. I. (2012). *Interactive learning online at public universities: Evidence from randomized trials*, May 22. Retrieved from http://www://www.sr.ithaka.org.

Bransford, J., Barron, B., Pea, R., Meltzoff, A. N., Kuhl, P. K., Bell, P., Stevens, R., Schwartz, D., Vye, N., Reeves, B., Roschelle, J., & Sabelli, N. (2006). Foundations and opportunities for an interdisciplinary science of learning. In K. Sawyer (Ed.), *Cambridge handbook of the learning sciences* (19–34). New York: Cambridge University Press.

Bransford, J. D., Brown, A. L., & Cocking, R.R. (Eds.) (2000). How people learn: Brain, mind, experience, and school. Washington, D.C.: National Academies Press.

Brennan, K. (2012). Best of both worlds: Issues of structure and agency in computational creation, in and out of school, Ph.D. thesis. Cambridge, MA: Massachusetts Institute of Technology.

Brooks, D. (2012). The campus tsunami. *The New York Times*, May 3.

Brown, E. (2011). Questions about virtual schools' effectiveness. *Washington Post.* Retrieved from www.washingtonpost.com.

Brynjolfsson, E. & Hitt, L. (2000). Beyond computation: Information technology, organizational transformation and business performance. *Journal of Economic Perspectives, 14*(4), 23–48.

Campbell, J. P. & Arnold, K. (2011). *Course Signals: A student success system.* Paper presented at EDUCAUSE annual meeting, Philadelphia, PA.

Campbell, J. P., DeBlois, P. B., & Oblinger, D. G. (2007). Academic analytics: A new tool for a new era. *EDUCAUSE Review.*

Carpenter, T. G., Brown, W. L., & Hickman, R. C. (2004). Influences of online delivery on developmental writing outcomes. *Journal of Developmental Education, 28*(1), 14–18.

Caulfield, M. (2012). *Why we shouldn't talk MOOCs as meritocracies.* Blog at http://mikecaulfield.com/2012/09/01/why-we-shouldnt-talk-moocs-as-meritocracies/

Cavanaugh, C. (2009). *Online course funding: The influence of resources on practices.* In J. Watson & B. Gemin (Eds.), *Keeping pace with K-12 online learning: A review of state-level policy and practice* (39–40). Vienna, VA: iNACOL.

Cavanaugh, C., Gillan, K. J., Kromrey, J., Hess, M., & Blomeyer, R. (2004). *The effects of distance education on K-12 student outcomes: A meta-analysis.* Retrieved March 5, 2009, from http://www.ncrel.org/tech/distance/index.html.

Chafkin, M. (2013). Udacity's Sebastian Thrun, godfather of free online education, changes course. *Fast Company*, November 14.

Chapman, C., Laird, J., & Kewal Ramani, A. (2010). *Trends in high school dropout and completion rates in the United States 1972–2008: Compendium report.* Washington, DC: National Center for Educational Statistics.

Cheung, L. & Kan, A.(2002). Evaluation of factors related to student performance in a distance learning business communication course. *Journal of Education for Business, 77*(5), 257–263.

Chiu, J. L. & Linn, M. C. (2012). The role of self-monitoring in learning chemistry with dynamic visualizations. *Metacognition in Science Education*, 133–163.

Christensen, C. M. & Horn, M. B. (2013). Innovation imperative: Change everything. *New York Times*, November 1.

Christensen, C. M., Horn, M. B., & Johnson, C. W. (2008). *Disrupting class: How disruptive innovation will change the way the world learns.* New York: McGraw-Hill.

Christensen, C. M., Horn, M. B., Caldera, L., & Soares, L. (2011). *Disrupting college: How disruptive innovation can deliver quality and affordability to postsecondary education.* San Mateo, CA: Innosight Institute.

Christensen, C. M., Horn, M. B., & Staker, H. (2013). *Is K-12 blended learning disruptive?: An introduction to the theory of hybrids.* Retrieved from Clayton Christensen Institute for Disruptive Innovation website: http://www.christenseninstitute.org/wp-content/uploads/2013/05/Is-K-12-Blended-Learning-Disruptive.pdf.

Clark, D. (2012). Udacity builds bankroll for online learning. *Wall Street Journal*, October 25.

Clark, D., Tanner-Smith, E., Killingsworth, S., Bellamy, S. (2013). *Digital games for learning: A systematic review and meta-analysis (executive summary).* Menlo Park, CA: SRI International.

Clark, R. E. (1994). Media will never influence learning, *Educational Technology Research and Development, 42*(2), 21–29.

Cohen, J. (1988). *Statistical power analysis for the behavioral sciences.* New York: Routledge.

Cole, R., Kemple, J., & Segeritz, M.(2012). *Assessing the early impact of School of One: Evidence from three school-wide pilots.* New York: Research Alliance for New York City Schools.

Collins, A. & Halverson, R. (2009). Rethinking education in the age of technology: The digital revolution and schooling in America. New York: Teachers College Press.

Columbaro, N. L. & Monaghan, C. H. (2009). *Employer perceptions of online degrees: A literature review.* Retrieved from http://www.westga.edu/~distance/ojdla/spring121/columbaro121.html.

Conklin, K. A. (1997). Course attrition: A 5-year perspective on why students drop classes. *Community College Journal of Research and Practice, 21*(8), 753–759.

Conner, M. (1997–2013). Introduction to informal learning. Retrieved from http://marciaconner.com/resources/informal-learning/.

Crowley, K. & Jacobs, M. (2002). Islands of expertise and the development of family scientific literacy. In G. Leinhardt, K. Crowley, & K. Knutson (Eds.), *Learning conversations in museums* (333–356). Mahwah, NJ: Erlbaum.

Cummings, J. (2011). Online learning challenges: State authorization, federal regulation. *EDUCAUSE Review*, November/December, 110–111.

D'Angelo, C., Rutstein, D., Harris, C., Bernard, R., Borokhovski, E., & Haertel, G. (2013). *Simulations for STEM learning: Systematic review and meta-analysis (executive summary).* Menlo Park, CA: SRI International.

Dawley, L. (2009). Social network knowledge construction: Emerging virtual world pedagogy. *On the Horizon, 17*(2), 109–121. doi: 10.1108/10748120910965494.

Dede, C. (2009). Immersive interfaces for engagement and learning. *Science, 323*, 66–69.

Dessoff, A. (2009). Reaching graduation with credit recovery. *District Administration.* Retrieved from http://www.districtadministration.com/article/reaching-graduation-credit-recovery.

DeVane, B., Durga, S., & Squire, K. (2009). Competition as a driver for learning. *International Journal of Learning and Media, 1*(2). doi: 10.1162/ijlm.2009.0018.

Duncan, A. (2010). *The new normal: Doing more with less.* Remarks of Secretary Arne Duncan at the American Enterprise Institute. November 17.

Dupin-Bryant, P. (2004). Pre-entry variables related to retention in online distance courses. *American Journal of Distance Education, 18*(4), 199–206.

EdSurge. (2013). *Core skills mastery.* Retrieved from https://www.edsurge.com/core-skills-mastery.

EDUCAUSE. (2010). *7 things you should know about analytics.* Retrieved from educause.edu/ir/library/pdf/ELI7059.pdf.

Engelbart, D. C. (1962). *Augmenting human intellect: A conceptual framework.* AFOSR Summary Report. Menlo Park, CA: Stanford Research Institute.

Evergreen Education Group. (2012). *Keeping pace with K-12 online and blended learning: An annual review of policy and practice.* Durango, CO: Evergreen Education Group. Retrieved from http://kpk12.com/reports/.

Evergreen Education Group. (2013). *10-year anniversary issue: Keeping pace with K-12 online and blended learning: An annual review of policy and practice.* Durango, CO: Evergreen Education Group. Retrieved from http://kpk12.com/reports/.

Fain, P. (2013a). Kaplan 2.0. *Inside Higher Ed.* August 15. Retrieved from wwhttp://www.insidehighered.com.

Fain, P. (2013b). Possible probation for Phoenix. *Inside Higher Ed.* February 26. Retrieved from http://www.insidehighered.com.

Fast Company. (2012). *Can Google's Thrun create the first real online college degree?* Retrieved from fastcoexist.com/1679192/can-googles-thrun-create-the-first-real-online-college-degree.

Figlio, D. N., Rush, M., & Yin, L. (2010). *Is it live or is it Internet? Experimental estimates of the effects of online instruction on student learning.* NBER working paper 16089. Cambridge, MA: National Bureau of Economic Research.

Fishman, B. & Dede, C. (in preparation). Teaching and technology: New tools for new times. To appear in D. Gitomer & C. Bell (Eds.), *Handbook of research on teaching*, 5th edition. Washington, DC: American Educational Research Association.

Florida Tax Watch. (2007). *Final report: A comprehensive assessment of Florida Virtual School.* Tallahassee, FL: Florida Tax Watch. Retrieved from http://www.inacol.org/docs/FLVS_Final_Final_Report(10-15-07).pdf.

Florida Virtual School. (n.d.). Florida Virtual School district enrollment summary: 2011–2012.

Fujimoto, K. & Cara, E. (2013). Massive open online courses (MOOC) mashup: San Jose State University: Udacity experiment with online courses fizzles. *San Jose Mercury News*, July 25.

Gallagher, L., Michalchik, V., & Emery, D. (2006). Assessing youth impact of the Computer Clubhouse Network. Menlo Park, CA: SRI International.

Gee, J. P. (2009). Deep learning properties of deep digital games: How far can they go? In U. Ritterfield, M. J. Cody, & P. Vorderer (Eds.), *Serious games: Mechanisms and effects* (67–82). New York and London: Taylor & Francis.

Gee, J. P. (2013). Digital media and learning: A prospective retrospective, unpublished paper. Tempe, AZ: Arizona State University.

Gibbons, J., Pannoni, R., & Orlin, J. (1996). Tutored video instruction: A distance education methodology that improves training results. Paper presented at the international conference of the American Society for Training and Development, Orlando, FL.

Glass, G. & Welner, K. (2011). *Online K-12 schooling in the U.S.: Uncertain private ventures in need of public regulation.* Boulder, CO: National Education Policy Center.

Glass, G. V. (2009). *The realities of K-12 virtual education.* Retrieved from http://nepc.colorado.edu/publication/realities-K-12-virtual-education.

Graesser, A. (2009). Inaugural editorial for Journal of Educational Psychology. *Journal of Educational Psychology, 101*(2), 259–261.

Graf, S. & Kinshuk. (2013.) Dynamic student modeling of learning styles for advanced adaptivity in learning management systems. *International Journal of Information Systems and Social Change, 4*(1), 85–100.

Graham, C. R., Allen, S., & Ure, D. (2005). Benefits and challenges of blended learning environments. In M. Khosrow-Pour (Ed.), *Encyclopedia of information science and technology* (253–259). Hershey, PA: Idea Group.

Grimes, S. K. & Antworth, T. (1996). Community college withdrawal decisions: Student characteristics and subsequent reenrollment patterns. *Community College Journal of Research and Practice, 20*(4), 345–361.

Grubb, W. N., Boner, E., Frankel, K., Parker, L., Patterson, D., Gabriner, R., Hope, L., Schiorring, E., Smith, B., Taylor, R., Walton, I., & Wilson, S. (2011a). *Understanding the "crisis" in basic skills: Framing the issues in community colleges.* Basic Skills Instruction in California Community Colleges Report No. 1. Sacramento, CA: Policy Analysis for California Education.

Grubb, W. N., Boner, E., Frankel, K., Parker, L., Patterson, D., Gabriner, R., Hope, L., Schiorring, E., Smith, B., Taylor, R., Walton, I., & Wilson, S. (2011b). *Basic skills instruction in community colleges: The dominance of remedial pedagogy.* Basic Skills Instruction in California Community Colleges Report No. 2. Sacramento, CA: Policy Analysis for California Education.

Hachey, A. C., Conway, K. M., & Wladis, C. W. (2013). Community colleges and underappreciated assets: Using institutional data to promote success in online learning. *Online Journal of Distance Learning Administration, 16*(1).

Hagedorn, L. S. (2010). Introduction to the issue: Community college retention— an old problem exacerbated in a new economy. *Journal of College Student Retention, 12*(1), 1–5.

Hanford, E. (2013). *The story of the University of Phoenix.* Retrieved from http://americanradioworks.publicradio.org/features/tomorrows-college/phoenix/story-of-university-of-phoenix.html.

Harasim, L. (2001). Shift happens: Online education as a new paradigm in learning. *Internet and Higher Education, 3*, 41–61.

Hattie, J. (2009). *Visible learning: A synthesis of over 800 meta-analyses relating to achievement.* London and New York: Routledge.

Haynie, D. (2013). What employers really think about your online bachelor's degree. *U.S. News and World Report*, July 1.

Heller, N. (2013). Laptop U. *New Yorker*, May 20, 80–91.

Heppen, J. B., Walters, K., Clements, M., Faria, A., Tobey, C., Sorensen, N., & Culp, K. (2012). *Access to Algebra I: The effects of online mathematics for grade 8 students.* NCEE 2012–4021. Washington, D.C.: National Center for Education Evaluation and Regional Assistance, Institute of Education Sciences, U.S. Department of Education.

Herald, B. (2013). Florida Virtual School, other e-schools face difficult times EdWeek, blog, Digital Education: Vienna, VA. Retrieved from http://www://blogs.edweek.org/edweek/DigitalEducation/2013/08/Florida_Virtual_School_Other_E-Schools_Face_Difficult_Times.html.

Herrera, L. (2011). In Florida, virtual classrooms with no teachers, *New York Times*, January 17.

Hidi, S. & Renninger, K. A. (2006). The four-phase model of interest development. *Educational Psychologist, 41*(2), 111–127.

Hill, P. (2012). Online educational delivery models: A descriptive view. *EDUCAUSE Review*, November/December, 85–97.

Hill, P. & Roza, M. (2010). Curing Baumol's disease: In search of productivity gains in K-12 schooling. CPRE White Paper 2010_1. Center for Reinventing Public Education. Seattle, WA: University of Washington. Retrieved from http://www.crpe.org/cs/crpe/download/csr_files/whp_crpe1_baumols_jul10.pdf.

Hollands, F. (2012). *Using cost-effectiveness analysis to evaluate School of One (So1).* New York: Center for Benefit-Cost Studies of Education, Teachers College, Columbia University.

Horn, M. B. & Staker, H. (2011). *The rise of K-12 blended learning.* Innosight Institute. Retrieved from http://www.innosightinstitute.org/innosight/wp-content/uploads/2011/01/The-Rise-of-K-12-Blended-Learning.pdf.

Hubbard, B. & Mitchell, N. (2011). Achievement of online students drops over time, lags state averages on every indicator. *Education News Colorado.* Retrieved from www.ednewscolorado.org.

Ingersoll, R. M. (2003). *Is there really a teacher shortage?* Philadelphia and Seattle: Consortium for Policy Research in Education and Center for the Study of Teaching and Policy.

International Telecommunications Union. (2013). ICT Facts and Figures. Geneva: Telecommunication Development Bureau, ICT Data and Statistics Division.

Ito, M., Horst, H., Bittanti, M., Boyd, D., Herr-Stephenson, B., Lange, P. G., Pascoe, C. J., & Robinson, L. (2009). Living and learning with new media: Summary of findings from the Digital Youth Project. Chicago: MacArthur Foundation.

Ito, M., Baumer, S., Bittanti, M., Boyd, D., Cody, R., Herr-Stephenson, B., & Tripp, L. (2010). *Hanging out, messing around, and geeking out: Living and learning with new media.* Cambridge, MA: MIT Press.

Ito, M., Gutiérrez, K., Livingstone, S., Penuel, B., Rhodes, J., Salen, K., Schor, J., Sefton-Green, J., & Watkins, C. (2013). *Connected learning: An agenda for research and design.* Irvine, CA: Digital Media and Learning Research Hub.

Jaggers, S. S. (2011). Online learning: Does it help low-income and underprepared students? CCRC Brief 52. New York: Columbia Teachers College, Community College Research Center.

Jaggers, S. S. & Bailey, T. (2010). Effectiveness of fully online learning courses for college students: Response to a Department of Education meta-analysis. New York: Columbia Teachers College, Community College Research Center.

Jaggers, S. S. & Xu, D. (2012). Predicting student outcomes from a measure of course quality. Paper presented at the annual meeting of the American Educational Research Association.

Jenkins, H. (2006). *Confronting the challenges of participatory culture: Media education for the 21st century.* Chicago, IL: John D. & Catherine T. MacArthur Foundation.

Johnson, L., Adams Becker, S., Cummins, M., Estrada, V., Freeman, A., & Ludgate, H. (2013). *NMC Horizon report: 2013 Higher education edition.* Austin, TX: New Media Consortium.

Johnson, L., Smith, R., Willis, H., Levine, A., & Haywood, K. (2011). *The 2011 Horizon report.* Austin, TX: New Media Consortium.

Jones, D. (2001). *Technology costing methodology handbook.* Boulder, CO: Western Cooperative for Educational Telecommunications.

Kafai, Y. B. (2010). The world of Whyville: Living, playing, and learning in a tween virtual world. *Games and Culture, 5*(1).

Kali, Y. & Linn, M. (2010). Curriculum design as subject matter: Science. In B. McGraw, E. Baker, & P. Peterson (Eds.), *International encyclopedia of education* (3rd edition) (468–474). Oxford: Elsevier.

Kalyuga, S., Chandler, P., Tuovinen, J., & Sweller, J. (2001). When problem solving is superior to studying worked examples. *Journal of Educational Psychology, 93*, 579–588.

Kamenetz, A. (2013). San Jose State MOOC missteps easy to see. Retrieved from http://diverseeducation.com/article/54903/#.

Kelderman, E. (2011). Online programs face new demands from accreditors. *Chronicle of Higher Education*. Retrieved from http://chronicle.com/article/Online-Programs-Face-New/129608/

Kennedy Martin, C., Barron, B., Austin, K., & Pinkard, N. (2009). A culture of sharing: A look at identity development through the creation and presentation of digital media projects. International Conference on Computer-Supported Education (Lisbon).

Kim, P., Kim, F. H., & Karimi, A. (2012). Public online charter school students: Choices, perceptions, and traits. *American Educational Research Journal, 49*(3), 521–545. doi: 10.3102/0002831212443078.

Kluger, A. N. & DeNisi, A. (1996). The effects of feedback interventions on performance: A historical review, a meta-analysis, and a preliminary feedback intervention theory. *Psychological Bulletin, 119*(2), 254.

Koedinger, K. R. & Corbett, A. (2006). Cognitive tutors: Technology bringing learning sciences to the classroom. In R. K. Sawyer (Ed.), *The Cambridge handbook of the learning sciences* (61–77). New York: Cambridge University Press.

Koedinger, K. R., Corbett, A. T., & Perfetti, C. (2012). The Knowledge-Learning Instruction (KLI) framework: Bridging the science-practice chasm to enhance robust student learning. *Cognitive Science, 36*(5).

Koller, D. & Ng, A. (2012). Log on and learn: The promise of access in online education. *Forbes*, September 19.

Koller, D., Ng, A., Do, C., & Chen, Z. (2013). Retention and intention in massive open online courses: In depth. *EDUCAUSE Review Online*.

Kolowich, S. (2013a). The professors who make the MOOCs. *Chronicle of Higher Education*, March 18.

Kolowich, S. (2013b). San Jose State U. puts MOOC Project with Udacity on hold. *Chronicle of Higher Education*, July 19.

Kozma, R. B. (1994). Will media influence learning? Reframing the debate, *Educational Technology Research and Development, 42*(2), 7–19.

Kronholz, J. (2011). Getting at-risk teens to graduation. *Education Next, 11*(4), 24–31. Retrieved from http://educationnext.org/files/ednext_20114_feature_kronholz.pdf.

Kulik, C. L. C., Kulik, J. A., & Bangert-Drowns, R. L. (1990). Effectiveness of mastery learning programs: A meta-analysis. *Review of Educational Research*, 60(2), 265–299.

Lack, K. A. (2013). *Current status of research on online learning in postsecondary education*. ITHAKA. Retrieved from http://www.sr.ithaka.org/research-publications/current-status-research-online-learning-postsecondary-education.

Lacy, S. (2013). Udacity's answer to Silicon Valley's computer science problem. Video interview with Sebastien Thrun. *Pandodaily.com*, April 29.

LeBlanc, P. (2013). Accreditation in a rapidly changing world. *Inside Higher Ed.* Retrieved May 26, 2013, from insidehighered.com/views/2013/01/31/competency-based-education-and-regional-accreditation.

Leckhart, S. & Cheshire, T. (2012). University just got flipped: How online video is opening up knowledge to the world. *Wired Magazine*, May.

Leddy, T. (2013). Are MOOCs good for students? *Boston Review*, June 14.

Lederman, D. (2006). In search of "big ideas." *Inside Higher Ed.* Retrieved from http://www.insidehighered.com.

Levin, H. & McEwan, P. (2001). *Cost-effectiveness analysis: Methods and applications.* 2nd edition. Thousand Oaks, CA: Sage.

Lewin, T. (2011). Official calls for urgency on college costs. *New York Times.* November 29.

Linn, M. C., Lee, H. S., Tinker, R., Husic, F., & Chiu, J. L. (2006). Teaching and assessing knowledge integration in science. *Science, 313*(5790), 1049–1050.

Lipsey, M. W. & Wilson, D. B. (2001). *Practical meta-analysis* (Vol. 49). Thousand Oaks, CA: Sage.

Littlefield, J. (n.d.). Cisco Networking Academy: A model for blended, interactive learning. About.com Distance Learning. Retrieved from http://distancelearn.about.com/od/onlinecourses/a/Cisco-Networking-Academy.htm.

Liu, S., Gomez, J., & Yen, C. (2009). Community college online course retention and final grade: Predictability of social presence. *Journal of Interactive Online Learning, 8*(2), 165–182.

Liyanagunawardena, T., Williams, S., & Adams, A. (2013). The impact and reach of MOOCs: A developing countries' perspective. *eLearning Papers, 33*, 1–8.

Lovett, M., Meyer, O., & Thille, C. (2008). The Open Learning Initiative: Measuring the effectiveness of the OLI statistics course in accelerating student learning. *Journal of Interactive Media in Education*, May.

Lundh, P., House, A., Means, B., & Harris, C. J. (2013). Learning from science: Case studies of science offerings in afterschool programs. *Afterschool Matters, 18*, 33–41.

Macfadyen, L. & Dawson, S. (2010). Mining LMS data to develop an "early warning system" for educators: A proof of concept. *Computers & Education, 54*(2), 588–599.

Mandernach, B. J., Donnelli, E., & Dailey-Hebert, A. (2005). Learner attribute research juxtaposed with online instructor experience: Predictors of success in the accelerated, online classroom. *Journal of Educators Online, 3*(2).

Marshall, J. (2012). Victory for crowdsourced biomolecule design. *Nature*, January 22. doi:10.1038/nature.2012.9872.

Maxwell, W., Hagedorn, L. S., Cypers, S., Moon, H. S., Brocato, P., Wahl, K., & Prather, G. (2003). Community and diversity in urban community colleges: Course taking among entering students. *Community College Review, 30*(4), 1–21.

Mayer, R. E. (2008). Applying the science of learning: evidence-based principles for the design of multimedia instruction. *American Psychologist, 63*(8), 760–769.

McKinsey Global Institute. (2000). *US productivity growth 1995–2000: Understanding the contribution of information technology relative to other factors.* San Francisco: McKinsey Global Institute.

McKinsey Global Institute. (2002). How IT enables productivity growth: The US experience across three sectors. San Francisco: McKinsey Global Institute.

Means, B. & Harris, C. J. (2013). Standards of evidence for design-based implementation research. In B. Fishman, W. R. Penuel, A. Allen, & B. H. Cheng (Eds.), *Design-based implementation research: Theories, methods, and exemplars* (350–371). National Society for the Study of Education Yearbook, 112th Yearbook, Issue 2. New York: Teachers College Press.

Means, B., Shear, L., & Roschelle, J. (in press). *Using technology and evidence to promote cultures of educational innovation: The example of science and mathematics education.* Paper commissioned by the Organisation for Economic Co-operation and Development.

Means, B., Shear, L., Zheng, Y., & Deutscher, R. (2013). *Next generation learning challenges: Evaluation of Wave I.* Menlo Park, CA: SRI International.

Means, B., Toyama, Y., Murphy, R., & Bakia, M. (2013). The effectiveness of online and blended learning: A meta-analysis of the empirical literature. *Teachers College Record, 115*(3).

Melendez, L. (2013). Governor Brown pushes for more online courses in CA. KGO TV-San Francisco, January 16. Retrieved from abclocal.go.com/kgo/story?section=news/education&id=8957088.

Miron, G. & J. L. Urschel (2012). *A study of the student characteristics, school finance, and school performance in schools operated by K12 Inc.* Boulder, CO: National Education Policy Center.

Miron, G., Horvitz, B., & Gulosino, C. (2013). Full-time virtual schools: Enrollment, student characteristics, and performance. In A. Molnar (Ed.), *Virtual schools in the U.S. 2013: Politics, performance, policy, and research evidence* (22–36). Retrieved from http://nepc.colorado.edu/files/nepc-virtual-2013.pdf.

Molnar, A. (2013) *Virtual schools in the U.S. 2013: Politics, performance, policy, and research evidence.* Retrieved from University of Colorado, Boulder, National Education Policy Center website: http://nepc.colorado.edu/publication/virtual-schools-annual-2013.

Mullins, C. (2013). 2012 distance education survey: Trends in elearning: Tracking the impact of elearning at community colleges. Reno, NV: Instructional Technology Council.

Murphy, E. & Coffin. G. (2003). Synchronous communication in a web-based senior high school course: Maximizing affordances and minimizing constraints of the tool. *American Journal of Distance Education, 17*(4), 235–246.

National Academy of Engineering. (2004). *The engineer of 2020: Visions of engineering in the new century.* Washington, D.C.: National Academies Press.

National Center for Public Policy in Higher Education and Southern Regional Education Board. (2010). *Beyond the rhetoric: Improving college readiness through coherent state policy.* Washington, D.C.: National Center for Public Policy in Higher Education.

National Research Council. (2009*). Learning science in informal environments.* Washington, D.C.: National Academies Press.

National Research Council. (2011). *Learning science: Computer games, simulations, and education.* Washington, DC: Board on Science Education, Division of Behavioral and Social Sciences and Education.

Neulight, N., Kafai, Y. B., Kao, L., Foley, B., & Galas, C. (2007). Children's participation in a virtual epidemic in the science classroom: Making connections to natural infectious diseases. *Journal of Science Education and Technology, 16*(1), 47–58.

Noer, M. (2012). One man, one computer, 10 million students: How Khan Academy is reinventing education. *Forbes*, November 2.

Norvig, P. (2012a). Panelist remarks for the Evidence Framework for Innovation and Excellence in *Education Technical Working Group.* Menlo Park, CA: SRI International, January 24.

Norvig, P. (2012b). Personal communication. March 14.

Oliver, K., Brady, K., Patel, R., & Townsend, T. (2009). *Formative evaluation report: North Carolina Virtual Public School.* Retrieved from http://www.ncvps.org/docs/results/09_report_final.pdf.

Papert, S. (1993). *The children's machine.* New York: Basic Books.

Pappano, L. (2012). The year of the MOOC. *The New York Times*, November 2.

Paradise, A. (2008). *2007 State of the industry report.* Alexandria, VA: American Society of Training and Development.

Parker, A. (2003). Identifying predictors of academic persistence in distance education. *USDLA Journal, 17*(1). Retrieved from http://www.usdla.org/html/journal/JAN03_Issue/index.html.

Parry, M. (2010). Online, bigger classes may be better classes. *Chronicle of Higher Education*, August 29. Retrieved from http://chronicle.com.

Parsad, B. & Lewis, L. (2008). *Distance education at degree-granting postsecondary institutions: 2006–07.* Washington, DC: National Center for Education Statistics, U.S. Department of Education.

Pearson Foundation. (2011). Community college student survey: Summary of results. Retrieved from http://www/pearsonfoundation.org/downloads/Community_College_Survey_Summary_201102.pdf.

Pellegrino, J. W., Chudowsky, N., & Glaser, R., eds. (2001). Knowing what students know: The science and design of educational assessment. Washington, D.C.: National Academies Press.

Picciano, A. G. & Seaman, J. (2007). *K-12 online learning: A survey of U.S. school district administrators.* Retrieved March 5, 2009, from http://www.sloan-c.org/publications/survey/K-12_06.asp.

Picciano, A. G. & Seaman, J. (2008). *Staying the course: Online education in the United States.* Retrieved March 5, 2009, from http://www.sloanc.org/publications/survey/pdf/staying_the_course.pdf.

Plass, J. L., Goldman, R., Flanagan, M., & Perlin, K. (2009*). RAPUNSEL: Improving self-efficacy and self-esteem with an educational computer game.* In S. C. Kong, H. Ogata, H. C. Amseth, C. K. K. Chan, T. Hirashama, F. Klett, J. H. M. Lee, C. C. Liu, C. K. Looi, M. Milrad, A. Mitrovic, K. Nakabayashi, S. L. Wong, & S. J. H. Yang (Eds.), Proceedings of the 17th International Conference on Computers in Education (CDROM). Hong Kong: Asia-Pacific Society for Computers in Education.

Project Tomorrow. (2011). *The new 3 E's of education: Enabled, engaged and empowered: how today's students are leveraging emerging technologies for learning.* Congressional Briefing—Release of Speak Up 2010 National Data for Students and Parents. Retrieved from http://www.tomorrow.org/speakup/speakup_reports. html.

Queen, B. & Lewis, L. (2011). *Distance education courses for public elementary and secondary school students: 2009-10, First Look.* U.S. Department of Education, National Center for Education Statistics. Washington, D.C.: U.S. Government Printing Office.

Rainie, L. (2010). Internet, broadband, and cell phone statistics. Washington, DC: Pew Internet. Retrieved from http://pewinternet.org/Reports/2010/Internet-broadband-and-cell-phonestatistics.aspx.

Rainie, L. (2012). *Changes to the way we identify Internet users.* Pew Research Center. Retrieved July 12, 2013, from http://www.pewinternet.org/Reports/2012/Counting-internet-users.aspx.

Ramage, T. (2005). A system-level comparison of cost-efficiency and return on investment related to online course delivery. *E-Journal of Instructional Science and Technology, 8*(1). Retrieved from http://spark.parkland.edu/ramage_pubs/2.

Renninger, A. (2000). Individual interest and development: Implications for theory and practice. In C. Sansone and J. M. Harackiewicz (Eds.), *Intrinsic and extrinsic motivation: The search for optimal motivation and performance* (375–404). New York: Academic Press.

Resnick, M., Maloney, J., Monroy-Hernández, A., Rusk, N., Eastmond, E., Brennan, K., & Kafai, Y., (2009). Scratch: Programming for all. *Communications of the ACM, 52*(11), 60–67.

Richards, J., Stebbins, L., & Moellering, K. (2013). *Games for a digital age: K-12 market map and investment analysis.* New York: The Joan Ganz Cooney Center.

Robinson, B. L. & Moore, A. H. (2006). Chapter 42. The Math Emporium. In D. G. Oblinger (Ed.), *Learning spaces.* EDUCAUSE.

Roblyer, M. D. & Davis, L. (2008). Predicting success for virtual school students: Putting research-based models into practice. *Online Journal of Distance Learning Administration, 11*(4).

Rusk, N., Resnick, M., & Cooke, S. (2009). Origins and guiding principles of the Computer Clubhouse. In Y. Kafai, K. A. Peppler, & R. N. Chapman (Eds.), *The Computer Clubhouse: Constructionism and creativity in youth communities.* New York: Teachers College Press, 17–25.

Russell, A. (2008). *Enhancing college education success through developmental education.* A Higher Education Policy Brief. Washington, D.C.: American Association of State Colleges and Universities.

Salmon, F. (2012). *Udacity and the future of online universities,* Web log post. January 23. Retrieved from http://blogs.reuters.com/felix-salmon/2012/01/23/udacity-and-the-future-of-online-universities/

Sefton-Green, J. (2004). *Literature review in informal learning with technology outside school.* FutureLab Series Report 7. Bristol: FutureLab.

Sefton-Green, J. (2010). *Learning at not-school: A review of study, theory, and advocacy for education in non-formal settings.* Cambridge, MA, and London: MIT Press.

Shectman, N., DeBarger, A., Dornsife, C., Rosier, S., & Yarnall, L. (2013). *Grit, tenacity, and perseverance in 21st-century education: State of the art and future directions.* Menlo Park, CA: SRI International.

Sheehy, K. (2013). Online course enrollment climbs for 10th straight year. *U.S. News & World Report.* January 28. Retrieved from http://www.usnews.com.

Shullenberger, G. (2013). The MOOC revolution: A sketchy deal for higher education. *Dissent Magazine*, February 12.

Siemens, G. (2012). *MOOCs are really a platform.* Elearnspace. Retrieved from http://www.elearnspace.org/blog/2012/07/25/moocs-are-really-a-platform/

Silva, E. & White, T. (2013). *Pathways to improvement: Using psychological studies to help college students master developmental math.* Stanford, CA: Carnegie Foundation for the Advancement of Teaching.

Sitzmann, T., Kraiger, K., Stewart, D., & Wisher, R. (2006). The comparative effectiveness of Web-based and classroom instruction: A meta-analysis. *Personnel Psychology, 59*, 623–664.

Slemmer, D. L. (2002). The effect of learning styles on student achievement in various hypertext, hypermedia, and technology-enhanced learning environments: A meta-analysis. Unpublished doctoral dissertation, Boise State University, ID.

Sloan, J. & Mackey, K. (2009). VOISE Academy: Pioneering a blended-learning model in a Chicago public high school. Innosight Institute. Retrieved from http://www.innosightinstitute.org.

Smerdon, E. T. (1996). Lifelong learning for engineers: Riding the whirlwind. *The Bridge, 26*(1/2).

Smith, D. & Mitry, D. (2008). Investigation of higher education: The real costs and quality of online programs. *Journal of Education for Business, 83*(3), 147–152.

Smith, M. L. & Glass, G. V. (1977). Meta-analysis of psychotherapy outcome studies. *American Psychologist, 32*, 752–760.

Smith, M. S. (2009). Opening education, *Science, 323*(89).

Smith, R., Clark, T., Blomeyer, R. (2005). *A synthesis of new research on K-12 online learning.* Learning Point Associates.

Spielhagen, F. R. (2006). Closing the achievement gap in math: The long-term effects of eighth-grade algebra. *Journal of Advanced Academics, 18*, 34–59.

Squire, K. & Durga, S. (2013). Productive gaming: The case for historiographic game play. In R. E. Ferdig (Ed.), *Design, utilization, and analysis of simulations and game-based educational worlds.* Hershey, PA: Information Science Reference.

Staker, H. & Horn, M. (2012). *Classifying K-12 blended learning.* San Mateo, CA: Clayton Christensen Institute for Disruptive Innovation.

State Higher Education Executive Officers. (2013). *State higher education finance: FY 2012.* Boulder, CO: State Higher Education Executive Officers.

Steinkuehler, C. & Duncan, S. (2008). Scientific habits of mind in virtual worlds. *Journal of Science Education and Technology, 17*(6), 530–543. doi:10.1007/s10956-008-9120-8.

Strother, S., Van Campen, J., & Grunow, A. (2013). *Community College Pathways: 2011–2012 descriptive report.* Stanford, CA: Carnegie Foundation for the Advancement of Teaching.

Stuiber, P. K., Hiorns, K., Kleidon, K., La Tarte, A., & Martin, J. (2010). *An evaluation of virtual charter schools.* Wisconsin Department of Public Instruction. Retrieved from http://www.legis.wisconsin.gov/lab.

Summerlin, J. A. (2003). *A comparison of the effectiveness of off-line Internet and traditional classroom remediation of mathematical skills.* Unpublished doctoral dissertation. Baylor University, Waco, TX.

Suppes, P. (1965). Computer-based mathematics instruction: The first year of the project. *Bulletin of the International Study Group for Mathematics Learning, 3,* 7–22.

Swan, K. (2003). Learning effectiveness: What the research tells us. In J. Bourne & J. C. Moore (Eds.), *Elements of quality online education, practice and direction* (13–45). Needham, MA: Sloan Center for Online Education.

Swan, K. & Shih, L. F. (2005). On the nature and development of social presence in online course discussions. *Journal of Asynchronous Learning Networks, 9*(3), 115–136.

Sweller, J. & Cooper, G. A. (1985) The use of worked examples as a substitute for problem solving in learning algebra, *Cognition and Instruction, 2,* 59–89.

Thomas, D. & Seely Brown, J. (2011). *A new culture of learning: Cultivating the imagination for a world of constant change.* Create Space Independent Publishing Platform.

Thrun, S. (2012). *University 2.0.* Presentation at the Digital Life, Design 2012 conference. Munich.

Trautman, T. & Lawrence, J. (n.d.). *Credit recovery: A technology-based intervention for dropout prevention at Wichita Falls High School.* Retrieved from http://www10. ade.az.gov/AIMSDPToolkit/TrautmanAndLawrenceFormatted.aspx.

Twigg, C. A. (1999). *Improving learning and reducing costs: Redesigning large-enrollment courses.* Troy, NY: National Center for Academic Transformation, Rensselaer Polytechnic Institute. Retrieved from http://www.thencat.org/Monographs/ImpLearn.html.

Twigg, C. A. (2003). Improving learning and reducing costs: New models for online learning. *EDUCAUSE Review, 38*(5), 28–38.

Twigg, C. A. (2004). *Improving quality and reducing costs: Lessons learned from Round III of the Pew Grant Program in Course Redesign.* National Center for Academic Transformation. Retrieved April 6, 2011, from http://www://www.thencat.org/PCR/RdIIILessons.pdf.

Twigg, C. A. (2005). *Course redesign improves learning and reduces costs.* Policy Alert. National Center for Public Policy and Higher Education. Retrieved from http://www.highereducation.org/reports/pa_core/.

Twigg, C. A. (2011). The Math Emporium: Higher education's silver bullet. *Change,* May–June.

Tyler-Smith, K. (2006). Early attrition among first time e-learners: A review of factors that contribute to dropout, withdrawal and non-completion rates of adult learners undertaking e-learning programs. *Journal of Online Learning and Technology,* June.

U.S. Department of Commerce. (1995). *Falling through the net: A survey of the "have nots" in rural and urban America.* Retrieved from National Telecommunications & Information Administration website: http://www.ntia.doc.gov/ntiahome/fallingthru.html.

U.S. Department of Education. (2010a). *Evaluation of evidence-based practices in online learning: A meta-analysis and review of online learning studies.* Washington, D.C.: U.S. Department of Education.

U.S. Department of Education. (2010b). *Transforming American education: Learning powered by technology.* National Education Technology Plan 2010. Washington, D.C.: U.S. Department of Education.

U.S. Department of Education (2012). *Enhancing teaching and learning through educational data mining and learning analytics.* Washington, D.C.: U.S. Department of Education.

U.S. Department of Education. (2013). *Expanding evidence approaches for learning in a digital world,* Washington, D.C.: Office of Educational Technology.

U.S. Department of Labor. (2003). FY2003–2008 strategic plan. Retrieved from http://www.dol.gov/_sec/stratplan/strat_plan_2003-2008.pdf.

Utman, C. H. (1997). Performance effects of motivational state: A meta-analysis. *Personality and Social Psychology Review, 1*(2), 170–182.

Vesselinov, R. & Grego, J. (2012). Duolingo effectiveness study: Final report. Retrieved from roumen.vesselinov@qc.cuny.edu.

Walsh, T. (2011). *Unlocking the gates: How and why leading universities are opening up access to their courses.* Princeton, NJ: Princeton University Press.

Walston, J. & Carlivati McCarroll, J. (2010). *Eighth-grade algebra: Findings from the eighth-grade round of the early childhood longitudinal study, kindergarten class of 1998–99* (ECLS-K). NCES 2010-016. Washington, D.C., Institute of Education Sciences.

Wang, A. & Newlin, M. (2000). Characteristics of students who enroll and succeed in web-based classes. *Journal of Educational Psychology, 92*(1), 137–143.

Wang, H. & Woodworth, K. (2011a). *Evaluation of Rocketship Education's use of DreamBox Learning's online mathematics program.* Menlo Park, CA: SRI International.

Wang, H. & Woodworth, K. (2011b). *Evaluation of Rocketship Education's use of the reasoning mind online mathematics curricula.* Menlo Park, CA: SRI International.

Warschauer, M. (2012). The digital divide and social inclusion. *Americas Quarterly.* Retrieved from http://www.americasquarterly.org/warschauer.

Warschauer, M. & Matuchniak, T. (2010). New technology and digital worlds: Analyzing evidence of equity in access, use, and outcomes. *Review of Research in Education, 34*(1), 179–225.

Waschull, S. (2005). Predicting success in online psychology courses: Self-discipline and motivation. *Teaching of Psychology, 32*(3), 190–192.

Watson, J. (2004). *Report to the Joint Budget Committee of the Colorado State Legislature on the cost of online education.* Denver, CO: Colorado Department of Education.

Watson, J. (2007). *A national primer on K-12 online learning.* International Association for K-12 Online Learning (iNACOL). Retrieved from http://www.inacol.org/research/docs/national_report.pdf.

Watson, J. & Gemin, B. (2008). *Using online learning for at-risk students and credit recovery.* Retrieved from http://files.eric.ed.gov/fulltext/ED509625.pdf.

Watson, J., Gemin, B., Ryan, J., & Wicks, M. (2009). *Keeping pace with K-12 online learning: An annual review of state-level policy and practice.* Durango,

CO: Evergreen Education Group. Retrieved October 29, 2011, from http://www. kpk12.com/cms/wp-content/uploads/KeepingPace09-fullreport.pdf.

Watson, J., Murin, A., Vashaw, L., Gemin, B., & Rapp, C. (2010). *Keeping pace with K-12 online learning: An annual review of state-level policy and practice*. Durango, CO: Evergreen Education Group. Retrieved October 29, 2011, from http://www. kpk12.com/wp-content/uploads/KeepingPaceK12_2010.pdf.

Watson, J., Murin, A., Vashaw, L., Gemin, B., & Rapp, C. (2012). *Keeping pace with online and blended learning 2012: An annual review of policy and practice*. Evergreen Group, Colorado. Retrieved from http://www://kpk12.com/

Watters, A. (2012). *The LMS infrastructure enters the MOOC fray*. Web log post. October 31. Retrieved from http://blogs.reuters.com/felix-salmon/2012/01/23/ udacity-and-the-future-of-online-universities/

Webley, K. (2012). University uproar: Ouster of UVA president draws fire. *Time*, June 20. Retrieved from http://content.time.com/time/nation/article/0,8599,2117640,00. html.

Wenglinsky, H. (1998). *Does it compute? The relationship between educational technology and student achievement in mathematics*. Princeton, NJ: Educational Testing Service.

Wenglinsky, H. (2005). Technology and achievement: The bottom line. *Educational Leadership, 63*(4), 29–32.

Werquin, P. (2010). *Recognition of non-formal and informal learning: Country practices*. Organisation for Economic Co-operation and Development.

Wicks, M. 2010. *A national primer on K-12 online learning. Version 2*. Retrieved from http://www://www.inacol.org/research/docs/iNCL_NationalPrimerv22010-web.pdf.

Wise, R. & Rothman, R. (2010). *The online learning imperative: A solution to three looming crises in education*. Issue Brief. Washington, D.C.: Alliance for Excellent Education.

Wojciechowski, A. & Palmer, L. B. (2005). Individual student characteristics: Can any be predictors of success in online classes? *Online Journal of Distance Learning Administration, 8*(2). Retrieved from http://www.westga.edu/%7Edistance/ojdla/ summer82/wojciechowski82.htm.

Wu, J. (n.d.). Revolutionize education using learning analytics. University of California, Berkeley School of Information.

Xu, D. & Jaggers, S. S. (2011a). Online and hybrid course enrollment and performance in Washington State community and technical colleges. CCRC Working Paper 31. New York: Columbia Teachers College, Community College Research Center.

Xu, D. & Jaggers, S. S. (2011b). The effectiveness of distance education across Virginia's community colleges: Evidence from introductory college-level math and English courses. *Educational Evaluation and Policy Analysis, 33*, 360.

Yuan, L. & Powell, S. (2013). MOOCs and open education: Implications for higher education. JISC CETIS Centre for Educational Technology & Interoperability Standards. Retrieved from http://publications.cetis.ac.uk/2013/667.

Zhao, Y., Lei, J., Yan, B., Lai, C., & Tan, H. S. (2005). What makes the difference? A practical analysis of research on the effectiveness of distance education. *Teachers College Record, 107*(8), 1836–1884.

Zucker, A. & Kozma, R. (2003). The virtual high school: Teaching generation V. New York: *Teachers College Press*.

Zuckerman, M., Porac, J., Lathin, D., Smith, R., & Deci, E. L. (1978). On the importance of self-determination for intrinsically motivated behavior. *Personality and Social Psychology Bulletin, 4*(3), 443–446.

Index